Sensing the Self

Sensing the Self

Women's Recovery from Bulimia

SHEILA M. REINDL

HARVARD UNIVERSITY PRESS

CAMBRIDGE, MASSACHUSETTS   LONDON, ENGLAND   2001

Library of Congress Cataloging-in-Publication Data
Reindl, Sheila M., 1958–
    Sensing the self : women's recovery from
    bulimia / Sheila M. Reindl.
      p. cm.
    Includes bibliographical references and index.
    ISBN 0-674-00487-6 (alk. paper)
      1. Bulimia.   2. Women—health and hygiene.
    3. Eating disorders.   I. Title.
    RC552.B84 R45 2001
    616.85'263—dc21

                        00-050582

To my mother, Phyllis Reindl,
and to the memory of my father, Donald Reindl,
with ever deepening appreciation
for their senses of generosity, goodwill,
gratitude, humility, and pride in work well done

and to the memory of Joan Erikson,
with gratitude for her sense of wisdom
and her wisdom about the senses

CONTENTS

Sensing the Self

Introduction

When someone is ill, we assume she wants to be well again. But a person with an eating disorder is typically ambivalent about recovering. While others are struck by her obsession, compulsion, and apparent misery and think she would surely prefer wellness and freedom to the tyrannical rule of her illness, a person in the throes of a serious eating disorder is, at best, profoundly ambivalent about getting help and getting well.

Looking back on her recovery from bulimia nervosa, a woman I call Isabella describes such ambivalence: "You've used it, and it's worked for a time, and you don't know what else to do. It's at that point where you know that this is bad, and you've felt bad afterwards, but it's been something that's helped you through . . . I guess deep down you know that it's harming you. Because it doesn't feel good. So that's the part that I think initially motivates you to want to change. But you can't imagine when you feel so bad about yourself that there are, what the other ways are to cope."

For all their destructiveness, a person's eating-disorder symptoms are also creative expressions of something essential about her experience, and they can therefore be indescribably difficult to give up. She may not even be able to imagine who she would be without her eating disorder, much less that who she would be is someone worth being.

A person with bulimia nervosa typically fears she is hollow, bad, even rotten at her core and works hard to avoid experiencing a core sense of shame. Isabella had feared that if she stopped her frenetic activity and her bingeing and purging she would be faced with empty time and psychic emptiness, which she found as unbearable as physical fullness:

> I would never allow myself to be alone. I couldn't be alone, had to be constantly with people or doing things. I never sat down. Myself.
>
> *Do you have a sense of why you didn't?*
>
> I was running.
>
> *And why were you running?*
>
> 'Cause I was afraid to deal, or face anything, face myself. I didn't want to face myself.
>
> *For fear—?*
>
> 'Cause I didn't think anything was there. There was nothing worth working for.

A bulimic person's shame may lead her to try to hide not only her eating-disorder behaviors but also her basic needs and yearnings. She may wish that her needs and desires did not exist and may try to act as if she does not need or want anything or anyone. When that attempt inevitably fails, she may wish that others could magically read her mind and respond to her needs and wants without her having to ask for anything. To avoid the shame of expressing her needs and desires, she turns to food, rather than relationships, for comfort. Isabella recalls: "Eating was a way to comfort myself. Instant gratification. That you couldn't often find in other places."

A bulimic person may be so disconnected from her experience that she does not even know what she needs or wants. If she does know, needing something or someone only confirms her sense that she is weak and inadequate. She believes her needs are not legitimate and therefore finds it difficult to seek care or to engage with any care she does manage to seek. In fact, she is likely to greet others' expressions of concern with contempt, the very contempt with which she views herself.

Purposes and Paradoxes

Yet because her needs and yearnings are real and pressing, she must find some way to express them: she puts into body what she cannot yet put into words. Her eating disorder serves as her voice, her attempt to express and meet her needs and desires without directly asking for anything. By "attempt," I do not necessarily mean a conscious or instrumental effort. Someone with bulimia nervosa may be unaware of her emotional experience and its role in motivating and perpetuating her behavior, with the result that she herself is baffled by her inability and reluctance to simply stop her bulimic behaviors. Isabella felt she was "this person who was alone and crazy. I really thought I was crazy. 'Cause I did some pretty nutty things. It just wasn't rational at all."

A bulimic's symptoms of bingeing, purging, fasting, excessive exercising, and other compensatory behaviors serve multiple purposes and present multiple paradoxes. Even as they express her needs, the symptoms punish her for trying to acknowledge her neediness. But even as she suffers her own punishment and self-contempt, she fiercely protects her right to her symptoms, which serve as declarations of her selfhood: "Mine." "No." "Keep out."

In yet another paradox, bulimia nervosa serves as both an expression of feelings and a defense against experiencing feelings, particularly shame, anger, loneliness, sadness, envy, and guilt. A person with bulimia nervosa fears, whether consciously or unconsciously, that painful feelings would be unbearable, even annihilating. For her, emotional pain confirms her belief that she is bad and weak. For example, if she feels lonely, her loneliness confirms that she is unworthy of company. If she feels sad, her sadness proves what a pathetic creature she is.

Because painful feelings accentuate her core sense of defectiveness and shame, and because she does not know how to tolerate psychic pain or to seek effective and nondestructive relief from it, she feels unable to bear the disappointments, hurts, rejections, injustices, frustrations, losses, and limitations that are inevitably part of human life. She tries to escape from painful emotions and fundamental needs because to experience them is to feel even greater self-contempt. The behaviors, preoccupations, and pain of the eating disorder consume her attention and energy and thereby distract her from or numb her to emotional pain and its attendant shame and self-loathing. Isabella remembers her efforts at such escape: "I was always trying to fill that void with something. Whether it was men or drugs or food or activity. Whatever it was. Shopping. That would be a way to make myself feel better . . . It was a way to escape from myself, from whatever I had to deal with . . . When I would eat like that, I would get so foggy and out of it that I would just go to sleep."

What perpetuates a person's eating disorder may include the factors that led to its development as well as other factors. For instance, her behaviors turn her psychic pain, which she fears is not legitimate, into physical pain, which is indisputably real. Over time, having an eating disorder and being ill may make her feel special and thereby become an essential aspect of her identity. In addition, her eating-disorder behaviors become loyal friends, dependably available in moments of distress or emptiness.

If bulimia nervosa allows her to be thinner than she could naturally be without it, her thinness can become a source of pride and a basis for her sense of self. She then remains devoted to her eating-disordered identity because she cannot yet imagine a sense of worth based in authentic aspects of herself beyond her appearance, accomplishments, and ability to please others. She avoids seeking help because she fears that caregivers would insist that she give up the sense of specialness she derives from the disorder. She fears that recovering, which entails becoming more accepting of one's authentic self, including one's naturally maintainable weight, would leave her with no sense of distinctiveness or worth.

The physiological consequences of eating-disordered behaviors can perpetuate further disordered eating and exercising and promote a more general disconnection from self. Physical deprivation sets someone up to binge, which in turn sets her up to feel compelled to compensate for the binge. Inadequate nutrition, purging, and excessive exercising can lead to electrolyte imbalances and low blood glucose levels, which impair her perception, mental processing, and mood regulation (Keys et al., 1950; Mitchell, Pomeroy, and Adson, 1997). The opioids released by the body during purging and exercising can be, in a certain sense, addicting. As she continually disregards and overrides her body's signals of hunger, fullness, and fatigue, a bulimic woman becomes increasingly disconnected from her subjective experience. Because she does not heed her own needs, desires, preferences, and limits, she grows ever more reliant upon external gauges to guide her life.

LEARNING FROM THE EXPERTS

In the face of such powerful intrapsychic and physiological forces, how do people manage to recover, and what is helpful to them as they do so? To address this question, I talked with women who have recovered from bulimia nervosa. If recovering is, in part, a process of becoming able to put into words the experience a woman once put into body, then we have much to learn by listening to those who have recovered, or discovered, a voice with which to tell their stories.

I base this book on my interviews with thirteen such women. They had had a fairly typical course of bulimia nervosa: they had been, on average, 17 years old when they developed the disorder, and they had been bulimic for on average five years (longer if one counts years of subclinical bulimia nervosa). All of the women had at some point been very ill. (For more about the women and about my research see the Appendix.)

The women teach us that recovering is a process of coming to experience a sense of self. More precisely, it is a process of learning to sense one's self, to attune to one's subjective physical, psychic, and social self-experience. These women's core sense of shame and their difficulty in tolerating painful emotions had led them to avoid turning their attention inward to their internal sense of things. In recovering, they "came to their senses" and learned to trust their sensed experience, in particular

5

their sense of "enoughness." In recovering, they also became better acquainted with and more accepting of the aggressive, needy aspects of self which they had previously rejected and tried to keep hidden for fear of exacerbating their sense of shame. To my surprise and theirs, many express gratitude for having been bulimic because the symptoms gave concrete form to their psychic distress and brought it to such a pitch that they had to reckon with it. In so doing, they came to feel more whole and to live life with a fuller sense of self.

The women teach us that even though they have recovered, some aspects of bulimia nervosa persist, particularly a vulnerability to shame and difficulties with enoughness—fears that they are not good enough, will not get enough, and cannot tell when enough is enough. But they no longer feel controlled by their vulnerability and difficulties. Their experience deepens our understanding of how treatment works, how and why people develop eating disorders, and how we might prevent eating disorders.

To understand how people recover, we need to integrate the experiential expertise of those who have had the disorder with the expertise of researchers and clinicians. This premise is inspired and informed by the work of Hilde Bruch, whose work with anorexics is regarded as fundamental for all who care for people with eating disorders. When traditional psychoanalytic approaches to treatment proved disappointing in her work with anorexic patients, Bruch rethought her efforts and assumptions in light of her and her patients' actual experience. Her genuine desire to learn from anorexics how they experienced themselves and their lives not only allowed her to discover an effective therapeutic approach but was a major ingredient of that approach. She relied upon what she called "the constructive use of ignorance" (1973, 338)—that is, her willingness to learn from and with patients in a joint effort to help them "become aware of self-initiated feelings, thoughts, and behavior" (1988, 8). She regarded the patient as "the significant explorer who was listened to, not only as a recounter of events but with encouragement to draw conclusions" (1988, 9).

She found that "patients respond well to this objective fact-finding attitude when they recognize that the therapist regards them as true collaborators in the search for unknown factors" (1973, 338). To Bruch's mind, true collaboration "implies that the therapist does not know and can find out only with the patient's active participation in the inquiry" (1985, 17). Collaboration requires that the therapist maintain an abiding curiosity, as opposed to a foreclosed certainty: "A therapist who assumes that he understands the patients' problems is not quite so alert and curious in unraveling the unclear and confused periods. He may be tempted to superimpose his prematurely conceived notions on the patient" (1973, 338).

My work was also inspired and informed by a study of the process of recovering from anorexia nervosa conducted by Eugene Beresin, Christopher Gordon, and David Herzog (1989), who interviewed thirteen recovered anorexics. They noted: "In the effort to obtain quantifiable, replicable outcome measures, somehow the phenomenology of the subject's experience was lost . . . We began reexamining the question of recovery by relying on a basic clinical principle: First and foremost, listen to and understand the patient from her perspective" (106). Impressed by their work, I decided to conduct a similar phenomenological study with women who had recovered from bulimia nervosa.

This book also has roots in the clinical and research traditions of the Bureau of Study Counsel of Harvard University, a campus counseling center founded by William G. Perry in the mid-1940s. I have been a counselor at "the Bureau" since 1985. Although the office now comprises clinicians with a broad range of theoretical orientations, the Bureau's historical roots are in client-centered counseling and existential psychology. While I integrate various theoretical perspectives—from object relations to relational theory—into my clinical work and research, I feel as if I enter those domains on a visa, my clinical passport having been issued from the realm of client-centered counseling and existential psychology. What grounds me in any given clinical moment is an effort central to those orientations, namely to stay closely attuned to a person's subjective experience. Attunement and empathy are essential to all effective therapy, regardless of the therapist's training and orientation. But empathic resonance and responsiveness were the heart of my early training and remain a core effort of my work. As Kiyo Morimoto, a former director of the Bureau, used to say, "People are experts on their own experience."

My understanding of the process of recovering relies upon what I have learned from all the people with eating disorders whom I have met in my clinical work. In my research, I did not select as a participant anyone who was or had been a client of mine or who was at the time eligible for the services of the Bureau. But in my effort not to create any impression that clients were expected to serve as research subjects, I nearly failed to recognize that my clients wanted to know that they had contributed to my understanding. Time and again, when a bulimic client learned that I had written a book about bulimia, she said, "I hope I helped you write it." And of course the truth is that I could not have written this book without my clients.

1

Coming to Their Senses

Friends, relatives, and caregivers of a person with bulimia nervosa may wish they could rouse her from her condition by saying "Come to your senses!"—as if she were not in her right mind and needed to be jolted from her folly. In fact, the women I interviewed indicate that recovering *is* a process of coming to one's senses—where the word *senses* refers, however, not to sound mental faculties but to one's sensed experience. It is by sensing our experience that we develop and recognize a sense of self.

The essence of recovering is the development of a sense of self, and here the word *sense* is as important as the word *self.* When we use the phrase *a sense of self,* we are apt to put the emphasis on *self:* "She has no sense of self." "She has a real sense of self." But if we place equal stress upon *sense* and *self,* the term takes on new meaning: to sense oneself. The noun, *sense,* suggests the verb, *to sense,* and the verb suggests a question: How do we sense self? It is this verb and this question to which these women drew my attention, and it is this process of coming to sense one's self that I explore in this book.

The following excerpt from an interview with Abigail, age 30 and a psychiatrist, conveys some sense (pun inevitable) of the phenomenon of coming to one's senses:

> I spent so many days counting calories all day, worrying about my weight. To the extent that I still do that, it's a lot less. But there's so much more to me than that. And I guess all that there was, I felt, was to be in college, being thin, getting the right

grades, getting a boyfriend, and making people happy, or something. I was able to do that, and I guess that's good, but it doesn't mean that I'm satisfied or something. So I really feel, I think, I really feel like the stuff I've been doing has been creating more of a real knowing, really trying to cultivate this development of my instinct and trusting my instinct. And knowing what I need, what I want. And not measuring it, like if someone else says it's good, then it's good. So it also has to do with trusting your appetite that "Today I'm hungry, I can trust that this is what I need to do is that I need to eat." Instead of struggling with that hunger. And it's really hard. But getting acquainted with different parts of me.

As Abigail indicates, women with bulimia nervosa tend to be profoundly disconnected from their subjective psychic and physical experience and to rely on external gauges to guide their actions. To recover, they must learn to attune to their own experience. As Suzanne Repetto Renna once said to me, they must shift from being a *censor,* or judge, of their experience to being a *sensor,* or experiencer, of their own life. Abigail's "real knowing" derives from "getting acquainted" with her feelings, instincts, needs, and desires.

When I ask Meg, age 23 and a secondary school teacher, what she has gained in recovering, she says with a laugh: "Everything." She continues: "Really, I've gained a life in which I am an active participant. I've gained a sense of self. I've gained just the ability to influence other people because I'm okay enough with myself that I can focus on others and effectively help them." When I ask what led to her bulimia, she talks about a profound disconnection from self: "It's all very much of a blur. Which is something that makes me a little bit sad because I don't have a lot of memories from high school and college, like specific memories. I think that I was so much not—I didn't have that much of a self. I think I was just whatever people wanted me to be, and I feel like that's one reason why I don't have memories."

Meg hopes that by talking with people who were her friends at that time, she can recall and reconstruct some sense of herself during her college years: "I'd really like to piece together some memories a little bit more. About specific incidents and things. Try to remember those years in terms of events as opposed to achievements. 'Cause at the time all I thought about was what I was achieving or what I was doing, not who I was." Meg's yearning for memories indicates that she now knows what it means to remember her experience from within herself, with a sense of having lived it.

SENSE OF SELF AND SENSING SELF

While the literature on the concept of self tends to refer to the self as an entity or a construction (Hartmann, 1958; James, 1890; Kegan, 1982; Kohut, 1971, 1977; Mead, 1934), I address not *the self* but the experience of *a sense of self* and the activity of *sensing self.* The accounts of the women I interviewed emphasize not the nature or construction of the self they sensed but the activity of sensing.

Erik Erikson and Daniel Stern both take particular note of the phrase *a sense of.* Erikson (1959/1980), in presenting the Eight Ages of Man, says: "In describing this growth . . . we take recourse to the term 'a sense of.' Like a 'sense of health' or a 'sense of not being well,' such 'senses' pervade surface and depth, consciousness and the unconscious" (58). Stern (1985), in writing about infant development, attempts not so much to define the term *sense of self* as to describe it:

> While no one can agree on exactly what the self is, as adults we still have a very real sense of self that permeates daily social experience. It arises in many forms. There is the sense of a self that is a single, distinct, integrated body; there is the agent of actions, the experiencer of feelings, the maker of intentions, the architect of plans, the transposer of experience into language, the communicator and sharer of personal knowledge. Most of these senses of self reside out of awareness, like breathing, but they can be brought to and held in consciousness. We instinctively process our experiences in such a way that they appear to belong to some kind of unique subjective organization that we commonly call the sense of self. (5–6)

Like Erikson, Stern stresses the experiential nature of the sense of self: "A crucial term here is 'a sense of,' as distinct from 'concept of' or 'knowledge of' or 'awareness of' a self or other. The emphasis is on the palpable experiential realities of substance, action, sensation, affect, and time. Sense of self is not a cognitive construct. It is an experiential integration" (71).

Sensing self-experience is both a conscious, intentional process, by which we focus inward and consult our own experience, and a subconscious and unconscious process. It involves our five primary senses (J. Erikson, 1988)—hearing, sight, smell, touch, and taste—but is not limited to them. When we feel relief, regret, pride, or contentment, we draw upon our capacity to sense self-experience beyond the primary senses. To sense something is to know it not just physically, not just mentally, but with body, mind, and spirit.

I use the phrase *sensing self-experience* to mean attuning to one's subjective, felt experience. I use the phrase *sensing self* to refer to the cumulative effect of continually sensing self-experience. That effect is the awareness of, to repeat Stern's words, "some kind of unique subjective organization that we commonly call the sense of self."

Eugene Gendlin and Marsha Linehan are among the few clinician-writers who specifically consider the verb *to sense*. For Gendlin, *"The 'motor' that powers psychotherapeutic change is a direct sensing into what is concretely felt (not emotions, but implicitly complex felt sense) . . . A felt sense is both psychic and bodily, but not in a way in which the two are separate"* (1974, 240–241). In explicating a psychotherapeutic method called focusing, Gendlin describes sensing as "a mode of inward *bodily* attention" which "begins with the body and occurs in the zone between the conscious and the unconscious" (1996, 1). He contends that it is by exploring this "border zone" that one experiences true, deep therapeutic change.

My definition of *sensing* is broader than Gendlin's. I use the term to mean not only the experience of an "implicitly complex felt sense" but also a more general process of referring inward to consult and know and trust one's subjective experience.

Linehan, in a training manual on dialectical behavior therapy, refers to "sensing" in advising therapists how to educate people about emotions: "Emotions involve sensing. When people have emotional feelings, they are actually sensing their body and brain changes. This is usually what is meant by an 'emotional experience'" (1993, 88). She suggests that therapists tell their clients: "Sometimes the problem in emotions is that you cannot sense your body and body changes. To regulate emotions, you have to be pretty good at sensing your body. If you have been shutting off all sensations for years, this can be difficult" (88). Linehan's model is designed for use with people with borderline personality disorder, not bulimia nervosa, but her approach, which integrates aspects of cognitive-behavioral therapy, dialectical thinking, and Zen mindfulness practice, comprises many of the ingredients that the women found helpful as they learned to sense and tolerate self-experience.

IMPEDIMENTS AND IMPAIRMENTS

The women's accounts suggest several factors that might explain their difficulties in sensing self-experience: an internalized sense of shame, deficits in self-structure and self-regulatory capacities, the use of dissociation as a defense, and sociocultural influences. Each of these factors, as well as developmental demands and biological vulnerability, might have contributed to the development of bulimia nervosa.

A CORE SENSE OF SHAME

The women had avoided sensing their self-experience in large part because it was characterized by a sense of being fundamentally inadequate and bad. Their attempts to refer inward to consult their own experience were associated with intolerable shame and with the anxiety naturally attendant to shame. Their eating-disorder behaviors were in part a way to avoid such negative self-experience.

Beth, age 27 and working as a case manager in a mental health clinic, describes this phenomenon:

> I guess always feeling like I'm not good enough, and I feel like that was part
> of how I grew up. And also the self-hate was, it became "Which came first,

the chicken or the egg?" Did I hate myself because I binged and threw up? Or did I binge and throw up because I hated myself? And after a while, feelings of inadequacy would lead me to binge, which would lead me to more feelings of inadequacy and then throwing up, and all of it just became such a cycle, waking up in the morning, having binged and thrown up the night before, and hating myself, and then hating myself so I didn't wanna see people, and then hating myself 'cause I didn't have friends, and feeling like I was inadequate and a loser because I didn't have friends. And it was all so connected, it just all fed on itself to the point where, before I went into treatment, I was isolated, I didn't have friends, and I hated myself so much. How can you go to a party and have a good time when you hate yourself and you can't talk to people or look them in the face?

———

All the women appear to have experienced covert shaming in the form of chronic emotional neglect. Several also suffered overt shaming in the form of emotional abuse (ridicule, mean teasing, contempt, blaming, unkind criticism) or in the form of physical or sexual abuse or trauma. From early in their lives, adults were not attuned and responsive to their emotional worlds. Without emotionally attuned responsiveness, a child does not learn to identify and tolerate her emotions. Because she experiences herself as unable to recruit an attuned response, she feels as if she makes no impact, as if she does not matter. She develops a deep sense of shame.

Gershen Kaufman, drawing upon the work of Sylvan Tomkins, argues that shame results when we are experiencing interest, concern, or enjoyment and wish to be acknowledged or joined in our experience but instead feel unheard or unnoticed by the person whose attention and affirmation we were seeking. We feel as if someone has turned away from us in disdain. In Kaufman's terms, "the interpersonal bridge" is broken, and we feel deflated, unworthy of the affirmation for which we had hoped (1980/1992, 13–14).

When a need or yearning goes unnoticed by someone whose "caring, respect, or valuing matters," we feel shame because we interpret the neglect as a rejection and an exposure of our deficiency (14). The neglected need or yearning is typically basic: a need to be heard or seen, a yearning for someone to recognize or join in an experience. Shame is induced not because a need or yearning goes *unmet* by a valued other but because it goes *unacknowledged* or receives only half-hearted acknowledgment. We do not need to be judged or mocked to feel shame: being ignored or slighted, whether intentionally or inadvertently, is sufficient. Nor does emotional neglect presume physical neglect: a child can suffer emotional neglect even when her physical needs are well met.

No one avoids shame altogether. It is natural and inevitable to have our needs go unacknowledged at times. The consequent sense of shame is diminished when the valued person accurately senses our shame and rage resulting from the lack of acknowledgment and openly admits having failed to recognize our need. According to Kaufman, such an undefensive acknowledgment is healing because it restores the interpersonal bridge: "We carry within us always the deep emotional impact of shame, and yet when someone deeply valued risks his own exposure to become vulnerable and openly acknowledges his imperfect humanness, his part in making us feel shame, we are carried beyond shame. The growth impact of having someone take that risk with us is far greater than if he or she had never triggered off a shame experience in the first place" (1974, 574).

Kaufman (1980/1992) distinguishes between interpersonally induced shame and internalized shame: if someone has repeated, shame-inducing interpersonal experiences in childhood which are not followed by restoration of the interpersonal bridge, shame is internalized and becomes an enduring, core sense of shame. Once shame is internalized, "the self is able to activate shame without an inducing interpersonal event." Internalized shame is thus persistent and "can spread throughout the self, ultimately shaping our emerging identity": "Our identity is that vital sense of who we are as individuals, embracing our worth, our adequacy, and our very dignity as human beings. All that can be obliterated through protracted shame . . . Contained in the experience of shame is the piercing awareness of ourselves as fundamentally deficient in some vital way as a human being. To live with shame is to experience the very essence or heart of the self as wanting" (8–9).

In writing about shame in bulimia, Kaufman distinguishes between its role in bingeing and its role in purging. When a person's basic interpersonal needs go unacknowledged, she feels shamed, and bingeing numbs her to that shame: "Bingeing on food is a substitute for interpersonal needs which are shame-bound. When one feels empty inside, hungry to feel a part of someone, desperate to be held close, craving to be wanted and admired, respected and loved—but these have become taboo through shame—one turns instead to food. But food can never truly satisfy the inner need. Longing turns to shame. And so one eats more to anesthetize the longing" (1980/1992, 186). By bingeing a person not only numbs herself to shame but also displaces the shame, shifting the object of shame from her self to her behavior. It is less painful to bear the shame of bingeing than the original shame of needing and wanting.

Purging adds a new element: "During the bingeing cycle, shame intensifies. The purge cycle adds something crucial to this: the affect of *disgust*. Vomiting is frequently resorted to by bulimics to purge themselves of the shameful food they so shamelessly devoured. Vomiting is the *disgust reaction* experienced on the drive level" (186). Yet the intensification of shame leads, paradoxically, to "a sense of cleansing":

> Why vomiting? Why such an intense form of purging? There is a kind of emotional cleansing that occurs if one literally bathes in shame. Magnifying the intensity of shame will rapidly bring it to its peak intensity, imploding the self and thereby automatically reducing shame. This is Tomkins' concept of *affect magnification* applied to bulimia . . . When the shame peaks, there is a "bursting effect," and one feels purged, cleansed, even purified. Self-purging through vomiting continues until defeat and humiliation are complete . . . By magnifying feelings of humiliation in intensity and duration, they are finally spent, their fire burned out. This is what creates the sense of cleansing. (186–187)

Ana-Maria Rizzuto (1991) identifies a phenomenon she calls "pathological shame," which she defines as "a persistent predisposition" to intense shame (299) and which seems to be what Kaufman refers to as internalized shame. Rizzuto traces the development of a core sense of shame to infancy and early childhood. We experience shame when we do not elicit from someone who matters to us a response that is complementary to our affective communication. Complementary communication exists long before we use spoken words, through skin contact between parent and child as well as through eye contact and nonverbal aspects of voice such as pitch and modulation. These elements of affective communication "seem to provide both parent and child with a feeling of contact with the infant as a total being" (301). But when a child repeatedly fails to elicit an affective response that complements her own affective communication, she is apt to develop an unconscious representation of herself as someone who is "exposed, defective, a failure, unable to exert self-control; . . . an individual who is unappealing to the object, unable to excite it to respond in a particular manner" (301). Chronic early experiences of emotional non-attunement leave a child with "beliefs and unconscious fantasies about [her] own worth, defectiveness, or unlovability" (302), which are "the main source of the painful sting of shame" (304).

The concept of shame sheds light on the way bulimic women experience their family environments. Clare Murray, Glenn Waller, and Charles Legg (2000) have found that "shame plays a central but complex role in the link between perceived parental style and bulimic psychopathology" (88). Internalized shame (defined as "internal attributions about the self resulting from chronic exposure to shameful situations over time") is "a perfect mediator," meaning that it accounts for much of the statistical association between bulimic attitudes and family characteristics—in particular, perceived paternal care and protection (85). Shame-proneness (defined as "oversensitivity to experience shame in social situations") appears to be a moderator, meaning that it influences the intensity of the effect of paternal overprotection (defined as "control and intrusion") on bulimic attitudes (85). Murray, Waller, and Legg speculate that one mechanism linking paternal behavior and internalized shame is that "paternal behavior has the impact of making the individual feel defective (either as someone who needs to be strictly controlled, or as someone not worth the father's attention)" (88).

Parents of bulimic women have been described as emotionally neglectful or underinvolved and critical (Root, Fallon, and Friedrich, 1986;

Johnson, 1991; Humphrey, 1988). Bulimic families have difficulty tolerating and modulating powerful feelings, "particularly anger, resentment, jealousy, grief, depression, anxiety, and insecurity" (Root, Fallon, and Friedrich, 1986, 35). These families tend to declare painful emotions unacceptable: "Direct messages are, for example, 'Of course, you can't possibly feel that, you're not that kind of person,' 'If you can't show a happy face, don't show your face at all,' 'People who are emotional are weak,' or 'Apologize for what you said (or did); you didn't really mean that.' Indirect but equally powerful messages about expressing feelings are given through teasing, degrading a person for crying, or threats to physical safety" (36). When a child's emotional connection with the parent is repeatedly broken, whether by neglect or abuse, and not rebuilt, she experiences chronic invalidation of her core yearnings and needs. If that which derives from the core of her is deemed unworthy of attention or unacceptably bad by the parent, she experiences her very self as unworthy and unacceptably bad.

The women's accounts suggest that once they had developed an internalized sense of shame about themselves early in their lives, within the context of the family, they were especially vulnerable to later experiences of overwhelming shame in contexts beyond the family. Situations that might provoke minimal or manageable shame in most people left them feeling devastated. Each woman describes childhood experiences that appear to have led to an internalized sense of shame, and each marks the onset of her disorder with precipitating experiences in adolescence that evoked a profound sense of inadequacy. I draw upon the experiences of Beth and Gita to illustrate this sequence.

———

Beth grew up in a family of four girls and felt there was never enough attention to go around. She did not receive from her parents confirmation that she was already, inherently enough:

> All through high school, I'd danced and run. On Saturday mornings, I would teach dance classes all morning. And then my dad would pick me up and bring me to a track meet. And then I'd run two or three races, long-distance

races in the track meet. And my track coach would tell me I should quit dancing and just do track. And my dance teacher would tell me I should quit track and just do dancing. And I couldn't quit either one. So I would do that every Saturday.

I think I used to have like miniature mental breakdowns. 'Cause I wrote for the school newspaper, and I taught dancing on Tuesdays and Saturdays, I ran track every day. My senior year, I was Latin Club president. Every night of the week, I was doing something. I became a lifeguard. It was like, no matter what I did, my parents would say, like my mom'd say, "Well, why don't you become a lifeguard?" And I'd be like, "Okay, I'll be a lifeguard. Sign up for licensing." And I took CPR.

You name it, I've done it in my life. I've taken Irish dancing, Scottish dancing. I took guitar lessons, bagpipe lessons. I competed in all these competitions with dancing. And also in track, I would go away for weekends and stuff. And write for the school newspaper. And I was being tutored twice a week, in math and in chemistry. I was confirmed, so we had to go to confirmation classes. So every single night of the week, I'd be out doing something. And my parents didn't think there was anything weird about it. They just thought you should do that. And I remember one night, just crying, I couldn't stop crying.

Beth's long list of activities indicates her inability to sense when enough was enough. Although her parents did not explicitly tell her she had to do more, she learned that their admiration depended upon her activities and accomplishments.

Beth recalls an incident of invalidation by her father:

My track coach used to say to me, "Your father puts so much pressure on you." And I'd be like, "No he doesn't." 'Cause he never said "You have to do this" or "You have to do that." But I do remember my freshman year of high school, one of the first races that I ever ran. I came in second. And I was pretty proud of myself. I remember feeling really good about it . . . I thought he was gonna say, "Good job!" And I remember him saying, "Oh, maybe if you lost five pounds, you'd win next time." And I remember, I was devastated . . . I just remember being really devastated by it.

Her father's criticism of an experience in which Beth took pride made her feel shame. She had hoped he would share in her sense of triumph and mastery. But instead she heard him say, "It is not good enough." He also communicated that her body was not good enough. In the face of such chronic invalidation, she felt that "I, Beth, am not good enough." She began bingeing at age 12 and purging at age 14.

Beth's early experiences at college reinforced her feeling of inadequacy:

> When I went away to college, I had a hard time because it was an Ivy League school, and I felt really inadequate. All these people had had computers, and I never had, I didn't know the first thing about computers . . . And I didn't go on a freshman trip—most people go on a freshman trip—because I was afraid. I was afraid to go on a trip in the woods with ten people I didn't know . . . I was too afraid, and I thought, "I won't know anybody." And my whole life, I had had friends who I had known since kindergarten. And so I just didn't go. And my father was all upset that I didn't go. 'Cause he was like, "Oh, that's one of the big experiences at the college" and stuff. So he sent in my registration late, but it was too late to sign up. So. And then everybody at school either knew friends from prep school or else knew people from their freshman trip. And I didn't know anybody. And it was really, really hard.

What was shame-inducing and shame-intensifying for Beth was not only being at college with people who seemed more comfortable and competent than she felt but also her father's lack of attention to her emotional experience. He did not acknowledge her fears, much less legitimate them or empathize with them. Instead, he acted as if her fears did not exist (were not real), should not exist (were not legitimate), and were not worthy of concern (did not matter). By his inattention and criticism he created a barrier where Beth had hoped for a bridge. Her eating disorder became markedly more severe during college.

Beth remembers many instances of being unable to evoke her parents' acknowledgment that something was wrong. Her bulimic symptoms got so out of control that her counselor recommended to the college dean that she be required to take a medical leave of absence. She left school, returned to her parents' home, and saw a therapist who referred her to an inpatient program. She attributes her failure to pursue the referral to her parents' attitude: "My father was so judgmental of therapy. The only people who were in therapy were nuts. And it was like a moral weakness. If you were, you were totally cracked . . . I felt like my parents didn't want me to get help."

As her bulimic symptoms worsened, she felt more and more desperate. The night after her twenty-first birthday, she overdosed on her antidepressant medication. Even the overdose failed to elicit an acknowledgment of her need for help. The emergency room clinicians focused on assessing her risk of suicide and did not respond to her effort to communicate that she needed care for her eating disorder: "They're just looking at me, 'Well, do you still wanna do it?' And I know if I say to them, 'Yes,' they're not gonna let me go. So I'm like, 'No, no, no. It was all a mistake.' And they're like, 'Well, why did you do it?' and I'm like, 'Well, I'm bulimic.' And they had no concept of what that meant. It was like they were so cold and noncompassionate and just clinical. It almost felt like they were typing it into a typewriter. I just remember feeling, 'What a joke.'"

Her parents, too, refused to acknowledge her need for help. Beth describes the morning after her overdose:

> My mom came in and was like, "Are you going to work?" And she wanted to know if I'm gonna go to work that day. I couldn't believe it. I'd just taken a bottle of pills, been in a psychiatric ward all night, and she's waking me up two hours later to see if I'm gonna go to work. I'm like, "Mom, I don't think so." And she's like, "Well, you're not gonna go to work?" I was working at a day camp as a counselor, and I was dating this guy, he was a lawyer, he was like 28, and I was working for his father. And she was like, "What's Dan's father gonna think?" and all this stuff. "What are you gonna tell them?" And I'm like, I just couldn't believe that.

As Beth's story illustrates, repeated refusals by the important people in one's life to acknowledge one's emotional experience can lead to an ever deepening sense of shame, illegitimacy, and ineffectualness and eventually to desperation and rage.

––––––––

Gita, age 31 and an elementary school teacher, when asked about her experience of recovering, describes having had, then lost, and then reclaimed a sense of self:

I think the bottom line was learning to trust—and I use that word a lot, I know—myself, my feelings, and my body, and me. I think I lived a lot of my life very outwardly. I tried to please people all the time around me and never thought of myself. I thought that was the way to be. My parents had often said to me, "Never be selfish." "If you think about yourself, you're selfish." "If you do things for yourself, you're selfish." "If you spend money on yourself, you're selfish." And I think I had really overly absorbed that and felt that anything I did for me or listened to me or was focused on me was selfish. And then finally I realized that I couldn't be good to anyone, or myself, or anything unless I did care and sort of grow that center of self.

Do you feel like you had to grow it, like it wasn't—?

Yeah. I had killed it. I had denied it. I had tortured it. I had hated it. I hated it, I hated it, I hated it.

Do you know why?

Many, many reasons, but I think part was not being perfect. And maybe losing my parents' love for me if I wasn't good. "Good," quote unquote. I don't know.

Did you always hate it?

No. I don't think so. I was thinking about first grade and kindergarten. I was really tough, and I was the leader of the girls in first grade—where you play these tag games, I'd be the leader. And I remember being very strong then . . . I just was really, I was me then. I remember I was strong, and I didn't really worry so much, and I was really in love with living and myself.

And then, I don't know how it all turned around. We did move when I was 7. But I still was pretty strong at 7. But somehow along the line I just got very shy and very quiet and very worried about what other people thought of me. And if I was doing things right. And I just sort of sunk inside. Or the person who was, who I wanted to be, or who I thought of as myself was sort of way in there surrounded by all this gibbly goosh outside, and I had forgotten about it. I forgot that that was in there . . .

Sometimes I'd see that somewhere. Sometimes in dance. I loved to dance. And all of the sudden sometimes I would just be inspired in modern dance, to be somewhere else. And I loved it. And oh, what other times? And sometimes just listening to music, and sometimes I would hit that running, too, when I was way out in the woods and it was beautiful and I was running. Or, in nature a lot I'd find it again. But then there was this hatred, too, that would come back and I'd have to be the person again, another person.

When I ask when she started hating herself, Gita recalls that she still had herself at age 7, and still at age 10. Then she pauses:

> What happened when I was 11 and 12? Oh, I switched schools when I was—this is pretty interesting. I switched schools for seventh grade. My mom had gone to this private school, and she really wanted me to go there. So I left the public schools in our town and went to private school in another town. And there I had to work really, really hard, and what I had been able to do in public school I wouldn't get by with that, and I had to really become a hard-driving student. And in some ways now I look back at that as very important. It was a good experience for me 'cause I wasn't motivated to pursue it unless I'd been forced to. But I think then it became clear to me that there was an outward person, I think that's when it started. Maybe, so 11, 12? And then, but still not so bad. I can still, if I think back on those times I still see images of Gita. But starting to fade. And definitely by 15, 14, 15, it, she was going.

When she no longer felt adequate, Gita stopped consulting her internal experience. Her excessive concern with her weight began around age 15. She began bingeing and vomiting when she was a freshman in college.

The shame Gita felt as a student in her new school was not interpersonally induced shame but rather the shame attendant to the struggle for mastery (von Stade, 1986). She no longer felt adequate to the task of her schoolwork. But we might ask why she was so easily toppled by that shame. It appears that she, like Beth, had arrived at adolescence with a core sense of shame attributable at least in part to emotional neglect and criticism. Gita's father and mother divorced when she was 2, and she grew up living primarily with her father and stepmother. Her mother suffered from labile moods and possibly bipolar disorder. Gita describes everyday instances of emotional neglect and criticism by her father and stepmother that may have led to interpersonally induced shame and, over time, internalized shame:

> I was often sent to my room because I was acting like my mother. So being like my mother was a huge flaw, and I was punished for acting like her. And what they meant was I was being hysterical. And not in control of my emotions . . . I would not be rational. I am not totally rational all the time. And something would happen and I would get upset about it, and I certainly at that point did not have good communication skills about what my feelings

were, and so I'd hold things in and then I would sort of blow up. Basically crying and maybe saying things that were extremes, like "Oh, I don't really like coffee cake!" or something. Just sort of extremes about things. My father's extremely rational and logical and orderly, and he's a scientist, and everything has to follow and make sense.

I mention that she was, after all, a child at the time. She explains that being a child didn't keep her younger brother from rationally defending his point of view:

He could fight back, and I would just crumble. And the minute I would crumble, they just don't deal with tears or wimpiness or whatever—I don't know what you want to call it, but I would call it female behavior. They don't see that as appropriate. So off I go . . . If they disagreed with me, or if they didn't want me to do something, I would be devastated. I wanted them to want what I wanted. And please them. If they were mad at me for something, then I never handled that well either. I always would crumble again, and then they thought I was weak and hysterical.

It seems that her parents did not help Gita to know her emotional experience and to express her feelings effectively. Having never learned how to regulate, tolerate, and integrate emotional experience, in the face of powerful feelings Gita "would just crumble."

Gita's account, like Beth's, illustrates that someone who approaches adolescence with a fragile sense of self can feel annihilated by shame-inducing experiences in adolescence. When she entered a new, competitive school in which she felt she was not good enough, she tried to become the person she sensed others wanted her to be. When she stopped sensing self and primarily sensed other, she got disoriented and wandered far off the course of healthy self-development.

In college, Gita tried to signal to her parents that she had a serious eating disorder by showing them a project she had done for a course:

My senior year of college I actually did a slide-tape video with one of my good friends about eating disorders. At this point, pretending, or talking as though I wasn't one of them. But I was really heartfelt when I wrote it. It was really "This is me," but—. And then I presented it to my parents, and I said, "Well, I think I have some of these tendencies," and they go, "Oh, no, no, no, no. You're not anything like this." And I just remember falling apart inside that they wouldn't hear what I was saying through the slide-tape, and that they thought I was perfectly okay. That just crushed me. And I think then I took a big dip, too, "Maybe I'm not, maybe I'm just being selfish," and "I really don't have a problem."

Her parents' refusal to acknowledge her eating disorder left her doubting that her problem was real or important and thereby exacerbated her sense of inadequacy.

———

Beth's and Gita's accounts reveal the insidious nature of emotional neglect and abuse. Like a toxic, invisible, odorless gas, emotional invalidation may be virtually undetectable except for the effect it has on living things. Invalidation of one person by another can occur without either party being aware of it at the time. For instance, in the case of Beth's parents, one might assume that a neglectful father would not attend his daughter's track meet or urge her to go on a freshman trip and that an underinvolved mother would not be so mindful of her daughter's work schedule. In fact, Beth's father may have believed he was responsibly challenging his daughter to reach for her potential as a runner and to test her wings as a college freshman, and Beth's mother may have believed she was responsibly teaching her daughter to honor her commitments in life.

Beth herself was probably unaware that the reason she felt so bad in her interactions with her parents was that she had been shamed. When her track coach observed that her father put a lot of pressure on her, Beth denied it because she assumed that parental pressure would be obvious: "He never said 'You have to do this' or 'You have to do that.'" But despite her parents' physical presence, their involvement in her life, and what may have been their good intentions, Beth's experience was that they did not acknowledge her needs, fears, interests, and yearnings.

Similarly, Gita's parents may have had good intentions. In arranging for her to attend private school, they may have intended to be responsible about her education and her future opportunities. In sending her to her room when she was "being hysterical," they may have been attempting to teach her self-control and socially appropriate behavior. But well-meaning intent did not spare Gita invalidation and shame. Gita learned that her emotional experience was not worthy of acknowledgment, and she came to believe she was not acceptable or lovable as she was.

It is precisely because emotional invalidation occurs *in the presence of* the valued other, the one from whom one yearns for validation, that it is so insidiously potent. The breaking of an interpersonal bridge implies that such a bridge did once exist: a parent must have been involved enough in the child's early life to have fostered a sense of desired connection. If a parent were entirely uninvolved—completely absent from birth—there would be no such bridge and no persistent yearning for a connection. Rebecca, age 27, a graduate student preparing to be a dietitian, says that if she had not had a father at all, she would not have kept hoping for more from him and thus would have been less vulnerable to perpetual disappointment and humiliation:

> My father never really gave me much recognition or reinforcement. He wasn't there, he was off drinking and drugging and having extramarital affairs, and just wasn't a father. So I was always looking for that additional . . . You need a mother and a father in your life. Or even if you didn't, maybe if I didn't have a father in my life, I wouldn't have had such a problem because I would've found strengths in other things in my mother. But since he was present, but he was really nonexistent, I just wasn't getting out of the relationship what a daughter needed.

Emotional invalidation may be hard to spot. A person whose parent was absent in her childhood need not wonder why she felt so alone (although many people whose parents were physically absent nevertheless wonder that). A person who knows she was physically or sexually abused need not wonder why she feels so bad about herself (although many people who were abused nevertheless wonder that). But a person who suffers chronic emotional invalidation in childhood sees no obvious explanation for why she feels so bad and is therefore apt to doubt that her pain is legitimate.

For instance, Meg doubted whether she had good enough reasons to have developed an eating disorder, especially given that eight of the twelve women in her treatment program had been sexually abused while she had not:

> It also made me feel like these things are so much worse, just so beyond my experiences, that I don't deserve to have an eating disorder.

Because you were one of the four people who hadn't experienced—?

Who hadn't had that sort of experience, and that was a sort of an obstacle to my recovery, just actually believing that. And there were other things. I guess that I was like, "I don't deserve, I shouldn't have an eating disorder. There's no reason for me to have an eating disorder." And this was one of the major ones, like, "They've suffered so much more than I have, and I shouldn't be wasting people's time with my problems because they're nothing in comparison with this."

How did you deal with that?

I talked about it with my therapist, the individual therapist, and I guess, she just said, "It's all relative. And [your problems] may not seem as extreme, but a lot of what you've gone through is really difficult stuff." And I still don't feel like what I went through was really that big a deal.

So there's still some of that same feeling?

Yeah, that's still there a little bit. And sometimes when I have problems now, I just think about how lucky I am. That I should just deal. And I wonder why. I mean, I can fit all the pieces together, the low self-esteem, and family problems, and whatever, all the pieces, obsessive-compulsive [symptoms in other family members], and they all work to form an eating disorder. But somehow, if you just look at individual pieces, nothing really looks that bad.

Gita, too, describes feeling that her life was not difficult enough to warrant an eating disorder. This is a viewpoint she attributes to her father and stepmother, but one to which she herself is sympathetic:

> And part of it is that I actually am a very happy, successful person, relatively speaking. They've seen a lot of people really in the doldrums, and my father's lived through the Depression, and I really don't have it that bad, and it's true, you know, American society, "Here you live in this gluttony of material goods and food and love and da da da da, and how can you complain?" is their [attitude], "You've got everything, you've been to college, you're

educated, you have a nice life. You don't have any problems. And if you do, it's very small, and it's sort of psychological, and those aren't real problems anyway. Those are things you can control and that are mind over matter." And I understand where they're coming from. They had a very different life than I did, and it had not been as easy.

When a parent is physically present but emotionally absent or abusive, the situation is highly confusing for a child. She cannot account for why she feels so bad. She may resolve this confusion by deciding, consciously or unconsciously, that everything is really fine—everything, that is, except her feelings. She chastises herself: "You are not being beaten. You have not been sexually abused. No one has died. You have food, shelter, and amenities. Just who do you think you are to be wanting more? You should feel fine, even fortunate."

Meanwhile, because the parent's very presence perpetuates the child's yearning for connection, and because the child's interpretation is that everything is fine with her environment and that the problem is only her perception, the child is not likely to shield herself against perpetual disappointment. With her defenses down, she is continually hurt, and the hurt cuts deep, perhaps deeper than she realizes at the time. Years later, looking back, she struggles to identify why she felt so worthless. "It's not as if something awful happened," she says. She fears she is exaggerating her experience, even making it up, and this fear compounds her shame and self-doubt. Unable to trust her senses, she feels unsteady and unsafe in the world.

———

While overt shaming—via emotional, physical, or sexual abuse or trauma—is not necessary for the development of a core sense of shame, it is a powerful source of shame. The women's accounts drew my attention to the role of overt shaming in the development of body shame. Eight of the thirteen women spontaneously reported having been shamed by a parent for their body's shape or weight.

Rebecca was both let down by her father's inconsistency and put down by a remark he made about her body. His remark no doubt cut especially deep because she longed for his approval: "I remember distinctly when I was 13, he made a comment about my butt [*clears her throat*], that I had a big butt. And forever and ever I will never forget that. And then I'm sure that triggered off a lot of, 'Well, if I can lose weight, then maybe my dad will think I'm more attractive as a young woman.' So it had a great influence."

Beth's father, in saying that if she lost five pounds she might win her next race, shamed her for her body. Beth recalls other critical remarks he made during a time when she was not overweight but merely developing a woman's body: "My father used to make comments about how I looked. I did gain weight that freshman year . . . And I did put on some weight as an adolescent. And he used to make comments about how I looked like a peasant and stuff, and I filled out and everything. So I do remember feeling bad about my body."

Amy, age 26 and a supervisor in a corporation, recalls that her father criticized her eating and her body and yet set her up to overeat by stocking the house with foods he knew she found irresistible:

> He would make comments like "Stop eating all that chocolate, that's why you're fat," or something like that. "You should learn how to control yourself." And what he would do is he'd go out and buy—which used to bother my mother because we didn't have control, my mother didn't have control, and I didn't have control—anyway, so he would go out and buy all these cookies and chocolates and put them in the house and expect us to have control and not eat them all. But my mother and I, we'd eat them all. 'Cause we didn't have control.

When Amy's father learned that she had overdosed on laxatives, he responded with cruelty and abuse:

> We leave the hospital, and my mom was like, "I'm getting you into a counselor," and I'm like, "No, Dad would kill me." She comes back and tells my dad that I took laxatives, and he slaps me across the face and says what am I, a drug addict? He was very, very, very tacky about the whole thing. "How could you do that?" And my mom was like, "She's gotta go see a counselor." He's like, "I'm not payin' money for her to see a counselor, I don't believe in those shrinks," and just was really ugly.

It is not surprising that abuse, whether physical, sexual, or mental, contributes to a core sense of shame, because abuse, by its very nature, involves an effort to demean someone. And it is not surprising that trauma leads to a core sense of shame, because trauma, by its very nature, leaves one feeling out of control of oneself and therefore vulnerable to a sense of inadequacy. In the face of abuse and trauma, a person may protect herself by dissociating, or psychically disconnecting, from aspects of her experience.

But as Bessel van der Kolk (1996) observes, if abuse is happening in the home, that home is probably not a place where a child experiences attunement to her emotional needs. She suffers not only from the cruelty, abuse, and trauma but also from chronic emotional neglect. She therefore does not internalize a capacity to affirm, soothe, and enliven herself. Given a core sense of shame, as well as a reliance upon dissociation as a defense and a deficit of self-structure and self-regulating capacity (discussed later in this chapter), she does not learn to attune to her self-experience. She is therefore at great risk for self-neglect and loss of control because she does not accurately read and regulate her physical and psychological states.

Jessie, age 25 and a supervisor in a corporation, attributes the development of her eating disorders—first anorexia nervosa and then bulimia nervosa—to sexual abuse in her childhood: "If this is the right word, the crux of it all, would be sexual abuse by my father." She also recalls emotional abuse:

> My mother is overweight. And she was probably, back when I was a very young child, a size twelve or a size fourteen. Not what you would call fat, but large. And my father hated fat. And he would torment her to a degree, but because she was an adult and a strong woman, she could say to shut up. But to me, my mother at the time worked nights, and I would be alone with him, . . . and it was, "You're fat." "You're a fat pig." "Nobody's gonna love you as long as you're fat." Things like that. He'd make me do exercise, strenuous calisthenics, me, as a small child. And one incident stands out so vividly. We were watching *Willy Wonka and the Chocolate Factory* one night, and I had to do thirty extra sit-ups because I was watching *Willy Wonka and the Chocolate Factory*. He was—now I can say it: he had problems.

She believes she started eating compulsively to numb herself to the abuse: "I think what brought the overweight on was, and this is from what my mother tells me, I never wanted to really do anything. I was very content to stay in front of the TV with the bag of candy . . . And I have to think that that was a way to suppress what was going on mentally and physically with my father. So as I gained and gained and gained and became a fat child, so his abuse grew as well."

Despite the abuse, Jessie yearned to be adored as "Daddy's girl." She felt shamed both by her father's humiliating treatment of her and by his emotional neglect:

> I was this wonderful, innocent, little child, and he couldn't see that . . . I never recall a moment in my life where I can honestly say I loved my father. And felt comfortable with my father. And felt like, "Oh, I'm Daddy's girl." Never. It was, "Oh, my God, Dad's home. Oh, no, what's he gonna yell at me for?" Or "What's he gonna say mean to me?" Or "Is he gonna embarrass me in front of my friends?" Like if my friends and I were in the yard, he'd say, "Wanna go to the park?" And we'd say, "Yeah, let's go to the park!" And our town had this great park with this swing set and slides and everything. And he'd take us down there, and my friends would get to play, and I'd have to jog laps around the park.

Someone who suffers early abuse and neglect can perpetuate mistreatment of herself long after the original abuse has stopped. For years, Jessie put up with cruelty and neglect from a boyfriend. Not until she began to sense her own worth could she identify his treatment as demeaning and unacceptable:

> I think if I had been in a normal state of mind from the day we met to however long, the relationship would've ended much, much sooner. But I think because I was sick and in a weak state mentally, I wasn't feeling worthwhile, I wasn't feeling great about myself, I thought this guy was okay. "Well, he's kind of an asshole, but what else am I gonna get?" . . .
>
> 'Cause when you don't like yourself and you're in a relationship, I think you tend to focus more on the other person because you don't feel worthwhile, and so you focus your attentions on him, and it's fine if he doesn't focus his attentions on you 'cause you don't feel that you're worth it, so this is okay. And then as you begin to feel that you're worth it, and he's not focusin'

anything on you, you begin to think, "This isn't right. This is supposed to be give and take, fifty-fifty, and this isn't happening. This is 'Me, me, me, me.' Well, I'm here now. And I want a little me."

And ultimately it ended like that. We were engaged, and I broke the engagement . . . And there were absolutely no regrets at all. It was like that was the final piece of mending my life . . . I think so many people stay in bad relationships because they feel that's all they deserve.

Amy's experience, too, illustrates that abuse and neglect in childhood can contribute to a woman's staying in an abusive or exploitative relationship. Amy tries to explain why she got involved with a man who abused drugs, lied to her, pressured her to have sex, and borrowed money from her without paying it back: "He was such a smooth talker . . . He liked talkin' to me and asked me all kinds of questions and was being very complimentary. That's probably why, because he was so into me . . . No one had ever been like him. He was very into me like no one else had ever been." Because she had never felt special to a man, she was vulnerable to the first man who expressed interest in her. She was so starved for affirmation that she accepted it even from someone who offered it instrumentally in the service of his own needs. Because she did not know her own worth, she tolerated disrespect and thereby perpetuated her sense of unworthiness.

Isabella, age 31 and about to begin a master's program in social work, was molested around the ages of 14 and 15, first by her brother-in-law and then by a friend's father. After these incidents, she experienced shame and guilt:

> Especially 'cause it happened to me with two different people. I thought, "Well, what is it about me that makes people do this to me?"
>
> *There must be something—?*
>
> Wrong with me.

Shame-accentuating trauma can come in various forms, including physical infirmity. For Isabella, being diagnosed with diabetes at age 11 contributed to her feeling ashamed of her body: "I always felt, especially after the diabetes—I don't remember really anything before the diabetes, before I was 11—but when I first got that, I felt just dirty and would take three or four showers a day. So I didn't feel comfortable with myself." The effects of this trauma were exacerbated by emotional neglect. Isabella wished her parents would learn about diabetes and appreciate her experience of the disease. Instead, she felt they were entirely uninvolved and uninterested. When she began to date, she chose men who were overcontrolling but who initially seemed willing to get involved in her life. She mistook control for care:

> Basically, [my parents] don't know what I'm supposed to be doing. To this day, I've had it for twenty years. So when you're 11, that's hard. Now I can take care of myself and do it. So I was always trying to fill this need, did it with men a lot, I think. I was very promiscuous . . .
>
> *Sort of wanting a man to step in and take care of—*
>
> Take over, yeah, take care of me. And that's what happened with him, [my ex-husband], too, because he was very domineering.

DISSOCIATION FROM SELF-EXPERIENCE

Bulimics use bingeing in part to disconnect, or dissociate, from painful thoughts and feelings. Todd Heatherton and Roy Baumeister (1991) propose that "binge eating is motivated by a desire to escape from self-awareness":

> Binge eaters suffer from high standards and expectations, especially an acute sensitivity to the difficult (perceived) demands of others. When they fall short of these standards, they develop an aversive pattern of high self-awareness, characterized by unflattering views of self and concern over how they are perceived by others. These aversive self-perceptions are accompanied by emotional distress, which often includes anxiety and depression. To escape from this unpleasant state, binge eaters attempt the cognitive response of narrowing attention to the immediate stimulus environment and avoiding broadly meaningful thought. (86)

What Heatherton and Baumeister call "self-awareness" I would call self-consciousness. *Self-awareness,* as I use it, does not imply self-consciousness and shame but rather attuned connection to one's present, subjective experience. What they regard as an effort to "escape" I would call an attempt to defend against painful affect, including the pain of the shame that is inherent in self-consciousness. Heatherton and Baumeister's theory of escape is consistent with my understanding that the women had not been sensing self-experience because when they focused inward they felt unbearable inadequacy and shame and experienced unmanageable chaos and fragmentation. For instance, Jill, age 30, an officer in a bank, in explaining why she got stuck at the fourth step of her Alcoholics Anonymous program (making "a searching and fearless moral inventory"), suggests that taking the inventory aroused such overwhelming shame that each time she tried to do it she binged and purged to escape the shame. Jill's recovery from bulimia nervosa was entwined with her recovery from alcoholism:

> The steps after that are really looking at yourself, with the fourth step where you take a personal inventory, and the fifth step you tell someone. And then you start looking at your defects, character, and what you wanna change. I couldn't do any of that. Couldn't do it. Anytime I'd think about it, I'd start bingeing and purging. So I just couldn't make that next step. And I have a bad habit of comparing myself to my peers, and they were doing the steps, and how come I'm stuck and they're not? So it's time to look at what the problem is here. So when I started to deal with the eating, then I was able to work on those steps.

The theory of escape is also consistent with the observation that eating-disorder symptoms are in part dissociative defenses, constructed in response to deficits in self-structure and self-regulatory capacities. I use the term *dissociation* to mean, in the words of Etzel Cardeña, "that two or more mental processes or contents are not associated or integrated" (1994, 15), with the result that consciousness, memory, identity, and perception are to some extent disconnected and not experienced as a whole (APA, 1994). Dissociation exists on a continuum. In everyday life, we experience it as "spacing out"; in more profound forms, dissociation can result in radically unintegrated self-states. Although the links between bulimia nervosa and dissociation are not precisely understood, researchers and clinicians find that people with bulimia nervosa are prone to dissociation (Sands, 1991; Everill, Waller, and Macdonald, 1995).

Susan Sands points out that "many bulimic patients are expert at dissociation" and that bulimics "portray their bingeing episodes as one might describe a trance state, drug trip, or delirium. Most become wholly identified with—'taken over' by—the bulimic self-state" (1991, 40). Jessie describes dissociation:

> It served as a cover-up almost. Yeah, a cover-up I would say, because psychologically I didn't have to deal with all this shit that I knew was in here, in my head. This protected me. I knew that I didn't like myself very much. I knew that I didn't like the way I looked. I knew vaguely that somebody in a position of authority over me, my father, had already told me nobody was gonna love me, and this was covering it up. This was a way to deal with those feelings without actually having to deal with them, if that makes any sense at all. This dealt with it, but to a subconscious degree . . .
>
> You're almost in a trance, if you will, because you're living and you're participating in life, but there's a whole lot that you have to deal with emotionally, psychologically, that your mind isn't ready to deal with. So it kinda shuts off and says, "We're gonna do this now." And that becomes the primary focus. It forces you to have that as your primary focus. That's all you care about. Work is secondary, school is secondary, life is secondary. This is the most important thing, this eating disorder. Because if we don't have this to focus on, we're gonna have to deal with all the bad crap. So it becomes, not a distraction really, but a protective mechanism almost like your brain puts in place. "Do this, this'll get rid of that." And it does.

But, as Sands notes, people with bulimia nervosa rely upon the defense of dissociation to such an extent that they ultimately develop an established, dissociated, "split-off bulimic *self*, with needs, feelings, and perceptions quite different from the patient's ordinary self-experience" (1991, 34). When a child's genuine needs and affects are met with chronically inadequate empathy by caregivers, the "needs and affects are disavowed, repressed, or split off from the total self-structure" (35). As a result, the child not only fails to internalize self-structure but also, eventually, creates a new, separate self-system with the split-off aspects of self. Then, "when the individual later begins to experiment with bulimia, the biochemical effects of the binge-purge cycle create an altered state that serves to reinforce the already existing split in the psyche and further organizes the dissociated needs into a bulimic self. The split-off state becomes associated with the bulimia, and the bulimic behavior becomes a way of voluntarily accessing this hidden self" (39–40). That is, the person "invents a new restitutive system by which disordered eating patterns rather than people are used to meet self-object needs, because previous attempts with caregivers have brought disappointment, frustration, or even abuse" (35).

Rebecca's memory of the years during which she was bulimic conveys the unreal quality of a dissociated experience:

> I feel like it's somebody else's life that I'm reflecting back on, I don't feel like it's my own. Because the pain, I think, is the most real out of all of it, but the behaviors and a lot of the terrible things that I did, I think for my own healing purposes, too, I kind of have separated from it . . . I kind of don't even know that person, that feeling. I mean, I know it's me, and obviously I still feel a lot of pain and a lot of remorse about certain things about it, but in a lot of ways I feel kind of like it was somebody else. Living in that hell was—I know about it firsthand, maybe I read a novel that was very intense. That's how it feels, that it was an experience that I can identify with that someone else had gone through, but it was never actually me. Till I really go a little bit deeper, and obviously it was me.

When "eating rituals are substituted for self-object responsiveness," Sands argues, the person's development is "derailed" because "the early needs remain split off and cannot be integrated into the adult personality" (36–37). To foster integration, therapists must appreciate that the dissociated bulimic self is "at bottom a body self" and that it "is usually mute when therapy begins" because it does not believe that words can communicate internally felt experience (40–41): "Indeed, eating-disordered patients themselves indicate their lack of belief in verbal communication when, for example, they express the conviction that asking for what they want won't work. And it is precisely because they do not believe in the effectiveness of words that, when they do begin to assert their needs, they often either act them out or verbalize them in such a way as to insure that they do not get what they are asking for" (41).

Like Sands, Rizzuto (1988) notes bulimics' dissociation of language and affect:

> These patients are able to use language effectively in everyday life . . . Their speech is articulate and, at times, elegant. They are able to express emotion about events that do not concern them directly . . . What seems impaired in these patients is the affective and self-referential component of speech. They cannot use language to reveal themselves to others or to understand the intent of others to communicate intimately with them . . . Bulimarexics believe that their words have no impact on other people. (370)

Rizzuto attributes this disconnection of language and affect to the child's not having experienced complementary communication with a caregiver. The child's early success or failure at communicating her subjective experience to others shapes her attitude toward the usefulness or uselessness of language. When the child experiences herself as able to communicate effectively with her caregivers, she internalizes the sense of attunement and consequently develops a favorable attitude toward communication.

But if a child repeatedly experiences herself as ineffective in communicating her internal states to others, she eventually gives up on the effort. Without a sense of the effectiveness of her gestures, facial expressions, and sounds, she learns to dissociate language from affect. In her experience, a person's voice and words do not have the power to touch another person emotionally. She therefore does not attempt to let others in on her internal world or to let others' words make emotional contact with her. As Rizzuto points out, a bulimic uses words to hide rather than reveal her subjective experience: "Words can be used to refer to things— even to oneself as a thing—but not to understand or reveal oneself as a feeling individual. Similarly, words would be heard in the same dissociated manner to prevent them from making emotional contact . . . The child defends against the repetition of the trauma of failed affective contact . . . because he/she has already experienced the pain of words without affect. As a result, the child avoids communication" (374, 376).

Meg describes the dissociation of language and affect when she recalls convincing a psychiatrist that she was just experimenting with dieting and was not in serious trouble. When I ask if she thinks her eating disorder might have taken a different course if the psychiatrist had "gotten it," Meg replies:

> I don't know if she could've gotten it though. I don't think I was gonna let her get it. I didn't think that at the time, but that was just who I was. I knew that she needed to think that I was okay . . . And so I answered all the questions correctly. I was talkative enough that it didn't appear that I had canned responses. I even had appropriate emotions.

You kind of knew you were doing that?

> No, I didn't. But now I know. But now I see that the reason why it was so hard for me to see, and for anyone else to see, was because everything was appropriate. I remember in college feeling that I was having the correct emotions, but they weren't meaning anything to me . . . You couldn't tell that anything was wrong at all. People who have some sort of psychological problems, usually you can tell that they're depressed or they're moody. But I don't think there was any indication at all. I could cry at the right times. I could be sad about things. Appearingly. I could be happy. I could do anything. I was a really great little puppet. But it didn't mean anything.

DEFICITS IN SELF-STRUCTURE AND SELF-REGULATION

Bulimic women tend to have an impaired ability to regulate their physical and emotional states. As Alan Goodsitt (1983) notes:

> Be it food, impulses, moods, behaviors, or relationships, these patients either swing wildly from one extreme to the other, or they find one end of the spectrum and remain frozen there. They are deficient in self-esteem and tension-regulation. They rely on external cues such as obsessively counting calories to determine how much to eat. When they are unable to do this, they vomit to control their food intake. Internal psychic mechanisms of self-regulation are not reliable. If this disorder is anything, it is a disorder of deficient self-regulation. (54)

The women indicate that they avoided sensing self-experience because doing so would have elicited shame, and they did not feel able to regulate or tolerate shame and other painful feelings. Self-psychological concepts of self-structure and self-regulation help explain their difficulty in tolerating the painful affect attendant to sensing self-experience (Goodsitt, 1983, 1985, 1997; Geist, 1985, 1989; Sands, 1991). From a self-psychological perspective, eating disorders can be understood as "disorders of the self" which "develop due to chronic disturbance in the empathic interplay between the growing child and the caregiving environment" (Sands, 1991, 35). To develop a healthy sense of self, a child needs attunement and empathy from her caregivers, who must accurately read and respond to her basic narcissistic needs so that she experiences soothing when she needs calm, enlivening when she needs stimulation, and affirming when she needs coherence. Attuned, empathic responses to the child's basic narcissistic needs are called self-object functions: they are provided by the other, or object, but are experienced as part of the self and as essential to the self. Caregivers' attuned responsiveness need not be perfect, but, to use D. W. Winnicott's term, it must be "good enough" so that a child can internalize the self-functions that were originally served by her caregivers and thereby develop the capacity to soothe, enliven, and affirm herself.

When a child does not receive good enough empathy and attunement, she does not internalize self-soothing, self-enlivening, and self-affirming functions and does not develop the adequate self-structure that such internalization makes possible. Sands explains that when "the child's genuine narcissistic needs, as well as the affects that surround them . . . are not empathically responded to," the child is vulnerable to experiences of "fragmentation and depletion" (35). For someone who feels chronically chaotic or empty inside, the obsessions and compulsions of an eating disorder can provide a sense of internal coherence and can serve to calm, stimulate, and numb. As problematic as the symptoms are, they protect her from the disintegration and internal collapse she would otherwise experience.

Goodsitt proposes that people with eating disorders use eating-disorder symptoms and other intense physical experience to vanquish painful emotions: "Often these are emergency measures to drown out anguished feelings of deadness, emptiness, boredom, aimlessness, and the tension experienced concomitant with these feelings" (1983, 54). The women indicate that while their behavior did numb them to painful feelings, it also derived from an impaired ability to sense less intense self-experience. Beth says: "I never knew when I was full 'cause I always felt like I didn't know if I was hungry or full. My whole life I never knew when I was full or hungry unless I was really stuffed or really starving."

It appears that Beth's difficulty in sensing her own experience not only derived from her deficits in self-regulatory functions but also perpetuated her disconnection from her emotional and physical states and her difficulty in regulating those states: "Like that it's not normal to sleep four hours a night. I didn't know that. I just never thought about it. Nobody ever told me what normal was, and I just didn't know. Or that it can be abusive to drink that much caffeine. You can feel really awful. And you can not sleep well, too. And that contributes, for me it contributed to the bingeing and the being out of control."

We can understand a bulimic's increasingly intense affect and behavior as deriving from emotional neglect. If she chronically failed to elicit acknowledgment of her pain and to recruit comfort or relief, she may have learned that her only chance of getting someone to attend to her emotional distress was to make her distress visible and irrefutable. If even this did not work, she may have learned to keep upping the ante of her behavior and affect in hope of finally getting the attention she desperately needed. Having worked herself up into a state of intense distress but having failed to elicit attuned responses from others, and with no internalized capacity to tolerate distress or provide comfort or relief for herself, she may have needed to numb herself against her own experience because it would otherwise have felt unbearable. Once she had disconnected from her subjective experience, to reintegrate she would have had to increase the intensity of her physical and affective states in order to sense self-experience at all. Without an internalized self-regulatory capacity, and having disconnected from her felt experience, she would lack a working gauge of enoughness. She would know no limits. She would not know when enough was enough.

One way we internalize self-regulatory functions and build self-structure is through what Winnicott termed *transitional objects*. Transitional objects enable a child to move from depending upon an external person or environment to soothe her, enliven her, and organize her internal experience to relying upon internal psychic structure to fulfill those same self-object functions. Some object-relational theorists have proposed that people with eating disorders use the body as a transitional object (Sugarman and Kurash, 1982). But Goodsitt points out that eating-disorder symptoms do not foster the internalization of self-object functions and therefore do not promote the building of self-structure. Rather, he says, "the symptoms are misguided attempts to organize affects and internal states" (1983, 59).

Sands makes a similar argument: "The problem with the new restitutive system organized around food or other substances is that it does not 'work,' because the self-regulatory functions it provides, while often seductively powerful in the moment, are only temporary . . . The individual remains dependent on using an external agent or action to fill in for missing internal structure" (1991, 36). But Sands does not see the use of the symptoms as entirely misguided. By looking to food rather than people to meet self-object needs, "the eating-disordered individual tries to circumvent the need for human self-object responsiveness and to avoid further disappointment and shame. Food is seen as trustworthy, while people are not" (35). An eating disorder may actually be an effort to protect and preserve a relationship by "relieving the relationship of the burden of having to meet the individual's self-object needs" (35).

Beth's symptoms substituted for responsive human relationships when those were nowhere to be found:

> I needed [my eating disorder] in a way 'cause I didn't have other coping skills. I remember being in the college infirmary and walkin' out, and I was so lonely and in so much pain, and I didn't know what else to do besides go eat a bag of bagels, and that's what I went and did. And it was the only thing, I didn't wanna do it, but it was the only thing I knew how to do. I didn't have a friend to whom I could say, "I'm so lonely, I can't stop." I didn't have

parents to call who would support me and say, "We understand, we love you anyway." It was like I didn't have anything but that.

I feel like it was really a process of seeing that there was something else for me, that I couldn't stop the behavior when there was nothing else there for me, and that it was really a long process of people—a therapist, a best friend, people in OA, my husband whom I met—that there were a lot of things that started to replace that need for food, to be so skinny, or whatever.

Because bulimic women do not know how to soothe themselves in the face of painful feelings, they experience the feelings as intolerable. Because they do not know that all feelings are ultimately self-limiting, they experience feeling bad as an unbearable *chronic condition* that will never end. Given their core sense of shame, they interpret painful feelings as evidence of a permanent, unacceptable *character trait* ("Feeling angry just proves what an evil person I am"; "Being upset by this situation shows what a weak person I am"), rather than as a temporary emotional *state* ("I am angry and upset") with variable and manageable intensity. A bulimic woman experiences painful affect as unbearable and attempts to end it by employing major—and typically self-destructive—coping strategies that only leave her feeling worse about herself. Her structural deficits compound her sense of inadequacy because, in a very real way, she is not adequately equipped to regulate her internal states.

DEVELOPMENTAL DEMANDS

That the onset of bulimia nervosa typically occurs during late adolescence or early adulthood suggests that it is developmentally precipitated. For all young people, the physical changes of puberty and the developmental tasks of adolescence pose challenges to the sense of self. In Western and westernized cultures, the developmental tasks of separating from one's family of origin, asserting one's libidinal and aggressive strivings, defining one's identity in new and competitive contexts, seeking belonging in new domains, and negotiating the world of sexual relationships all present situations in which adolescents are apt to be vulnerable to a sense of shame. Although adolescence is inevitably a time of heightened self-consciousness, for someone who arrives at adolescence with an internalized sense of shame and an impaired ability to remain connected to self-experience, awkwardness and uncertainty are especially difficult to tolerate. For such a person, normal developmental experiences of comparison, envy, and competition may overwhelm her capacity to tolerate shame and threaten to shatter her brittle sense of worth.

For instance, four women referred to their class background as having occasioned intense shame. Moving to a college or another new community in which they felt lower class precipitated feelings of inferiority, inadequacy, and shame. Being in a context in which unfamiliar, higher-class values and expectations prevail is a situation which might be difficult for any young person but which is devastating for someone with a core sense of shame about her self.

In an attempt to retain or regain some sense of control and worth, a girl with a core sense of shame who encounters adolescent challenges to her sense of worth may begin to diet. Dieting is a common, immediate precipitant for an eating disorder. Not all dieting leads to an eating disorder, but many if not most eating disorders are preceded by dieting.

SOCIALIZATION OF GIRLS AND WOMEN

In the United States, 1 to 3 percent of college-age women meet diagnostic criteria for bulimia nervosa (Drewnowski, Hopkins, and Kessler, 1988; Drewnowski, Yee, and Krahn, 1988; Pyle et al., 1991). Women are more at risk for bulimia nervosa than men, a fact that some attribute to sociocultural factors: the overvaluation of a thin, androgynous, prepubescent body-type for women; the devaluation of what is feminine, including the natural contours of women's bodies; the objectification of women, by which girls and women learn to regard their bodies as objects to be shaped and controlled; the internalization of a critical, objectifying gaze, by which girls and women continually evaluate their bodies as erotic objects; and the socialization of girls and women to respond to others' needs, desires, and expectations but not to recognize or meet their own (Orbach, 1986).

For young women, usual adolescent threats to the sense of self are exacerbated by cultural messages to conform to a standard of beauty that is impossible for most women to attain. The culture idealizes and even normalizes an extremely thin, childlike body-type for women, one very few women can naturally achieve and healthfully maintain. Given that the culture equates thinness in women with happiness, intelligence, success, and popularity, and given that it trains young men to find thinness and childlike features erotic, young women are especially at risk for trying to achieve thinness at any cost.

Abigail recalls envying anorexic women at college: "I also remember this woman I thought was just beautiful, and she was anorexic. And, Marlena was her name, and she lived in this dorm, and she had anorexia . . . Here are these people that I sort of admired in a way 'cause they seemed like they were socially desirable . . . like this anorexic woman just really getting this positive reinforcement or seeing other people get positive reinforcement for being really thin."

Isabella learned early on that her worth was based in her appearance: "I had really low, low self-esteem, and I thought the only thing that would keep me going is to look perfect. I've been told . . . since I was young, people always just said, 'Oh, you're so cute,' and blah, blah, blah, and that just kind of stuck, like that's my only worth."

Rebecca learned as a young woman that men valued her for her sexual appeal:

> That was what I thrived on all through college. I went out every single weekend and wore the most revealing outfit I could possibly get away with without being overly promiscuous about it. I just, I thrived on that. It was very fulfilling for me. And it reinforced me staying at such a low weight because I got the acknowledgment from men that I never got in other ways in the past, and I could make myself attractive . . . I remember going out and being at clubs thinking, "This is all worthwhile. I'll kill myself all week." Definitely demented when you look on it now, but I remember thinking that . . . And so all I learned through my four years of college is that you were kind of an item, you were an object, men were attracted to me because of the way I dressed and I appeared but not because they knew me.

Yet not all young women in this culture develop eating disorders. What distinguishes those who do from those who do not? Catherine Steiner-Adair (1984) suggests that girls who identify with society's image and expectations of women are more likely to have difficulty with their eating than are those who make their own independent judgments about what they value in women. Perhaps girls who can make independent judgments about what they value in women are better able to sense self-experience. Conversely, girls who identify with society's image and expectations of women may have difficulty sensing self-experience and may therefore be vulnerable to orienting to others' preferences rather than to their own. When they orient solely by the compass of others' needs, expectations, and approval and do not consult their own needs, interests, and desires, these young women get dreadfully lost. When they orient to a culture that objectifies women and expects women to conform to an impossible standard of beauty, young women are at risk for turning off onto a path that leads to an eating disorder.

Lyn Mikel Brown and Carol Gilligan (1992) observe that between the ages of 11 and 16 girls tend to lose their voice and their trust in their perceptions of themselves and their world. I hear this theme of the loss of self-trust and the silencing of self in the accounts of the women I interviewed. Brown and Gilligan and other researchers (Gilligan, Rogers, and Tolman, 1991; Jack, 1991) and clinicians (Pipher, 1994) have found that girls and women come to believe they need to silence their authentic experience to preserve their relationships. In my research and clinical work, I have found that while women with eating disorders locate the beginning of their symptoms around ages 14–18, they typically identify an earlier age—between 8 and 13—as the point at which they began to develop disabling self-doubt and self-condemnation. As third and fourth graders, they began to believe they needed to be other than who they were. Self-doubt and self-condemnation perpetuate disconnection from self-experience.

Katy Aisenberg (1994) claims that the culture has normalized girls' disconnection from their own experience: "For girls in this society, to become engendered is to become able to dissociate from our experiences, our opinions, our emotions, bodies, and voices . . . I believe that our culture promotes, represents, and rewards dissociation in women and that the idealized state of femininity is itself a fugue state." Aisenberg, who attributes dissociation in women not only to culture but also to relational experiences, sees dissociation as a continuum and proposes that eating disorders can be described as dissociative disorders.

The culture has also normalized a way of regarding women's bodies as assemblages of reshapeable parts. Jean Kilbourne (1979, 1987) finds that printed advertisements tell a story of how women are objectified in our culture. In particular, women are portrayed as part objects; that is, a part of the person—hair, breasts, legs—is used to represent a whole person. Kilbourne argues that objectification and part objectification are first steps toward dehumanization of the other, which is the first step toward violence. Given that eating disorders are a form of self-destructive behavior, of violence against the self, they can be understood as girls' and young women's internalization of a dehumanizing regard.

Anne Becker (1997) points out that an extremely thin body-type has become normalized in American culture—and in many other Americanized cultures—in part because of a deeply rooted cultural belief that anything is attainable. We have been taught the myth that we can do or acquire or be anything we want. This myth can lead us to focus on constructing the self we want to be rather than on being who we are. In this era of bodysculpting, liposuction, and plastic surgery, we may get the impression that we can mold our bodies to the culture's specifications—trim here, build there, firm here, tone there. The culture promotes denial of the reality that many aspects of our bodies are not reshapeable, are reshapeable only to a limited extent, or are reshapeable only by extreme, unnatural, unhealthy means. The cultural belief that we can acquire or do or be anything perpetuates intolerance of diversity. A climate of intolerance exacerbates shame and doubt about the body self and promotes violence toward the self.

The culture of the family is a main means by which the larger culture's values are transmitted to children. Young women who grow up in a larger culture and a family culture which regard them as part objects and as inherently not good enough may be especially vulnerable to experiencing a dissociated and fragmented sense of self. Richard Geist (1989) notes that eating-disordered women experience a "shattered sense of wholeness":

> Patients report a long history of fragmentation-producing responses. These responses include overattention to bodily appearances with total or partial disregard of inner feelings; scrutiny of momentary behaviors, but a denial of their temporal or spacial relativity; and preoccupation with negative aspects of their performance while denying the joy and pride inherent in the total production. In other words, when the eating-disorder patient peered into the mirror of the parents, she perceived not the sustaining reflection of her whole body self, but a prismatic image of isolated parts. (17)

Jessie's account suggests that disordered eating results from complex interactions among social values, social pressures, body-type, and a child's experience in the family. Her father's shaming of her body during her childhood affected Jessie's interpretations of social experiences in adolescence, and her interpretations confirmed and perpetuated her sense of shame and inadequacy:

> I think great pressure is put on young women. And even small kids. I think there's too much emphasis on body image . . . 'Cause I remember, what he'd say to me: "You're fat and nobody's ever gonna love you." When I was 4, sittin' on the couch and eatin' a Snickers bar, I didn't care. When I was 14 and startin' high school, that's what immediately popped into my head . . .
>
> I don't know if it's because around that age I was very heavy. And all my friends were dating, your little eighth-grade and ninth-grade dates to the dance or whatever. And I wasn't. And clothes were becoming more important. When you're a teenage girl, clothes are important. When you're 8 or 9 or 10, you're out swingin' off the tree, you don't care what you look like. But now you're goin' to the dance, and you wanna look nice. And you wanna wear the good styles that all your friends are wearin'. And you're set apart.
>
> I was set apart. I was fat. I was different. I didn't wanna be different . . . And I think those words started to echo in my mind. I was beginning to realize that I was different. 'Cause for a long time, when I was maybe 9, 10, 11, I thought I was wonderful. I loved myself, I thought I was great, I would get up and do anything, and play anything, and I thought I was fantastic . . .

'Cause I didn't know I was different then. It didn't matter. And then I got to realize that I was different and then the words came back. "You're fat. Nobody's gonna love you." And certain things came back, and I think that mighta triggered it . . . Boys didn't wanna dance with me. And then you look around and say "Oh, what's wrong? Must be me."

Joan Jacobs Brumberg (1997) has used diaries written by American girls between the 1830s and the 1990s to trace and illustrate the historical changes that have contributed to girls' learning to hate their bodies. She observes that medicine and the media have "created a new, more exacting ideal of physical perfection" (xxv). Girls today "make their body their central project," and the body "is at the heart of the crisis of confidence" that researchers of girls' development have documented (xxiv). Brumberg links girls' tendency to regard the body as a project with the prevalence of eating disorders: "Adolescent girls today face the issues girls have always faced—Who am I? Who do I want to be?—but their answers, more than ever before, revolve around the body" (xxiv).

BIOLOGICAL VULNERABILITY

Biologically based aspects of temperament, neurobiological sequelae of trauma, and neurobiological effects of emotional neglect may all leave one vulnerable to being emotionally overwhelmed to the point of needing to disconnect from self-experience.

Biologically based aspects of temperament may affect how readily one is physiologically aroused by stimuli, how easily one is soothed, and how readily one recruits attuned, empathic responses from caregivers (Kagan, 1989). For instance, if a child has a physiologically based temperamental proclivity to be fearful of unfamiliar stimuli, she may not only be prone to being emotionally overwhelmed, but her parents may experience her as frustrating and find it difficult to remain attuned to her, especially if they do not understand her temperamental predisposition and if they themselves have a different temperament (Chess and Thomas, 1987). Thus both her temperament and the responses to it may impair her ability to experience and internalize self-soothing functions.

Her parents' difficulty in attuning to her may also leave her feeling emotionally neglected and shamed.

Trauma alters the brain's structures and neurochemical functioning, and therefore its biological effects persist long after the actual traumatic event. Memory, learning, the capacity to use emotions as signals, the ability to regulate one's state of arousal, and the ability of one's body to modulate the stress response may all be impaired (van der Kolk, 1996). People who have suffered trauma may have a biological vulnerability to emotional dysregulation—that is, difficulty in modulating their emotional states—because their ability to soothe and enliven themselves is weakened and consequently their ability to tolerate the affect attendant to sensing self-experience is impeded. To the extent that trauma interferes with one's ability to consolidate a memory of experience, it may undermine one's sense of self-continuity and identity.

Allan Schore (1994) emphasizes that from the beginning, our experience affects our brain's development and our brain's development in turn affects the way we experience things. Early development occurs in the relational context of infant and caregiver, and therefore "the infant's affective interactions with the early human social environment directly and indelibly influence the postnatal development of brain structures that will regulate all future socioemotional functioning" (xxx). That is, the caregiver's ability to serve as an attuned mediator and modulator of an infant's experience of her physical and social environment not only affects the child's subjective experience in any moment but also influences the development of her brain and therefore affects how her brain will process experience in the future. According to Schore, our experience affects even the expression of our genes: "It is now accepted that early postnatal development represents an experiential shaping of genetic potential" (16).

An Insubstantial Sense of Identity

Although bulimic women are clinically observed to suffer from disturbances in identity, there is little empirical research on identity in bulimic women. One exception is a study by Erika Schupack-Neuberg and Carol Nemeroff (1993), who found that bulimic women are more likely than either women who binge eat but do not purge or normal controls to show identity disturbance and to use bingeing as an escape from self-awareness.

The work I find most useful in thinking about the women's experience of identity is by Erik Erikson and Gershen Kaufman. Erikson uses the phrase *a sense of identity* to refer to three senses: (1) a sense of individuality or self-specificness, which one of his patients called "oneliness" (1959/1980, 149); (2) an experience of "selfsameness," which he describes as "a *subjective sense* of an *invigorating sameness* and *continuity*" in time and space (1968, 19); and (3) a mutual recognition of one's identity, the sense that significant others recognize one's uniqueness and continuity. Thus for Erikson "an optimal sense of identity" involves soma, psyche, and social context: "Its most obvious concomitants are a feeling of being at home in one's body, a sense of 'knowing where one is going,' and an inner assuredness of anticipated recognition from those who count" (1959/1980, 127–128). In describing the fifth age of man, Erikson calls the virtue that derives from the tension between identity and role confusion *fidelity*, by which he means "something and somebody to be true to" (1968, 235). In the process of recovering, the "something and somebody" to which the women needed to be true was their own self-experience. Being faithful to themselves required high fidelity, the ability to accurately receive and respond to the signals of oneself.

A core sense of shame can lead to perfectionism and to what might be called *infidelity* to self. Kaufman (1974) notes that when we feel defective, "awareness of difference between self and other becomes translated automatically into a comparison of good versus bad, better versus worse" (572). Our differentness is then a danger: "Rather than valuing that difference, we feel obliged to stamp it out and strive instead for perfection, that last hope of making up for our basic underlying sense of being defective" (572).

Rebecca developed a false identity based on pseudomaturity. She says: "One of the ways of becoming mature is knowing yourself and becoming familiar with yourself and more comfortable with yourself. And I think in a lot of ways I was very immature . . . looking back, I think I was very, very mature for my age because I always had to be very responsible and just took on those outward characteristics of being a very responsible young adult or teenager or whatever. But I don't think I was very mature in how I dealt with myself and how I saw things." She learned from her mother's example that it was important to be perfect even though that required creating an inauthentic self: "My mother is very much a perfectionist, and I see a lot of my qualities that are similar to hers now as I have more of a perspective on things . . . those are a lot of the things that drive you into trying to change yourself or make yourself to be something that you may not be."

Many of the women report problems with memory, including Amy, who says, "My whole childhood experience is a complete blank to me." If one's ability to sense self-experience is impaired or impeded, one may not remember one's lived experience and may therefore have a disrupted sense of self-sameness and self-continuity, that is, an impaired sense of identity.

An impaired ability to sense substantial aspects of self may in turn leave one vulnerable to defining oneself by superficial aspects of self such as appearance and achievement. One may learn to live life from the outside in, rather than from the inside out. When one's sense of identity and worth is based in achievements, even seemingly minor "failures" can lead to internal collapse.

Sarah, age 24 and a student in a master's degree program in psychology, had sought a sense of self-worth through being a good student:

> Through high school I thought that I was gonna graduate first or second in my class. And it was getting toward the end of senior year, and it wasn't looking like I was gonna graduate first. And I was feeling at a loss for anything, because at the time, it was all or nothing. Either I was first in my class or I wasn't smart. And if I wasn't smart, then what was I? Because I certainly, I didn't feel like I was popular, and I didn't have a boyfriend. So I didn't feel like I had anything else going for me except being smart, and now I wasn't smart . . . And so that was slipping away, and so I went on this diet.

She began a very restricted diet and soon thereafter started to binge and purge.

When she learned she would be neither valedictorian nor salutatorian, Sarah felt inadequate and worthless. At the same time, she felt secondary shame about feeling so distressed: "I was just totally crushed. And the other thing was that I knew at the time that it was silly to be that upset. That's what I felt. And so I couldn't even be upset about it because all my friends were like, 'Give me a break, you have a 98 average, just because it's not a 98.02, you're upset?' But I was. I had already started feeling like I didn't have anything to hold on to."

Rebecca recalls that in college her identity was based on her ability to attract men's attention:

That was what was familiar to me, that's how I got my sense of self-esteem, was how I looked. It was from nothing else. It's very powerful to have people looking at you and having positive recognition, attractive men looking at you . . . That's kind of what I lived for. 'Cause I walked around school really shabby, oversized jeans and sweaters, and then on Friday and Saturday night we used to do up the town, and I used to just live for that. Literally live for that, to get out and be somebody else. People that knew me really well would say, "There's Rebecca One and Rebecca Two."

In referring to Rebecca One and Rebecca Two, she indicates that she did not have the sense of self-specificness and self-sameness that fosters a sense of identity. She came to regard her eating disorder itself as essential to her identity:

I still never really ever thought I would not be bulimic. All my life, this is all I knew, this is my forming of adulthood, this is the only person I knew . . . Even though it was negative, it was still kind of a positive thing for me 'cause it's all I knew. But I never thought, even when I was in group, and in individual counseling, that I would ever get over it. I said, "There's no way possible. I just, I need to do this. I just need to purge" . . . And I just figured, "Nobody can help me. I can't be helped, I'm not supposed to be helped. I'm supposed to be like this. This is what I am. This is what I'm meant to be . . . Rebecca is bulimic. Being bulimic is Rebecca." I never thought there would ever be a difference, and I thought this was a problem or a situation that I would have to live with for the rest of my life. And I had gotten to the point that I had come to accept that.

Looking back to chart the loss of her sense of identity, she remembers her long hair, which she cut when she started college, and her horse, which was sold when she was 16:

> It's like meditation, it's just therapeutic to go riding. It's just you and your horse. And I miss that tremendously . . . Rebecca was thought of with her long blond hair—because I always had straight blond hair down past my waist—and her horse. That's what I was to people, friends and neighbors and relatives. So me selling my horse, I lost half my identity. And then when I was in college and I cut my hair, I lost the other half of my identity. Because I had always had these things, that's what people knew me as and what had created that sense of who I was.

She had once felt that she and others had a shared sense of her Rebeccaness. But when she sold her horse, and again when she left her community and cut her hair, she lost her sense of self-specificness, self-continuity, and mutual recognition of her Rebeccaness.

As they recovered, the women gained a more substantial sense of identity and worth and a feeling of pride in having recovered. Pride, as Rizzuto (1991) points out, is the counter to shame: "Pride is the feeling on the other side of shame, frequently associated with feelings of joy, well being and social expansiveness and a communicative disposition. It is related to . . . a sense of being a worthwhile, respected, successful, strong, deservedly well liked person in charge of one's own life. Pride gives the body and the sense of self as much of an expansive feeling as shame moves them to shrink to their minimal size" (299).

Sensing When Enough Is Enough

In the interviews, I listened for, among many things, pivotal experiences that marked a definite shift toward a readiness to recover. I do not mean points at which a woman turned a corner and began running lickety-split down a path of recovering. Such dramatic turning points were rare to nonexistent in the women's accounts. Instead, these pivotal experiences were characterized by a manifest commitment to working toward wellness. The shifts were marked by the convergence of six essential elements:

1. A felt sense of enough.
2. A specific and intentional act directed toward getting help.
3. Others' timely, attuned response to the act directed toward getting help.
4. An abiding context conducive to sensing self-experience.
5. A belief that one will recover.
6. Investment in the process of recovering.

I do not claim that these elements caused a pivotal experience but rather that each pivotal experience comprised these elements. The absence or mistiming of even one or two elements was associated with a less complete recovery. Of the thirteen women, eleven experienced the convergence of all six elements. Amy and Claire, the two women whose recoveries are most fragile or incomplete, experienced the convergence of only four or five.

The first three essential elements worked together to create a *sense of self-agency* and a trust in an inner gauge of enoughness. The other three elements worked together to create a *context of commitment* that fostered recovering.

ELEMENTS OF SELF-AGENCY

Bulimia nervosa is characterized by dysregulation, that is, by bingeing and purging, and may be accompanied by other out-of-control behaviors such as fasting, excessive exercising, erratic sleeping patterns, stealing, compulsive shopping, and sexual promiscuity. Bulimic women do not readily recognize and respond to an internal gauge of what is enough. They do not know whether they have eaten enough or exercised enough, whether they are attractive enough or accomplished enough, whether they are distinctive enough or deserving enough.

While they have difficulty sensing self, women with bulimia nervosa tend to be skilled and practiced at sensing other. They over-rely upon external gauges—numbers of calories and grams of fat, clothing size and body weight, grades and awards, others' expectations and approval—to guide their determination of what is enough. Both the behavioral symptoms of bulimia nervosa (binge eating and purging or other compensatory behavior to counter the binge) and the psychological symptoms (including over-reliance upon body size and shape as determinants of one's sense of worth) indicate an absence (or abdication) of internally sensed gauges of enoughness and a reliance upon externally based, non-sensed gauges.

Beth provides some indication of how a young woman learns to rely on external gauges to guide her life:

> I was on the basketball team in the winter, and I remember that one of the reasons I joined the basketball team was so I wouldn't be home after school, and I wouldn't eat after school. So I thought, "Well, if I join the basketball team, I'll be structured and I won't come home and be bored and eat something" . . .
>
> In the spring, two of my friends wanted me to go out for track. And I didn't really wanna go out for track anymore. I was kinda sick of basketball, sick of having to stay till 5:30, 6:00 at night. And they were like, "Oh, come

on, just do it." And I'm like, "No, I really don't want to." And they're like, "Well, just bring your clothes tomorrow, and do it for one day. If you don't like it, you can quit." So I said, "Okay."

So I did, and I went out to run, and I beat everybody back. 'Cause I had danced all these years, so I had pretty good lungs. And I beat everybody, and I was like, "Oh, this is pretty good." 'Cause I would beat everybody, and it was like a breeze to me, and everybody else is dying. It was just a two-mile run, and like everybody else is stopping and walking. And I came back, and the coach was really excited, and he was like, "Oh, a natural!" And I kinda liked it, 'cause in my family I always tried, I mean there were four of us, and it just felt like there was never enough attention in my family. And so it felt really good, somebody'd approve of me, that I did something good. So I was like, "Oh, I'll keep doin' this." So then I started running.

Beth ran track not for her own pleasure or sense of competence but for others' approval of her performance. She therefore had no sense of how to tell when she had run enough. Her running became increasingly compulsive and excessive to the point of being self-harming.

Virginia Demos's model of how infants develop a sense of active agency illuminates the process by which the women began to sense an internal gauge of enoughness. Demos (1993) argues that affect helps us organize our experience and learn that we can have an effect upon our experience. To illustrate how affect leaves us feeling effective, she describes the role that crying serves for an infant. At first, "the crying neonate neither knows why she is crying, nor that there is anything that can be done about it . . . This initial experience of distress is as close to pure affect as possible" (15). Referring to Sylvan Tomkins's notion that the evolutionary function of affect is "to make the organism care about what is happening and to provide the motivation to organize a response," Demos explains that the distressed infant, "because she is crying, now cares about what is happening, is now motivated to pay attention to what happens next, to remember what these punishing sensations felt like, and to begin to connect them to antecedents and consequences" (15).

Demos considers how much crying is enough to motivate the infant to organize a response:

If affects have evolved in order to amplify experience and to motivate us by making us care about what is happening, then we must learn to be able to tolerate and endure our affects in order to use the information contained in them and to organize an adaptive response. I am suggesting that there is an optimal density of negative affect that is neither too low, thereby preventing the infant from exercising and developing his or her regulating capacities, nor too high, thereby overwhelming the infant and evoking defensive responses, but that ranges from moderate to moderately high. (17)

By experiencing this "optimal density of negative affect," the infant gets its own attention and makes connections among three elements which combine to form an experience of agency or effectiveness:

A = becoming *aware* of a distressed state

I = experiencing an *intention* to end it

M = *mobilizing* behaviors to achieve that goal

Demos applies the acronym "AIM" to the experience of these three elements and regards AIM as essential to the development of a "sense of active agency": "the knowledge that one's own efforts are effective in causing something to happen, or in recreating and prolonging a positive state, or in limiting, ending, or avoiding a negative state" (21). When the infant becomes aware of distress, experiences a wish to end that negative state (or prolong a positive one), acts upon her sense of intention, and gets a response to her action, she grounds the response to her crying in herself and experiences a sense of agency.

For the infant to experience a sense of agency, her caregivers must provide well-timed responses to her efforts to signal distress. If comfort comes at the first whimper, the affective experience is "too brief and weak for AIM to occur" (22). It is as if help came magically, out of the blue, and the infant therefore experiences herself as having had no effect in recruiting help or in ending her distress. If comfort comes after the infant is inconsolable, she is too distraught to make the connections that AIM requires. She must be responded to when the intensity of her affect is neither too low to get her attention nor so high that she is consumed by painful feeling.

Analogously, when the women made specific and intentional acts to get help because of an internally felt sense of enough and received timely and attuned responses to those acts, they grounded in themselves the experience of feeling a sense of enough, wanting something to happen, mobilizing their efforts to end their distress, and being effective in ending it. They experienced confirmation that their internal gauge of enoughness worked.

A FELT SENSE OF ENOUGH

All of the women suffered with bulimic symptoms for years before committing themselves to recovering. It is not the externally observed reality of misery but the *internally felt sense* of having reached one's limit of distress that characterizes this essential element. That sense was typically transient, not enduring. Before they could commit themselves to recovering, the women needed to experience, even if only briefly, a sense of enoughness. That sense of enoughness took various forms:

A sense of being sick and tired of the disorder: "Enough of this misery"

A sense of inevitability or ultimate necessity: "Enough of defying or denying the inevitable"

A sense of danger or impending loss: "This is risky enough that I could lose something essential"

A sense of desire and possibility: "This matters enough for me to get well"

A sense of reality and legitimacy: "I am sick enough to need help"

A sense of (particular) others' limitations: "Enough of trying to get them to acknowledge my needs"

A sense of limited ability to recover without others' help: "Enough of trying to do this alone"

A sense of self-determination: "Enough of letting others or circumstances be in charge of my life"

For any one woman, the felt sense of enough derived from a combination of these senses, but not necessarily all of them. True to real-life complexity, these felt senses are intricately interconnected.

"Enough of this misery"

Some women describe the felt sense of a limit as feeling "fed up" or "sick and tired" of the sheer misery and duration of their symptoms. Amy says:

> I did not want to continue feeling the same way that I had been feeling . . . I really wanted to stop talking and take action. Basically, I was just tired of talking, and tired of complaining about it, and tired of hearing myself . . . I was just really sick of myself, basically. I was just sick of the same old story over and over again. I was tired of me saying to everybody, "Oh, I'm so fat. I could never do this because I'm so fat. I could never wear that because I'm so fat." I was just tired of it . . . I was wasting so much energy thinking about how fat I am, how ugly I was, how much I ate. I was just, that's all I did was focus on food. That was it. Focused on what I was gonna eat for lunch, breakfast, dinner, snacks. What I was gonna eat on the weekends, that's all I focused on, was food and what I look like. And I was sick of it.

Jill, who is in recovery from alcoholism as well as from bulimia nervosa, says: "I was just tired of feeling sick all the time, of the behavior, of making myself throw up, bingeing, of all the craziness that came from it . . . I don't think there was one particular incident that made me say that, but I just reached the point where, as they say in AA, I was sick and tired of being sick and tired."

While all of the women look back with astonishment at how they managed to keep functioning even when their bulimic symptoms were wildly out of control, some did experience the limit of their ability to live a full life. Claire, age 25, a nurse who is now in a bachelor's program in psychology, describes the effects of abusing laxatives: "The gripes and pains you get in the night keep you awake. So you don't get the rest that you want . . . When you have nausea or diarrhea, your electrolytes are all over the place, and you just feel incredibly weird and lightheaded, and it wouldn't be until the afternoons that I would start to enjoy my days. Basically until 1:00 it was preoccupied with emptying yourself and feeling really bad, really bad . . . It was really tiring doing this to myself."

Because laxative abuse tethered Claire to her bathroom, it limited her social life: "I gave up seeing my friends. I would be asked to go out for meals, and I would always say, 'I'll meet you for coffee afterwards.' I'd say I couldn't afford it, but really I just couldn't sit at the dinner table with them. And when I would stay with friends for the weekend, I would always make it maximum one night because I had to go through my ritual, and I couldn't do that when I was in someone else's home."

Like Claire, Gita felt not only tired *of* the disorder but tired *by* it. Bingeing and purging increasingly drained her energy: "It just kept feeling worse and worse. In the beginning it was so easy, and I didn't feel it, and I had energy afterwards. And as I got older, I think part of it was just aging, my body couldn't take this anymore. The build-up of it all. I just couldn't take it physically, and so just the feeling so awful, I think that's probably part of it."

Gita also felt that her eating disorder had lasted long enough and was not appropriate to her professional phase of life:

> And maturing in some way, becoming more responsible and realizing that "Here I am, I have a job, I'm a teacher for children, how can I be doing this?" Realizing it was inappropriate in where I was in my life. When I went to the eating disorders group at the campus health center, I was the only graduate student there. I was embarrassed . . . "Now this is something that can be a problem in college, but now I've grown out of that phase." I was ashamed that I was achieving a status and being mature but still having what I considered a juvenile problem.

"Enough of defying or denying the inevitable"

Many of the women describe becoming aware that they had to accept the inevitable. For instance, when a nutritionist gave her a concrete lesson in body identity, Amy recognized that there was a real limit to how much she could reshape her body or lower her weight:

> She takes an apple, a pear, and banana out, and she explains how they're made up this way. And sure, you can trim the pear a little bit, or trim the apple a little bit to look a little bit like the pear, or maybe you can make the pear look a little bit like a banana, but it won't be as long as the banana . . . And she said, "Now, that's how human beings are. You have your body, and sure, you can exercise a little bit to make it a little bit firmer, but you can't necessarily make it look like a model that you're envious of, that you want

her body, you're not gonna be able to make it look like that. Everybody's made up differently. Some people don't even have to exercise a day in their life in order to look good, not to have cellulite." She said, "And laxatives, most definitely, it's not gonna help you shape your body a different way."

This demonstration marked a turning point for Amy: "That little speech with the little three pieces of fruit sitting there just did a tremendous amount of clicking for me. Made me realize, 'Geez, I'm a pear. And I'm never gonna look like an apple or a banana.' It just made me realize—even though I still have a slight obsession with it—I really do know that I'm never gonna look this particular way, even though I would like to." In response to this initial session with her nutritionist, Amy gave up laxatives cold turkey after having abused them for six years.

Beth felt a sense of inevitability when she recognized that she needed the abiding structure of a twelve-step program (Overeaters Anonymous) in her daily life: "'Cause I had done support groups, group therapy, individual therapy, two, three times a week. I had tried exercise, I had read every single book there was . . . I tried everything. And I think on some level I knew that there wasn't anything else there for me, that on some level I knew I needed to go to OA."

Jessie realized that she either had to give up purging or face inevitable, serious threats to her health: "Something in my mind told me it's time to get over this now. If you're gonna do it, it's now. Or you're gonna be like this forever . . . And more studies had come out about the dangers of this and what it does to your cardiovascular system and your stomach, and I was having little problems. I had a lot of cavities and was starting to get stomach problems. And I knew that I could get out now and probably be okay, or it would just get worse." It was Jessie's sense of inevitability that led her to begin therapy.

Kate, 32 and working as an administrative assistant, when asked what advice she would give to someone who is bulimic, replied: "You have to accept that if you keep on doing what you're doing, it's gonna kill you . . . You can do something to fix it, and if you don't do something to fix it, it's gonna kill you. If it doesn't kill you physically, it's gonna kill you emotionally. It's just gonna make you a shell of a person and you're never gonna realize everything that you could be as long as you've got this one secret from people."

"This is risky enough that I could lose something essential"

The sense of inevitability was typically associated with a sense of danger or the threat of loss, typically the threat of losing one's life, doing irreversible damage to one's body, or losing an important relationship. The women sensed that if they did not know when enough was enough they would almost inevitably cross the line and lose too much.

Kate recognized her laxative abuse as a threat to her life one morning after having taken many laxatives the night before:

> The reason that I went to see my therapist was, it's a long story, but I had a really bad attack one night—actually, it was early morning, like 5:00 in the morning—of cramps because I had taken, whatever, 30, 25, 30 laxatives that day. And my niece and nephew were sleeping over, and I sleep downstairs with them when they sleep over, and we have a downstairs bathroom. So I'm sitting in the bathroom in absolute agony, emptying my guts out, and all I could think of was, "They're going to find me dead on the floor in the morning. I'm not going to be able to stop. I'm absolutely going to drain every ounce of fluid out of my body, and the kids are going to get up and go to the bathroom, and they're going to find me down on the floor" . . . And then I called the hospital . . . and they referred me to Linda.

Kate's fear was initially more on behalf of her niece and nephew than herself. It was when she saw the dangers of laxative abuse spelled out in black and white that she fully registered the threat to her health:

> I don't think it was until—usually I have to read something in print to believe that it's going to happen. The first time I went to see Linda she gave me this whole write-up on how—'cause I always used to think that the vomiting part of it was much more dangerous than the laxative part of it. I figured, "Well, I'm only using laxatives, and it's a lot safer than the vomiting aspect of it, or the starving yourself to death aspect of it" . . . But she gave me this write-up about losing your electrolytes. And I think there were case studies of women who had actually, literally killed themselves from this because of the loss of body fluids and from the potassium being off balance

and all of that stuff. So I think that's when. And everything that they described in the article was exactly what I had felt that night, or that morning. And so I think it occurred to me then.

Jill sought help for her alcoholism before she sought treatment for bulimia nervosa. But she eventually found her eating disorder an obstacle to working the steps of AA. As mentioned in Chapter 1, she got stuck at the fourth step because every time she tried to take a moral inventory she binged and purged to escape the pain: "I still needed that outlet because it was very painful. Some of the stuff that you wrote down that you looked at, you were looking at yourself, and that's a hard thing to do. So I know I would wanna binge over stuff 'cause it brought up a lot of feelings, and I would binge over it and throw up over it."

Jill was afraid that if she stayed stuck at the fourth step she would eventually lose both her sobriety and the fellowship of AA. This fear led her to seek treatment for her eating disorder: "I just think that AA was working for me. I knew I didn't want to stop going. 'Cause it was the first place where I really felt accepted . . . So I didn't wanna stop going to AA, and I was afraid if I stopped, I'd start drinking . . . I didn't wanna go back to that life of drinking. I was two years sober. It was my anniversary date, that was the big event, it was right after that I just said, 'I gotta do something. I don't wanna give up the two years I have by drinking again.'"

"This matters enough for me to get well"

Attendant to a sense of danger and loss is a sense of desire and possibility. The felt threat of loss brings with it an awareness of what one does not want to lose. The women realized that someone or something mattered enough to them that they wanted to be well to enjoy that person or that experience.

Amy's decision to stop using laxatives was motivated by her desire to enjoy life: "I felt like I couldn't get on with my life until I got rid of this . . . There were so many other things that I wanted to do. I wanted to go out with my friends, enjoy myself, not be concerned about what I look like."

For some, wanting to have children was part of their motivation to recover. Meg's desire to be a mother and to participate fully in a marriage and in society gave her reasons to be healthy:

> I thought about getting older and not wanting to have this forever, be bulimic forever. And the prevailing thought most of the time when I was wanting to give up at points was just that "I don't want to be bulimic when I have children." And "I wanna get rid of this and get on with my life" type of thing, be a normal person. Just looking and saying, "Okay, this is what I want my future to be like. Then this is not a part of it." And actually, that's interesting because I couldn't say to myself, "My life is miserable now, I need to stop this now." But it was always, "I have to do this because my future won't be the way I want it to be" . . .

> *Why would it be more important not to be bulimic when you had children?*

> Well, because I couldn't, it takes up so much of your time and your energy, and you're just always focused on yourself and what you're eating and how much you're exercising, and it would just be ridiculous to try and have children and care about other people. And I think actually it was probably the idea of getting married, too, and being a contributing member of society. And being able to be much more of a giving person and not so self-centered. And children were part of that, and getting married.

Gita, the only one of the women who was a mother, had become pregnant late in her process of recovering, at a time when she was bingeing and purging only rarely. She says that her desire to have a child did not directly motivate her to recover but that being pregnant helped her consolidate the gains she had already made: "I was being very good to myself because I felt I had to. I wanted the baby to be healthy, and I was a perfectionist, and in turn, I had to take care of myself. 'Cause I was the bearer of the child. So I think those two attitudes really, and having to have them for nine months, you couldn't slip back. And being sort of healthy for nine months and really trusting my body for nine months was enough time to carry forward with that after I was done."

All of the women initially experienced the bulimic symptoms as a means to obtain something they wanted, typically as a means to lose weight or to eat what they wanted without gaining weight.* But most eventually recognized the disorder as a serious threat to something else they also wanted. The sense that their eating disorder threatened something they desired marked a shift in their readiness to change.

"I am sick enough to need help"

The senses of inevitability and danger contributed to the women's experiencing a sense of reality and legitimacy—that they *really did* have an eating disorder, that there *really was* something wrong in their lives, that there were *real consequences* to this illness, that they *really did* need help.

Gita, who was conflicted about whether she was legitimately ill, made a slide-tape video about eating disorders for a college course, in part to learn whether she really had an eating disorder: "I guess I was researching it because I really wanted to find out was there, should I be taking some medication, was I really bulimic? Was I really anorex—? What was I? Sort of figuring out what was going on or why it was going on." Looking back, she marks making the video as her acknowledgment "that it was a real problem for me." In making the video, she tried to make her illness real to herself and her parents and to establish that she was sick enough to need help. But her efforts failed. In fact, she came to doubt the legitimacy of her disorder even more:

> I'm like, "Well, gosh, I don't even have the right disease. I have bulimia instead of anorexia. Anorexics are the ones that are really suffering. They're the ones who really have a problem. Look at these poor people, and look what they do to themselves. I just go throw up, that's easy." And then I would say, "Oh, maybe I don't have that problem at all, I'm making this up. Compared to these other people I don't have it half as bad. Look at my life, I'm very lucky, I love my parents, I love my school, I love working."

---

*Bulimic behavior does not necessarily result in weight loss and in fact can result in weight gain. Vomiting does not rid the body of all calories consumed during a binge because many foods are broken down and absorbed too quickly to be purged. Laxatives do not rid the body of many calories because they work near the end of the digestive tract, and most calories have been absorbed before that point.

And so I got very angry at myself for having a problem, or thinking I had a problem.

Several years later Gita used the occasion of a physical exam at her university's health clinic to signal her disorder to a nurse practitioner, who acknowledged that her symptoms were worthy of clinical attention: "Then I went to graduate school, and that was a real beginning, a new opening. And I thought 'Well, this is the time to get real good help.' And I decided to be very honest about it and very direct. And they did this questionnaire for me, just in the normal physical. And it came out, the nurse practitioner goes, 'You know, I really think you should talk to somebody about this.'" When asked how the questionnaire was helpful, Gita says it made psychological concerns as legitimate as physical ones: "That they're prepared to hear about that as part of you, not just how are your ears and your stomach, that there's a psychological piece, too."

Sarah, like many women, found it difficult to believe she was sick enough to deserve help. She recalls "feeling like there was this voice in my head determined to prove that I was a good bulimic, or at least that I had a problem. Because I still wanted help. But I still didn't feel like I had enough of a problem to get help, and so I felt like I had to have it be bad enough."

Sarah wanted Lynn, a faculty adviser in her high school who was a mentor to her, to verify that her disorder was "bad enough" to warrant getting care: "But even though I could tell Lynn what was going on, I think I was just waiting for her to tell me, 'You need to go talk to somebody.' 'Cause I felt like I needed somebody to tell me that. 'Cause I didn't want to waste anybody's time if I wasn't really having a problem."

Lynn did encourage Sarah to seek counseling, but Sarah felt she expressed her concern more as a suggestion than as an imperative. When Lynn failed to increase the intensity of her concern as Sarah increased the intensity of her bulimic behavior, Sarah set standards of her own for what would qualify as sick enough. But her standards kept rising as she kept overriding her own gauge of "sick enough." Only when she found herself going to extreme lengths to conceal her symptoms—vomiting

into cups in her dorm room so as not to be heard in the common bathroom and throwing out the cups in the garbage room so her roommate
would not discover them—did Sarah recognize her disorder as serious
enough to warrant help: "My symptoms kept escalating. 'Cause I would
tell Lynn, 'I'm just throwing up,' and then I told her I was using laxatives,
and I always said, 'If I start using laxatives, that's when I need help.' I
went back to college . . . thinking, 'Well, if it keeps going in school, where
I really can't get away with it, that's when I know I'm in trouble.' I kept
having all these points that I kept going by, and that's when I started
throwing up in cups in my room." At that time, she found a therapist and
began individual therapy.

"Enough of trying to get them to acknowledge my needs"

Many of the women needed to give up their hope of getting help—or
even acknowledgment of their disorder—from the people from whom
they most wanted it, typically their parents. They had to face the reality
of others' limited willingness or ability to recognize and respond to their
distress. This realization was a prerequisite for seeking and accepting
help from those who were prepared to provide it. A sense of others' limitations was associated with a sense of inevitability, legitimacy, and self-
determination: the women realized that they would inevitably have to
stop waiting for others to decide that they were sick enough and would
have to determine for themselves that they needed care.

In Sarah's case, the person from whom she most wanted help was not
a parent or other family member but Lynn, her high school faculty
adviser. Even though Lynn did suggest several times that Sarah seek
counseling, Sarah kept wanting her to insist: "I also think if she had really
come down on me and said, 'This is serious, you need to go,' then I
maybe would have, the second time she said it, or sooner. Because I
wanted validation that I had a problem from somebody. And I think her
being wishy-washy about 'Maybe you should talk to somebody' wasn't, I
still wasn't getting confirmation of that."

Acknowledgment that her problem was "bad enough" to deserve
help was not the only thing Sarah wanted from Lynn: "And also I think,

now that I think about it, I probably wanted it from her, and so I was waiting for it to come from her, like, 'Why can't you just turn into my therapist?' And maybe I finally realized that I wasn't gonna get that, that she had her own life, and that she wanted to help me but I wasn't her daughter. As much as I probably wanted to be at the time. And that the best she could do was help me out in little chunks but tell me where I could get more help." Only after repeatedly trying and failing to recruit Lynn's fuller involvement did Sarah realize that Lynn was neither going to insist that she get help nor going to provide the help. Sarah recognized that she herself had to decide that she was sick enough to need care.

Gita had tried and failed to get her parents and a doctor to acknowledge that she had an eating disorder. She finally granted herself that acknowledgment: "So then I was starting that it was a real problem for me, I said, 'This is ridiculous, I can't live like this anymore, I'm really sick. No matter what anyone says I'm going to start getting help for this, or seeking some outward support.'" It was at that point that she arranged for a physical exam and communicated her symptoms to the nurse practitioner.

Recognition of others' limitations brings disappointment, anger, and grief. Isabella, who developed diabetes at age 11 and who regards her eating disorder as partly a response to feeling out of control of and ashamed of her body after the diagnosis, had, for many years, yearned for her parents to involve themselves in her care and in her feelings about the diabetes. Once she faced the fact that her parents were not going to offer her the support she wanted, she formed her own support group. But it was hard for her to stop expecting curiosity, concern, and coaching from her parents:

> I found my own sources to give me that coaching. Like at first I was just so angry that I wasn't getting it from where I wanted it . . . But I just sat in that anger. So then I knew that wasn't working, so I moved on, and I found my therapist and the support group, and I formed . . . a diabetes support group for women. And we meet every three weeks and just talking to them and getting people to support me, my sister and friends—

That sounds like a very big shift, saying, "I may never get this from where I most wanted it. I certainly won't get it when I most needed it. But where else can I get it now?"

Right. And I've still made the mistake of trying to get it from men, whether it's in sexual relationships or just trying to get that love from anybody I can. But I'm also working at that, and getting it more from myself and from people who I know really truly care about me for me.

Abigail recounts an incident by which she learned that she could not rely on her mother to support her efforts to recover. Her mother came to town to attend a wedding and was hurt and angry when Abigail chose not to sit with her at the wedding and to stay in her own apartment rather than in her mother's hotel room. In an attempt to clarify why she was putting her own needs above her mother's preferences, Abigail told her mother she was seeing a psychiatrist for an eating disorder. Late that night, her mother phoned Abigail and threatened to jump out the window of the hotel:

> She was just ragging on me about what an awful kid I am, and I'm ungrateful. I think over the years I've come to realize how troubled my mother is and that an adult mother might have been able to put her own needs aside. My mom, she's okay, but she has problems that stem from her own childhood, or whatever. But I feel that maybe this was an example of what had happened all along, was that this was a time when I was ready to use my voice and ask for support and in some way just to tell her "This is what this is about." I was trying to tell her, "I can't be with you. It's not good for my health, and I had to make this decision, and it's either my health or being with you, and I'm gonna choose my health." She went on and on, "Your health's not important." She'd say, "Family's the most important thing, family's the most important thing." And so I just had to show her that this was killing me. And she didn't even pay heed. She didn't ask me what it was about . . . So that's important. I guess over the past couple years, I've had to just say, "Well this is what I have, this is my mother. And I can't wait for her."

Abigail realized that she had to stop expecting help from her mother and to accept help instead from those who could give it, namely her boyfriend and her therapist. In doing so, she had to bear her anger and disappointment: "But it pisses me off . . . She never, ever will ask me how my eating disorder is . . . I just figure it's just my thing to work on, and I can't count on her to help with this . . . It infuriates me. But just seeing what it's about I guess can give me more power. I can see her as being less powerful and that my ideas are fine to live by . . . I think finally I'm developing a sense of 'I can rely on myself, and things are gonna be okay.'"

"Enough of trying to do this alone"

It may seem contradictory that the women had to sense both others' limited ability to help them and their own limited ability to recover without others' help. In fact, they had to accept the limitations of some particular others, accept the help of other others, and discriminate between types of others.

Jill describes wanting to recover on her own: "All I could think of was, 'This is really disgusting and I don't want anyone to know I do this, and I can stop it myself.'" After repeatedly vowing to stop and failing to do so, Jill realized that willful resolve was not enough to help her recover. She sought individual therapy and, on her therapist's recommendation, joined an eating-disorders group.

Sarah, too, recognized that she could not recover alone:

It was just like, "Forget it. I'm sick and tired of trying to pretend that I'm not dependent on anyone," and just giving it over finally so that eventually I could take some of it back. Just giving it over seemed like the thing that I had to do . . . See, Annie makes it easier because all the pretending, she calls it right on the line, then I don't have to pretend anymore . . . 'Cause my mother always said I was so independent, so I just thought I was. The problem was I felt like I was so dependent. So it looked like I was independent, and I was really so dependent. So to just stop pretending like I could handle everything by myself, that I could just do this life thing without any people involved in it.

Beth was in individual and group therapy, took a medical leave of absence from college, spent three months in an inpatient treatment program, and then attended Overeaters Anonymous meetings. During all this treatment her symptoms diminished, but throughout it all she kept trying to get her parents to take her illness seriously and kept being disappointed by their response. She suffered a serious, prolonged relapse:

> It got to the point where I was in the job that I'm in now, I work in a mental health center, and I was bringing in empty yogurt containers and throwing up into them in my office 'cause I knew if I did it in the hall of a mental health center, people would know. So it was so bad. So I'd been calling treatment centers, and I just remember lying on my floor and holding my arms out and saying, "God, show me the way." 'Cause all these treatment centers wouldn't take my insurance or wouldn't do this or that.

In her desperation, Beth came to understand that despite all her treatments, she had never fully let herself receive help from those who were prepared to help her. She recalls the day she decided to let God into her life:

> It was Veterans' Day. I had the day off, my husband did not, and I spent the day just bingeing and throwing up. And it was as bad as it was in college. I hadn't thought it could ever get that bad . . . And at that point, I just realized that I had to accept that I was—I don't know how to put this—I accepted that I was totally powerless over it, and that I needed God to help me . . . I just knew that I had tried to do this for so long by myself, and that the only thing that could help me was something that was greater than myself.

She also opened herself to letting people help her:

> And I guess it was just like I was overcome by that I wanted somebody to help me. And I got a sponsor from OA. I'd never wanted anyone to help me or to tell me what to do. I wanted to do it by myself. I got this person who had been a bulimic for years and had two years of recovery she hadn't binged, purged, thrown up in, and she was older than I was, but she just told me, "Do this and this and this and this." And I was just like, "I'll do whatever you tell me to do." For the first time in my life, I let somebody else try and help me.

Beth never binged or purged after that Veterans' Day. She had turned to God and OA as last resorts when she understood that she needed more sustained structure and consistent support than traditional treatment approaches could offer: "And for me it was just really like 'I can't keep on living like this, or I'm gonna die,' and believing that God was gonna help me to change this, and that people would help me, that I didn't have to do it all by myself."

"Enough of letting others or circumstances be in charge of my life"
Many women recall a point at which they recognized that they could live their own lives and took action on their own behalf. Such action involved leaving something that was not in their best interest, such as an abusive relationship, a college environment, a job or professional field, an urban environment, and moving toward something that was in their best interest, such as a loving relationship, a treatment program, a graduate program, a new job, a rural environment. Such acts were prompted by a strongly felt sense of "Enough!"

Claire's recovering from bulimia nervosa was entwined with her recovering, at age 23, from surgery to remove benign ovarian and uterine tumors. Because her doctors ignored what she told them about her medical history, she suffered life-threatening post-surgical complications. She felt disappointed not only by her doctors but also by her parents. While recuperating from the surgery and complications, she "did a lot of soul searching" and realized that she had to take charge of her life:

> My dad had always said when we were younger—my dad's a big, strong, six-foot, working-class man—"If anybody ever hurts you, I'm going to break their legs." And here were these doctors that had neglected me so that I nearly died, and then messed up so that I nearly died even when I was in the hospital, and my parents hadn't even asked the doctors how the surgery had gone because they knew I was very independent, and they thought I would do that. And I felt that they had let me down again. As well as the doctors who had let me down. So I was really wondering who I could trust . . . It took a long while to shift from kind of denying that anything really bad had happened or gone wrong—I kind of intellectualized a lot about it—to then being very, very angry. I was angry for a very long time.

> *As you look back, how do you see the role of that soul-searching and arriving at that anger as being connected to recovering from bulimia?*

> I gradually wanted to have more control over myself. I remember when the penny dropped, and I realized I had to look after myself. When I was going

back to the doctors every time and they were giving me a slap on the back, shakes by the hand, "You're doing so well." And I wanted to say, "You nearly killed me," but I couldn't. And they kept changing their medicines, my medicines, all the time, and couldn't get any that worked, and I started taking homeopathy. And having massages, and exercising more regularly. And I kept thinking that I couldn't rely on somebody else to look after me. I really had to look after myself because they'd all let me down. And it was now or never.

In mid-sentence, "their medicines" become "my medicines," and Claire associates to taking action on her own behalf. She shifted from being enraged, directing her anger inward against her body, to being outraged, directing her anger outward on behalf of her body.

Abigail recalls the day during her medical internship when she realized that she had no sense of how to choose a specialty and that she was not in the driver's seat of her own life:

I can almost think of the day where I was like, "I can't believe this. I haven't done anything that I've wanted to do, and I don't even know what I want." And it was at that point where I said, "I'm not putting up with this. I'm going to, I'll find out what I want."

I wonder what made it possible for you to realize that then . . .

I think on some level it was really being alone. I started to make money. I didn't need my parents. They didn't give me any money so I didn't have to answer to them with my pursuits. I think my financial independence was very important. That I could do what I wanted to do. I guess in college, I felt like, "Well, they're paying for this, so I should do what they would want me to do." And when I graduated medical school, I guess I just felt like it was so miserable for me that last year that I could not persist with the status quo. I remember sitting in the therapist's office, in the social worker's office, just couldn't believe that the misery that I was suffering was me . . . I felt really by myself. And as terrifying I think as that was, I remember thinking . . . "If I don't drive, no one else will." Like no one's gonna do this for me . . . And if I just leave it up to whoever, it's not gonna be what I want. And as hard as it was going to be, I was going to have to drive. I remember building that courage. 'Cause I would get scared, but I remember just that I had to, I had to do it.

When Beth, despite her parents' lack of support, entered an inpatient treatment program, her parents reacted with anger and concern about what others would think. In a self-liberating act, Beth told them not to hide the truth about her:

> When I told my parents that my therapist said to me that I needed more serious help, and I bought my own plane ticket to [the state where the hospital was], I did all the insurance work for it, they didn't wanna pay one penny. And they were really enraged with me, they were saying things like "What are we supposed to tell everyone?" . . . And I said, "Tell them the truth." And that was a real turning point for me 'cause I had always done whatever my parents wanted me to do to be the good daughter, and I always did what my father wanted me to do, it was really important for me just for his approval. And so when I did that, that was a major turning point in my becoming my own person.

A SPECIFIC AND INTENTIONAL ACT

For all the women, the manifest shift in readiness to change included a specific and intentional act directed toward getting help. This was in contrast to, for example, bulimic behaviors or impulsive behaviors, which could also be regarded as efforts to get help but which were general efforts rather than particular acts and which were not directed expressly toward getting help.

The women's specific, intentional, and directed acts included not only going to therapy or entering a treatment program but also smaller, prior acts: calling a hotline or hospital to ask for a referral to a therapist; accepting a friend's offer to find a referral; calling a therapist to make an appointment; calling a hospital, treatment center, or insurance company about an inpatient stay; making and keeping an appointment; and honestly reporting symptoms to a health care provider.

Five women took overdoses—of laxatives, antidepressant medication, insulin, or alcohol—that resulted in emergency room treatment or inpatient medical care. The overdoses could be considered specific efforts to recruit help, as opposed to general, ongoing efforts of bingeing and purging. They could be considered intentional efforts to get help, but that intention may not have been entirely conscious. The overdoses were in any event oblique efforts to get help, not directed specifically toward the help itself.

OTHERS' TIMELY AND ATTUNED RESPONSE

Every woman's account of recovering reveals the importance of someone's timely and attuned response to an effort to get help. Such responsiveness is doubtless an essential ingredient of any therapeutic relationship, regardless of a client's diagnosis. What is of particular interest, however, is *how* a timely and attuned response was helpful for women recovering from bulimia nervosa.

Here I draw upon the clinical observations of Richard Kadison (1993), who has found that psychological readiness to begin the work of recovering is not a stable *phase* but a highly transient *state* in which women with eating disorders are likely to seek help. It is important to respond to that state during the narrow window of opportunity it presents because otherwise that window closes and the opportunity is lost until the woman experiences that state again. Others have also described readiness as a state (Miller and Rollnick, 1991). For the women I interviewed, a felt sense of enough was one aspect of that state and was the motivator for their specific and intentional acts directed toward getting help.

A timely and attuned response to such an act confirmed their felt gauge of enoughness and thereby enabled them to experience themselves as effective agents. Because the felt sense of enough is typically temporary, the response to an attempt to get help must be timely in order for the person to experience the links between her sense of enough, her effort to act upon that sense, and her agency in recruiting a response. Because the effort to get help is typically tiny and subtle, someone responding to it must be attuned enough to notice it, interpret it accurately, and respond appropriately.

Gita's account points to how timely and attuned responsiveness fosters the sense of agency. After several indirect efforts to seek others' acknowledgment of her eating disorder, Gita sensed that she was sick enough to deserve help and made an appointment for a physical exam. She communicated her distress via her responses on a health questionnaire that was part of the exam. Although Gita was not entirely forthcoming, the nurse practitioner was attuned to her effort to signal distress and responded with what Gita perceived as real concern: "I don't know if I admitted to throwing up then, I think I still was in that denial stage, but I admitted to running in place for an hour and doing very obsessive things. She said, 'We have a great group here. Why don't you come see the guy and see how you like it' and was very encouraging. I'm like 'Fine. Yeah, I think that would be good.'"

Once Gita felt taken seriously, she was more resilient in the face of subsequent lack of attunement. Even though her parents continued to deny the reality of her eating disorder and even though she found that the group to which the nurse practitioner referred her was not a good match for her, she trusted her own sense that she was indeed sick enough to need help: "I was taking the first step, and I felt like I was doing something right, in the right direction."

Many of the women vividly remember phone calls they made in efforts to get help. Their accounts—and the fact that they remember the phone calls so clearly several years later—confirm the importance of timely and attuned responses. Meg says:

> I was at a friend's house . . . and I was calling some 800 numbers about the places, like the treatment center I ended up going to, and some other places. And I realized in talking to the people on the staff of this one treatment center about the programs there that that was exactly what I needed and wanted. And right after that I called my mom and told her, "This is what I want to do. This is what I need to do." Because just talking to them about it sort of soothed me and made me feel like that was exactly the right thing to do.

By contrast, Beth recalls phoning a mental health center on a holiday during her high school years and reaching an answering service:

> One time I remember—I think it was Easter Day—I'd binged, and I can remember throwing up caramel, something like that, and I remember

throwin' up a bunch of times. And I was lyin' on my floor, and I remember calling the local psychiatric center—and I didn't know anything about stuff like that—and I called, I was like, "I need help, I can't stop throwin' up," and the woman, I remember her saying, "I'm just an answering service." And I didn't even know what an answering service was, so I'm like, "Well, can't you help me?" And she's like, "No, I'm just an answering service." And so I remember, I just hung up, and I didn't feel like I could get help anywhere.

Timely and attuned responses to efforts to get help did not come only from health care professionals. For nearly all the women who had been in therapy, an intermediary—a boyfriend, husband, friend, or health care provider—had given them a referral timed to their state of readiness. Meg is grateful for her boyfriend's responsiveness to her sense of timing about seeking care:

He knew about my eating disorder when we started going out. And he didn't pressure me about it. I was able to talk to him and tell him when I had binged and purged. And I sort of trained him to ask the right questions so that I could talk about it. And he wasn't judgmental at all. And then when I really needed someone, when I decided that I wanted help, I went to him. And he, at that point, when I put the ball in his court, he did everything he could. He got numbers, he made calls for me, he stood by me when I made the calls, he drove me to my first meeting at the hospital for the outpatient groups, made me go in. He was there the whole time. And that was so important.

Timing was only one element of "a timely and attuned response." It was also crucial that the content and the affective tone of the response confirm a woman's gauge of enoughness: that she was sick enough, that she had suffered long enough, that she had tried hard enough to recover alone, and that she mattered enough to be worthy of care.

For instance, once Gita was ready to signal that she needed help, the nurse practitioner's active, straightforward, nonjudgmental manner enabled her to trust that she would be taken seriously without being shamed:

The woman there, I still vividly remember that day and that she said, "Well, you should maybe think about that this could be a problem for you," or "Would you like to be in a group?" She was the first one who really addressed it as an issue in a comfortable way. I don't think any other professional in health care had ever really listened about it. Or maybe I was ready to talk about it, too . . . But the woman, there was something about her, too, that I think was helpful to me, in that she wasn't threatening or making me feel bad about it. And I don't know how quite it is that that works, but that my sense of her was that I could tell her and that she would help me.

Leslie, age 25 and in her first year of a doctoral program, has a master's degree in social work and is credentialed as a psychotherapist although not currently in clinical practice. She describes her therapist's attuned response to her:

> I've never had that kind of connection with a client where I felt like I knew what they were going to say before it came out of their mouths. And she knew my story. From head to toe, she knew. Other than what my mother looked like, she could tell you everything about her. And I think maybe she had treated a lot of cases. But she really had a sense of what the dynamics looked like. Sometimes, when I couldn't say something, she could say it for me, and I could just nod my head. 'Cause there were a lot of times where I just couldn't get the words out, I was so choked up. There was a very special connection with her.

Leslie is not alone among the women in saying that she felt understood and in safe hands when her therapist seemed to know her experience even when she herself could not voice it. The women's sense of being understood may have been a result of the therapists' having heard what they were expressing concretely, through body and behavior, in the language of the bulimic self (Sands, 1991). As Suzanne Repetto Renna points out, "It is one thing to 'take the words out of someone's mouth' and another to 'give words' to something one has not yet learned to name." By reading their symptoms directly and by giving words to their experience, the therapists may have conveyed that the women's experience was legitimate and comprehensible and may thereby have countered their sense of shame. While such seeming omniscience might feel intrusive to someone who is able to sense and voice self-experience, for a woman who is not, this sort of response may be a form of attunement and mirroring, especially early in the therapeutic process.

The importance of timeliness and attunement is interesting in light of the women's having suffered chronic emotional neglect and the core sense of shame that derives from neglect. Chronic emotional neglect by definition implies untimely, unattuned responses. Timely and attuned responses served as powerful antidotes to a core sense of shame. Such responses did not necessarily meet a woman's need but rather acknowledged both her effort to get help and the sense of enough that had prompted her effort. Acknowledgment was the essential counter to a sense of ineffectiveness and unworthiness. In getting a timely and attuned response, the women received confirmation of their subjective gauge of enoughness and, in effect, confirmation of their core self: Yes, you matter enough to be worthy of a response.

ELEMENTS OF COMMITMENT

The women's greatest progress toward health came when they experienced three conditions that created a climate of commitment to recovering. These three conditions were an abiding context conducive to sensing self-experience, a belief that they would recover, and investment in their own recovering. The women's commitment was both active and requited: by their actions they manifested their own commitment to recovering, and they also experienced others' active engagement in their process of recovering.

AN ABIDING CONTEXT CONDUCIVE TO SENSING SELF-EXPERIENCE

We commonly refer to "getting support for oneself" or "being in a supportive environment." But "support" is a vague term. These women indicate that the specific, essential qualities of support are that it be an abiding context—meaning that it is identifiable, currently in place, and a consistent part of one's life, as opposed to amorphous, potentially in place, or inconsistently available—and that it enable or promote the sensing of self-experience.

Asked what advice she would give to people struggling with bulimia, Abigail says it is crucial to find time and space in which to know one's experience:

> My feeling, my fantasy is that I would tell them to take time out for themselves, but I don't know that they would know what that meant in the middle of it all . . . And you don't have the money perhaps to just stop whatever, if you're in school. So you have to find some way to give yourself a break from meeting other people's expectations and their needs. It's probably about different things for different people, but what would that be if you could? . . . Just to go somewhere, even if it's not changing your location, where you can discover who you are and what it's like to have your own needs. And see, I have this fantasy that you would go somewhere for a year and you'd be much better, but I don't know that that happens. So maybe it would just be then to take that time every day, twice a week. And I think that that maybe is what therapy represents for me in some abstract ways.

For Leslie, therapy was a context in which she felt free from judgment and shame and therefore felt safe enough to be authentic:

> I didn't have to care so much what she thought about me. I've always worried so much about what people think of the way I look or the way I talk or the way I act or what I do. That was gone with her, I didn't have to worry about that. And I also knew that everything I said was staying in that room. It was never going anywhere. So it was a safe place, but it also allowed me some flexibility that I hadn't had. I went to this very small college where everyone drove a Maserati or a BMW or a Mercedes, and I came from this working-class family, and really tried to hide that. For four years I didn't want anyone to know where I was from or what my family was like. And of course, like most college campuses, the girls were absolutely beautiful and skinny and wealthy. And I was trying to fit into that. And never felt like I fit. So I didn't really let anybody know me. Like really know me. And she gave me a place to really let that out and be myself. For the first time.

Beth's abiding context for recovering included the potential for round-the-clock support from people in Overeaters Anonymous: "And I'd been in therapy, oh, my God, therapy, therapy, therapy. But once I left the therapy, it was like, the next day, if I needed help, no one was there. And with OA, it was like I could call anybody at any time for help during the day. And there were all these people who were willing to listen to me." The availability of OA members and her belief that God was ever present enabled Beth to get more abiding support than a therapist could provide.

Several types of environments can be conducive to sensing self-experience: environments internal to the self (a well-nourished and well-rested body, a state of mind that allows one to slow down and consult one's self-experience); environments external to the self (one's actual physical environment, the structure of one's daily life); and relational environments. I consider the nature of these environments in Chapter 5. In Chapter 6 I discuss particular ways in which helpful relationships served as abiding contexts that supported self-sensing.

BELIEF THAT ONE WILL RECOVER

Except for Amy and Claire, all of the women experienced either a belief that they would recover or a sense of someone else's belief that they would do so. Many felt this belief when they encountered another woman who had recovered or was in the process of recovering from an eating disorder. Belief was thus literally embodied—by other members of a therapy group or a self-help group; by Geneen Roth, an author of several books on eating disorders who herself recovered from an eating disorder and now leads workshops on recovering from compulsive eating; by Roth's workshop participants whose narratives appear in her books; and by a health care provider who disclosed that she had recovered from an eating disorder. Identifying with people who had recovered helped the women move beyond the *hope* that they *could* recover to the *belief* that they *would* recover.

Jessie was one of those who felt belief after reading Roth's books: "She was very open in that book. It wasn't a this-is-what-you-should-do book. It was an I-was-there-too book. 'I was there. This is what my family did to me. This is how I felt. This is how I felt about myself. And this works. And look at me, I'm beautiful. I feel beautiful now.'"

Meg believed she would recover when she met women who were further along in the process of recovering than she was: "It was great because different people were at different places in their recovery. So I came in, was at one place and was able to see lots of different people at different places and the progression of where people who were leaving were and just look up to them, like, 'God, I can really get there.'"

Beth, too, began to believe in her capacity to recover by identifying with people in OA:

Seeing that people hadn't binged or thrown up in five or ten years. That amazed me. Without exception. Not that they binged once a month, or that they only binged once a year on their birthday. But that they hadn't done it for ten years. That gave me so much hope. And having a sponsor who had done the things that I did. And that she was abstinent, not bingeing, purging, throwing up, or doing any of that stuff. Those were the things that gave me the most hope, was seeing other people. That you didn't have to do this forever . . .

I just got to the point where I was like, "Well, I'm just going to have to accept that this is gonna be something that I'm going to have to live with, that a couple times a week, when my husband leaves, I'm going to binge on a bag of cookie dough, or whatever, and I'm going to have to throw it up, and then I'm just going to have to pick myself up and get my ass to work, work all day, and accept that this is part of my life." And when I heard people saying that they didn't do that, they didn't have to live with that, that they had a choice, that just gave me a lot of hope. People who had done things that I did, people had thrown up into bags and done the things that I had done.

The women's belief that they would recover resulted not only from identifying with others' experience of change but also from feeling believed in. While Rebecca thought she would always be bulimic, her husband and her therapist held on to a sense of possibility for her. She borrowed on their belief in her to make her own investment in therapy and in herself: "I'd have to say my husband, Robert, and Susan, my therapist, more than being just people, they're symbols that I could actually do it. I still didn't think I could, but I guess other people believed in me a little bit more."

Kate's therapist's belief in her inspired her belief in herself:

When I first went to counseling, when I first met Linda and when I first went to group, I think I was so impressed with Linda the first time I met her, that initially, I wanted to show her I could do this because she had such faith in people that they could overcome it. And I think a lot of us in the group felt that initially: "We want to show her that we can do this." Because she believed in us and in me so much, that I can do it, that initially you want to do it for her. It's like wanting to do something for one of your parents, it's like wanting to prove to your parents that you can do what they believe you can do.

One could interpret Kate's experience as compliance and approval-seeking. But it seems that Kate used her therapist, in the role of coach, as a self-object to help her internalize a sense of being believed in. Like Rebecca, Kate seems to have accepted her therapist's loan of belief as a means to believe in and invest in herself.

Belief in their capacity to recover was also gained through the accumulation of seemingly small experiences of agency. As discussed in Chapter 5, as the women discovered that they could affect their emotional and physical states in everyday life, they began to believe that they could live without their eating disorder.

INVESTMENT IN RECOVERING

Most of the women speak about a point at which they made themselves and their well-being a priority. Doing so typically involved clearing out other, competing commitments and treating the process of recovering as a project worthy of their best attention, effort, and resources. Such active prioritizing and investment enabled them to create for themselves an abiding context conducive to sensing self-experience.

Clearing out other commitments involved, for example, taking a leave of absence from school, entering an inpatient or residential treatment program, leaving (or losing) a stressful job, or distancing oneself from an unhealthy relationship. Reducing competing commitments was typically a conscious and deliberate effort, although circumstances (such as a summer break from school or work) and less consciously intentional efforts (such as losing a job or taking an overdose that led to hospitalization) also helped the women reset their priorities. Investment took various forms, including paying for therapy; devoting time, energy, and effort to therapy; attending sessions even when the going got rough; being willing to try a therapist's suggestions despite fear and doubt; and tolerating weight gain that resulted from normalizing eating patterns.

Rebecca, who twice chose to enter an inpatient treatment program, recalls being sad that she would be in the hospital on her birthday. She found it helpful when a nurse said, "Hey, it's probably the best birthday present you could give yourself." Rebecca's outpatient therapist used the metaphor of investment: "I was making very little money, and I was spending $65 a week to go see her. It was ridiculous. But she said, 'Think of it as investing in yourself, basically.' And that's what it was. I mean, I really needed to." Her nurse and therapist conveyed their belief that Rebecca was worth the investment.

Jill believes that using her own money to pay for therapy made her invest more effort in the therapy:

> My insurance doesn't cover it. I didn't ask my parents for any money . . . My father always wanted to support me and pay for everything and give me money for everything, and so that was a big thing for me to pay for it, too. So I think it made me work even harder.

> *Why had you chosen to do it that way?*

> Well, part of it was I was really encouraged by my therapist. I don't know if I would necessarily have done that, but I also knew she was right 'cause money was a real issue, and so, by paying for it myself, I would really own it.

Jessie's mother and grandmother paid for her therapy, but because this strained their financial resources, Jessie felt she had to invest her full effort:

> 'Cause we were payin' cash, my insurance wasn't covering it so it was $80 a visit, so that was all we could afford. Or that was all I would ask them to pay. I probably could've used once a week, but once every other sufficed. And I didn't feel right asking each to pay for two visits [per month]. And at the time, I couldn't afford it. So. But it was good enough . . .

Is there anything else that you feel like you did that really promoted that relationship?

The only thing that I did that promoted the relationship was I gave everything she said a chance. Once I gave her initial idea of not goin' on a diet a chance, and nothin' horrendous happened to me, I then gave everything she suggested a chance . . . We really did work at this fifty-fifty. We really did.

Jessie's investment was in the context of a requited commitment: her investment in herself and her well-being was matched by the investment of her mother, her grandmother, and her therapist. Jessie also invested her own honesty in her therapy with Helen: "I've been in therapy several times, and I didn't really try to combat it wholeheartedly the first couple of times . . . If I didn't go in to Helen and tell her everything and be completely honest with her and myself, I would still be bulimic. I could sit with her for four years and still be bulimic. And that poor woman would be beatin' her head against the wall wonderin' what the hell is goin' on and why I'm not making any progress. And I would know."

Kate invested in the process of change by paying close attention to her thoughts, feelings, sensations, and behaviors:

The actual having to think about eating, what I was eating and why I was eating it, that was very hard. It was also time-consuming. It takes a lot of energy, first of all, it takes a lot of time to have to stop and think about why you're doing this. Whereas before I would just pick up things and eat mindlessly. Now it was "When you're gonna eat something, sit down and eat it, and think about what you're eating." And my initial reaction was "I don't have time to sit down and think about what I'm eating. I just wanna eat it and move on to the next thing." But it was true, as time went on, that I came to realize that most of the time when I was eating before, I didn't know what I was eating, I didn't taste what I was eating, I didn't smell what I was eating. I knew nothing about the food I was eating.

Kate's investment also took the form of staying in therapy long enough to make progress: "I think that actually sticking with it until I reached what I considered to be a good resolution for myself was a big deal because I have a history of starting things and not finishing 'em . . . So I think actually just reaching an end and actually accomplishing something and getting over the eating disorder."

Some women thought they were committed to recovering when they first entered therapy, but had not realized just how much of an investment recovering would require. Meg, who began an intensive outpatient therapy program without clearing away other commitments, found herself overwhelmed:

> And I was still going to school, I was still rowing, I was still in ROTC. And then I had this outpatient stuff on top of it. And it didn't work at all. All these things were coming out . . . with the individual and the group therapy, all these feelings and stuff, things I had never thought of, like that I didn't get along with my mom. Big things that I had no idea how to handle. I had no coping mechanism other than my eating disorder, so my eating disorder continued to get worse, and I started to abuse laxatives, I started to sleep all day and cry all the time and just got really, really, really bad. I barely made it through that semester. Somehow I did. And I decided toward the end of the semester that the only way I was gonna get better was to make my eating disorder a priority because clearly it wasn't working that way. And I hadn't made it a priority even though I was going to the sessions . . . The fact that I was getting help was seeming to me like I was making it a priority. And I didn't realize till the end of that whole term, right before I decided that I needed to go into inpatient treatment, what it really meant to make something a priority.

Gita, too, recalls recognizing that she could not recover until she committed herself to the effort. As a teacher, she had the summer off, and she used that time to develop healthy habits:

> It almost needed a full-time solution. And I think that's what that summer was with my father-in-law, who helped me with caffeine, and Paul focusing me on the therapy. I really devoted a lot of time to it. And I couldn't solve it by letting it sit there and doing little pieces here and there. It took a huge investment of energy is the bottom line, and a lot of support from people in their various ways. Time to make a lot of changes, but, as I said, they were not true changes of myself anymore. It was impossible to try to keep changing myself by lifting more weight or running farther or trying a different diet or learning everything I can about it, being this research expert on the field, that didn't change it either. It took a commitment of myself to really change

my lifestyle but in a way that wasn't divorcing myself. So it was this complex realization, but, again, a commitment to it.

SUSTAINING A FELT SENSE OF ENOUGH

Several women used concrete tokens to evoke specific felt senses of enough. As mentioned earlier, Amy gave up laxatives cold turkey after a nutritionist showed her an apple, a pear, and a banana and pointed out that, like each type of fruit, Amy's body had an unavoidable identity. The image of the fruits helped Amy sustain her realization that there were limits to how much she could change her body weight and shape. Amy also used boxes of laxatives as tokens that reevoked her felt sense of enough:

> And now when I see laxatives in the store, I feel like throwing up, because I can actually, when I look at the laxatives I can envision and actually kind of taste the taste of the coated pill going down my throat when I see them. And I'll sometimes walk down the aisle and just look at them just because it amazes me that I used to do that . . . Even to this day when I see them, I can taste the coating of the pill going down my throat, and it's like . . . I would go and look at them but I would never buy them.

Kate, too, discontinued her laxative abuse cold turkey and used a box of laxatives as a concrete token to help her remain committed: "I actually kept the box of laxatives on my lamp table in my living room just so that I had to see them all the time. And I think that any time I felt the urge to reach for them, I just had to think back to that night and remember. The physical pain first of all. 'Cause I have a certain tolerance for pain, but not that much. And just that whole experience, all I basically had to do was think back to those fifteen or twenty minutes. That was enough."

Meg's concrete token was a list of medical complications of eating disorders that a friend had given her:

> Like a thing on the effects of bingeing and purging that someone gave to me that I put in my journal, and I used to look at it all the time, and it was an important piece of paper to me because it was something that made me realize that even though . . . there weren't any real repercussions at that

87

point from my bingeing and purging, that eventually there was going to be. And that was really something that I thought about when I was getting help was that, "Shit, I'm getting old, I could be really screwing up my body, I wanna have kids someday. I don't wanna be dealing with this and the health risks forever. It's just getting stupid."

These concrete tokens, by helping the women sustain a felt sense of danger, inevitability, and reality, helped them maintain their commitment to change. Tokens may also have been evocative of relationships: Amy's relationship with her nutritionist; Kate's relationships with her niece, nephew, and therapist; Meg's relationship with her friend. In their use of tokens and protective relationships, the women are like toddlers who, in the process of internalizing their parents' sense of danger and limit, walk up to electrical outlets or glass vases they have been told not to touch, point, and say, "No." They may repeat "No" several times, as if awaiting confirmation, sometimes even looking back toward a parent. Through such rehearsal and confirmation, a toddler internalizes a limit. Similarly, the women's use of tokens and of others' protective regard appears to have helped them internalize a sense of a limit.

MISSING AND MISTIMED ELEMENTS

The two women with the most fragile or least complete recoveries, Claire and Amy, are also the two who did not experience the convergence of all six essential elements. Claire, who no longer binges, reports that she has drastically cut down her use of laxatives and now uses them only as needed, but she wonders if she is being entirely honest with herself about that. Her exercising, although greatly reduced from previous levels, still verges on excessive. She appears to be missing two of the elements: a timely and attuned response and investment in the process of recovering. A third element, an abiding context conducive to sensing self-experience, was present for a time in her relationship with her boyfriend, but it was compromised by her boyfriend's attention to other women.

Amy has given up laxatives completely, but her exercising at times borders on excessive. Of all the women, she seems most preoccupied with her body shape and weight. She had little psychotherapy and is missing an abiding context conducive to sensing self-experience. A belief that she would recover was present in her conviction that she would stop the behaviors, but she lacked a belief that she would recover from psychological aspects of the disorder.

The other eleven women, who did have pivotal experiences defined by the convergence of all six elements, also recall experiences that included only some of the elements. Experiences in which all three elements of self-agency were present were remembered as positive even when they were not accompanied by all three elements of commitment. But experiences in which one or more of the three elements of self-agency were missing—typically, when someone did not receive a timely and attuned response to an effort to get help—were associated with discouragement, shame, or despair, as were repeated experiences of missing or mistimed elements of commitment. In talking about her parents' dismissal of her statement that she resembled the women in her video about eating disorders, Gita associates to another occasion when she did not receive an attuned response:

> I had actually, the year before, gone to a doctor and told her I had an eating disorder, I thought I did. And she goes, "Oh, that's too bad," and then had not said anything else to me. And I was like, "Oh. Maybe it's not a big deal." So I got a few kind of slaps in the face, I think, before I really got help . . . And maybe she thought it wasn't her field and it was the end of her day, like I sort of remember her being very hectic. And I sort of mentioned it, and it looked like she wasn't even listening to me. And I started crying. She goes, "Oh, that's too bad." But I guess I don't know what I expected. I sort of expected her to hug me or something and she just, it was not her thing at that point.

The women may have encouraged unattuned responses by making general, indirect, or poorly targeted efforts to seek help. For instance, Gita asked for help indirectly from her parents, and she "sort of mentioned" her eating disorder to a busy physician who, given her specialty (Gita thinks she was a gynecologist), may not have understood that Gita was asking for help for her eating disorder.

But even specific, directed, well-targeted efforts were sometimes met with misattunement. For instance, Abigail, while a medical student, sought psychological help after she realized that her swollen salivary glands were due to her vomiting:

> I didn't have any money, so I went to see the guy that [the medical school] had for us. So I went in his office and he asked me about how I was doing in school. And I was doing great in school. And he asked about relationships, and I had a relationship which was a reasonable relationship. And I was in tears, crying in this man's office. And he said to me, "You're the most mentally healthy person I've ever seen." I'm crying in his office. He was available mostly I think for people who were having difficulty in classes. People who were failing out. So he didn't ask, and I wasn't ready to say. I was crying and I wanted to say it but it didn't feel safe . . .
>
> If he had asked "How's your eating?" I think I would've been able to say it. But he didn't ask anything about that . . . So I didn't say anything. And I left. And I thought, I don't know what I thought. I guess I thought I can fool people into thinking I'm healthy, and they'll be surprised . . . So I gave up for a while, I guess, and I just kind of suffered.

Leslie reports a similar experience when she sought help but neither her mother nor her doctor acknowledged the seriousness of her disorder:

> I decided I had to tell my parents something, anything. And that didn't go over real well because they had no idea, my parents had never heard of eating disorders. I bought my mom a book that she could read about what they are. And all they could say was "How can someone so smart do something so stupid?" So it didn't get any better right away . . .
>
> My mother's answer to this whole thing, when I told my mom that I had a problem, she took me to our family physician . . . He went in and he checked my electrolyte balances and my iron count and that stuff. He came out in the waiting room and said to my mother, "She knows more about this than I do." And she figured, by him saying that, that meant I really didn't have a problem. Like, "Oh, if he's not thinking it's a big deal, and he's not making a huge deal out of this, then it can't be that big of a deal. If he doesn't know about it, I mean, he's a doctor." So, it took me a while, I really had to do most of it on my own for a while.

A Case of Convergence

Rebecca first experienced the convergence of the six elements when she realized that her relationship with her boyfriend, Robert, mattered enough for her to recover. When Robert asked her to move in with him, Rebecca decided to tell him she was bulimic. After doing some research on eating disorders, he "got totally blown away with everything, and just really scared to death that I was gonna die. And he basically said, 'You know that I love you, but if you don't get help, we're not gonna have a relationship.' So that was just like, 'I'd better get help.' 'Cause it was important enough to me. But I still really wasn't doing it for me per se, I was kinda doing it because I didn't want to not be a part of his life."

Rebecca's fear of losing the relationship led her to experience a sense of enoughness in response to Robert's ultimatum. She had been assuming that she would never recover, but once Robert set a limit, she realized that the relationship was "important enough" that she wanted to recover. Although she had already tried individual and group therapy, she decided to give therapy another shot.

Rebecca called a prospective therapist, Susan, whose number Robert had gotten for her. The timeliness and attunement of Susan's response in their first phone contact left Rebecca feeling hopeful, and she entered therapy with Susan. Drawing upon Robert's and Susan's belief in her capacity to recover, she was able to invest time, money, and effort in the process of recovering. Her relationships with Robert and Susan and her experience in a therapy group served as abiding contexts conducive to sensing self-experience.

Rebecca experienced the convergence of all six elements again when she sensed that she needed to do more intensive work than she could do in outpatient therapy, and she entered inpatient treatment:

> I was just like, "Susan I'm not getting anywhere. I come and see you every week, or go to group, and I just don't feel that—I'm at this plateau, and nothing's changing." And up to that point, things had been changing, and I had been working on things, and I had felt like I was getting somewhere in

therapy, and in recovery . . . And she had said at the beginning—and she never ever pressured you that you needed to go in the hospital, she made things your decision—"Rebecca, this is always an option. Let me know how you think about it." And I think I was the one who brought it up to her and said, "Susan, I think I should go in the hospital." And then with me saying that, she was all supportive. And made things very safe. And I was able to take the next step and actually get in there.

Rebecca experienced a felt sense of enough—specifically, a sense of having tried hard enough in outpatient care and a sense that getting well mattered enough for her to invest more. In entering an inpatient program, she made a specific and intentional act directed toward getting help. She was supported by Susan and readily admitted to the program and thereby experienced a timely and attuned response to her effort to get more intensive help.

Two critical features of this hospitalization, features above and beyond the inpatient treatment itself, allowed Rebecca to experience the convergence of the three elements of self-agency. First, the hospitalization was covered by insurance even though Rebecca did not need medical treatment and was able to keep herself safe. In the era of managed care, it is unusual for an insurance company to approve inpatient hospitalization in such circumstances. The hospitalization was crucial to Rebecca's recovering, both because it provided the structure and containment she needed to do more intensive therapeutic work and because its timeliness allowed her to trust her gauge of enoughness. Second, her outpatient therapist had, from the start, acknowledged that hospitalization was always an option. Rebecca knew that she could elect hospitalization without having to increase the intensity of her symptoms, without having to devalue or reject her therapist, and without having to fear abandonment by her therapist.

The convergence of the three elements of commitment enabled her to make recovering a priority. The hospital provided an abiding context conducive to sensing self-experience, in particular, a contained environment in which she could confront her own defensiveness in interpersonal relationships:

It was very humbling, basically. The therapists in there push you to the limit because you're in a safe place so it's not that you can leave that place and you're gonna go kill yourself, or you're gonna do something really self-destructive. So they would push you so far with all your issues. I really got pushed with my interpersonal behaviors. One of my mechanisms of self-preservation was being very intimidating. And really just making people back down. And that was my way of preserving myself. We worked a lot on that in the hospital. It was just very difficult 'cause I didn't like myself a lot of the times when I was in there because they made me see this person that I really, really didn't like.

The safety of the hospital enabled Rebecca to confront a deeper level of self-experience:

What Susan wasn't able to do was that extra push, that extra kick in the butt that I needed to really bring up a lot of things that I wasn't able to deal with because being with Susan wasn't a safe enough environment to do that in. Because, again, you only have an hour session, or a fifty-minute session, and you can only deal with so much then. And if you bring up a lot of garbage, it's just not safe to leave. If you could stay in that room for a day or two and bring up all that garbage and really work through all that pain and that hurt, then—but you can't. So the hospital was able to do that, and I saw a lot of things that I was not aware of at all up to that point.

While in the hospital Rebecca continued to feel believed in by her husband and therapist. She also entered the hospital with a belief in the process of therapy and in the value of more intensive therapy. By choosing to enter the hospital, to suspend her outside activities for three weeks, and to work hard once she was there, she made an investment in the process of recovering and in herself.

ENOUGHNESS

The experience of enoughness is a deeply resonant and recurring theme throughout the process of recovering. For instance, as discussed in Chapter 3, the women experienced enoughness in three domains: physical satisfaction (the sense of having eaten enough or exercised enough);

psychic legitimacy and adequacy (the sense that being human is good enough); and relational acceptance (the sense that they are good enough to love and be loved).

The concepts of enoughness, AIM, and self-agency not only help us understand how the women began to sense their own internal gauge of enoughness but also inform us about the functions bingeing and purging serve. Bingeing may serve for bulimic women the function that crying serves for an infant: it may intensify a distressed state and thereby call a woman's attention to her own distress. But bingeing also numbs a person to her experience. It both numbs one to painful emotions and converts an emotional state of distress to a physical state of being literally fed up and thereby makes possible a physical solution to the distress in the form of purging or other compensatory behavior. Whereas bulimic women feel unable to bear or relieve their emotional distress, they know how to do something physical to relieve physical distress.

By bingeing, the women translated psychic pain into physical pain. In making their distress physical, they made it real, legitimate, and manipulable. Gita talks about reading the transcript of our first interview:

> And I thought about some points that we came to and how the bulimia was kind of a way of making concrete feelings of something that I didn't understand. And I hadn't really looked at it clearly that way before, but that made a lot of sense. And I see that in a lot of things that I've done or not done in my life that, even just crying sometimes, the tears on your face is a concrete way of expr—of feeling, and that maybe the bulimia was a concrete way of understanding my feelings which I'm still trying to understand for me what, there's sort of this black place inside. And I remember the transcript describing that, too, that somehow the concreteness of bulimia and tears, it put the pain into something.

Sarah echoes this experience: "At the time I wouldn't have been able to say what it was, but there was this feeling like, 'If I start doing this and people find out, they'll know something.' I didn't know what I wanted them to know. But I knew that I wanted people to know something was going on. And I had no clue what it was and felt I needed something concrete and tangible to be able to tell people."

Jill prolonged her bingeing and purging to provide evidence that she needed more therapy: "I think that my eating disorder sometimes became a weapon in therapy with Jean because if I got better, if I got totally better, I was afraid I wouldn't be able to keep going . . . It got to the extreme where I would do things to make sure I could keep going to see her. So I think some of my behavior was prolonged, like I stayed in it longer than maybe I really had to."

The emotional-distress-made-physical is amplified by bingeing, which, like an infant's crying, helps the bulimic, in Demos's words, to "care about what is happening and to provide the motivation to organize a response" (1993, 15). When her physical distress reaches a high enough level, she purges. Purging might therefore be considered a well-timed response—albeit a problematic one—to a sense of "enough." Purging may allow one to provide for oneself a timely and attuned response to distress. Several women speak about feeling as if they "really had the timing down," and as if their bingeing and purging behaviors were "an art form." If bingeing allows one to convert psychological distress to physical distress and then to intensify the distress and bring it to a high pitch, and if purging allows one to relieve that distress, then the cycle of bingeing and purging creates a self-directed experience of AIM and self-agency.

As discussed in Chapter 5, the women express gratitude for having had bulimia nervosa because it concretized and intensified their psychological difficulties to the point where they had to address them. Just as a binge converts immediate psychic distress to immediate physical distress and makes the distress intense enough that it demands a response, so chronic bingeing and purging (or other compensatory behavior) convert chronic psychic distress to chronic physical distress and make the distress intense enough that it demands attention.

ANGER AND ENOUGHNESS

All the women mark a felt sense of enough as significant in their recovering. This is noteworthy given that binge eating involves either a lack or an overriding of a subjective gauge of enoughness. People with bulimia nervosa are often told: "You know no limits." "You take things to the limit." "You need to learn to set limits." The subjective signal that one has reached, or is reaching, one's limit is the felt sense of enough. That sense can range from comfortable satiation to discomfort to the intense distress of having gone beyond a limit. That distress typically manifests as anger: "Stop it—I am fed up." It is as if people with bulimia nervosa do not recognize their limit, as signaled by anger, until they reach the intensity of being more than fed up, about to explode.

One function of anger is to signal to the self and others that the self's interests and limits, whether physical or psychic, are threatened. Anger motivates us to protest when our needs, preferences, and limits go unheeded. Anger helps us set, hold, or reestablish the limits of what we will tolerate.

Abigail recalls using her anger to take a stand on behalf of an important limit:

> It was just realizing that when I got very depressed at the end of medical school that I hadn't ever done anything that I wanted to do. And just getting real angry about that. I was just really angry. So internship, I was carrying that around. And . . . when I went in to tell the Chair of Medicine that I was going to leave, and it was very hard for me to do, and he was very angry with me. It was really scary . . . I was able to stand there and say, "I need to do this." And he was saying, "You don't have any direction, you don't know what you want, psychiatry isn't what you want." And he was saying all these ridiculous things to me, and I was still somewhat, I don't know if I believed myself. But I felt a lot more secure, and also noticing it was like the father, it was like a parent saying, "You don't want to do this, you don't know what you want, you're acting like a child." And I kind of felt like, "Oh, no, I can stand on my own two feet here."

Women who do not sense their own anger, or who sense it but ignore or override it, are apt to have difficulty using anger to safeguard the self. In the terms of Demos's model of AIM, if they do not become aware of their anger, or if they disregard it, they do not form an intention to end it, and they therefore do not mobilize to protect the self's interests. As a result, their limits are inevitably transgressed. They perpetuate others' chronic underresponsiveness to their emotional reality by underresponding themselves to cues that their limits are threatened. When the transgression then occurs, they are likely to feel intense anger, even rage. The intensity can be overwhelming. As a result, they often express the anger explosively. Or they try to use bingeing and purging to vanquish or discharge the anger. They have not learned to tolerate their anger long enough to feel it, to understand what it is signaling to them, and to express it effectively on their own behalf. Instead, they experience anger as destructive—of the other, of the self, and of relationships.

Abigail's difficulty in knowing and asserting what she wanted contributed to anger, which she expressed by bingeing and purging:

> Regarding men, when they would leave, or when I was alone after being with them, I would engage in more [bulimic] behaviors when they left . . . I think it was so hard for me to be with people and be myself. When I'm with men, I can't identify what I want very easily. And so I end up doing what they want, and then when I'm by myself I think that I would get angry about that. So then there's the anger, and then there's finally this freedom to do my thing, which is the eating disorder itself . . . That the binge—the food is a silencer and that the purging is a fight back against. Like, "I'm not gonna take this. I'm not gonna be quiet." It is pretty angry . . . an angry thing to do, to make yourself vomit, or with force expel things that are inside your body . . . There is something that "I'm not gonna just sit and just be quiet," or something. But it's a struggle with that. I think it's a struggle with declaring yourself.

The anger of being fed up is distinct from yet related to the rage that is the defense against shame. If we have internalized a sense of shame, new instances of interpersonally induced shame leave us feeling annihilated. We speak of being mortified, as if we could die of shame. If a valued other fails to respond to us when we seek acknowledgment, we experience narcissistic rage as a defense to protect the self. According to Erikson (1963), "Shame is early expressed in an impulse to bury one's face, or to sink, right then and there, into the ground. But this, I think, is essentially rage turned against the self. He who is ashamed would like to force the world not to look at him, not to notice his exposure. He would like to destroy the eyes of the world. Instead he must wish for his own invisibility" (252–253). If we can bear shame and not defend against it with rage, we experience the adaptive anger of having reached and recognized a limit: "Enough of your failing to acknowledge me."*

Shame can be self-perpetuating. When our needs, preferences, and limits go unacknowledged by those we value, we learn to hide our feelings, whether consciously or unconsciously, so as not to leave ourselves open to the shame we would feel if we expressed them clearly and they were ignored. Hiding our feelings not only makes it hard for others to read our emotional cues but also makes it hard for us to sense our own internal states. When we hide our emotions, we have trouble identifying for ourselves what we need and want and what our limits are. We are then ill-equipped to communicate our needs effectively, and so we perpetuate situations in which our needs are not known or considered. Our unspoken needs go unacknowledged. Emotional neglect, even if it is neglect in which we collude, leaves us prone to intense anger. Our needs, preferences, and limits exist even if we are unaware of them, and when they go unacknowledged, anger is our natural, adaptive response, a protest from a self whose interests need protection.

---

*Kaufman (1980/1992) suggests that where we see shame, we should suspect hidden anger, and where we see anger, we should suspect hidden shame.

Physical, Psychic, and Social Self-Experience

The women learned to sense their physical sensations and needs as well as their emotional states and their connections to other people and to their own humanity. Like a symphony which begins with a few instruments and gradually builds to full orchestration, sensing self-experience was an additive and resonant expansion leading to an ever deeper and more complex sense of self.

KNOWING ONE'S BODY

The women had been radically disconnected from their physical selves, as Beth describes:

> I remember in the worst of my addiction, I couldn't go to bed. I could not make myself go to bed . . . It's really hard to eat sanely when your life is just totally insane, when you're sleeping two hours, you need to drink caffeine, a ton of caffeine to keep going. Otherwise, you'd collapse . . . And if you had asked me if I was tired, I would've looked at you like, "I'm never tired." "I'm never cold." "I'm never hungry."
>
> I think it's really important for therapists to help people to become more aware, like that I would be tired if I only slept two hours a night for the past week. That kind of stuff. I really, really and truly did not know what tired felt like. I didn't know what hungry was. I didn't know what any of those bodily— I didn't know that maybe a person would be tired if they ran

seventy miles a week. I just had no connection with my mind, with my body at all.

SENSING BODILY SENSATIONS AND NEEDS

Given how disconnected from physical self-experience the women had been, it came as a revelation to them that physical sensations and needs were essential sources of information and that their body was an organism with its own wisdom and competence. Beth had to learn to recognize and respect her body's need for rest:

> I would just get so tired. And then not wanting to rest. So it was the only time—back to a question of how else did I see my eating disorder—I used it as a way to rest. I always had to be doing something every moment. And I couldn't waste time . . . I would never let myself take a nap or something like that, or just take a half an hour of quiet time to just sit and be still. I always had to be doing something. Writing a letter to somebody, there was always an agenda. And so when I binged, it was like, "Ahhh." That's when I relaxed . . .
>
> I knew, well, at least I'd have a half an hour of just blitzing out. And then I'd go throw up, and it would be, "Ahhh. Okay." That was how I rested. So I had to learn it's okay to take a nap, it's okay to lie down in the middle of the day. It's okay, maybe you're doing too much. Learn stuff like that.

Many of the women emphasize that to sense their physical sensations and needs they needed to stop depriving themselves. Several found Geneen Roth's (1982, 1984) approach especially helpful. Roth believes that the counter to compulsive behavior is awareness of experience. To develop awareness, Roth contends, a compulsive eater must permit herself to eat whatever she truly wants whenever she wants it, because only when she feels entitled to respond to her hunger and appetites will she be able to let herself experience what she truly wants, with an emphasis on "truly." When someone eats food she does not truly want, or eats to fill emotional needs, or eats when she is not hungry, she will not stop eating in response to feeling full because she did not start in response to feeling hungry. Roth acknowledges that a person who tries her approach may initially gain weight, but asserts that she will ultimately experience the limits of her hunger and the natural regulation of her weight and size.

Jill participated in a group that drew upon Roth's approach and found it helpful:

> I really keyed in on the whole deprivation issue and that people are depriving themselves, and I really believe that's what sets you up to binge . . . And [Roth's] book wasn't based on that at all. It's like, "Eat what you want, eat what you like, eat when you want it, eat however much of it, eat whatever." There was no good person/bad person for eating this or not eating this. And so I did her exercise, I ate whatever I wanted whenever I wanted it, and I really tried to focus on "Why am I eating this? Is there something in particular I'm craving here? Why?" Focusing on "Am I really hungry? Do I really want this? Is there something else going on? Am I full? Have I had enough?" Those were all real exercises, things I had never thought about or focused on.

Gita learned to attune to her body when she lived with her boyfriend:

> He has a very nice eating style. If he's hungry, he eats, if he's not, we don't have to have a meal. So his patterns really helped me . . . I think it's in some ways a male way of dealing with it . . . The style of eating and exercising that they have was more compatible with my body than the female routine of always trying to cut back on little things and having three meals. If I have small, little things if I'm hungry, I do much better, and I don't have to eat as much. I don't feel starved at a meal, I don't feel like I have to overdo. So I think Paul's "I don't care if it's not dinnertime, I'm going to eat a sandwich now, I'm hungry," realizing that that was okay, and that he's fit—sometimes he's a little chubby in the belly, but it comes and goes, weight comes and goes. Just seeing a different way of living.

Gita was not alone in finding that adopting a man's healthy eating habits enabled her to practice eating in response to felt hunger and appetite rather than in response to imposed rules and restrictions.

A back injury forced Gita to take a break from exercising. Soon after the injury, she got pregnant. As a result of her injury and her pregnancy, she had to become attuned to what made her body feel "good and flexible and healthy." Previously, she had exercised with the intent of burning

101

fat and with the attitude of "pushing yourself so you can't breathe" because "you gotta do everything to make yourself perfect."

After Sarah recovered from her eating disorder, she developed a severely infected gallbladder which had to be removed. Her doctors suspected that some of the digestive difficulties and pain she had had for years had been due to gallstones. Looking back, Sarah realizes how out of touch she had been with her body:

> I think I have developed more of a respect for [my body] and what it went through. And what it gets me through. And ways that I can take care of it . . . I've started thinking about foods that are healthier than others in a very different way than I used to think about that. Not in terms of "I can't eat this 'cause it has fat in it" but "Well, I think I'd rather have this 'cause I know how it's gonna make me feel inside. It's not gonna sit as heavy, and I don't think I want it to sit as heavy." And definitely just more in touch with what I digest better than other things. And just definitely more aware of how different foods affect me and the times of day that I can eat them . . . I think it's just more of a connection.

TRUSTING ONE'S BODY

The women also found it helpful to learn to sense their body's competence and responsiveness. Meg recalls following a nutritionist's suggestion to take time before eating to gauge her level of hunger:*

> I had to completely relearn how to eat. And I had to trust my body. And those were two things that I still work on now. Believing that my body is a machine, and it's very scientific, and it's gonna work the right way, and it's gonna keep you at a set weight, at a set point, if you fuel it the correct way and if you listen to it and really hear what it's telling you. Trust that you're gonna be okay, and that you can eat too much one meal, and that if you listen to your body, the next meal you're just not gonna be as hungry. And it's all gonna balance out . . .

---

*Meg talks about a hunger meter that ranges from zero to ten. When I advise clients to use a hunger meter, I recommend calibrating it from negative five (uncomfortably hungry, famished) to positive five (uncomfortably full, stuffed), with zero being neither hungry nor full.

So the idea was, before you went into a meal, take some time and calm down. Not to just rush into it. But calm down and think about where you were on a scale from zero to ten—zero being absolutely starving, and ten being extremely full—and to find out where you were, and then you would eventually find out what it felt comfortable to eat, whether it was five or six or seven or whatever. And then think about how much food you needed to eat in order to get to the number you wanted. And take as much food as you wanted accordingly and have a plate, and sit down with it, and eat only when you were sitting down at this particular spot. And I still use that now.

When Gita talks about "trust," I ask, "Do you know what you're trusting to?" She replies: "Just sort of my body. Trusting my needs and feelings, trusting my feelings. If I feel hungry, or if I feel like I need to go out and walk or, just trusting what my body is saying to me."

Gita sees her pregnancy as a transforming experience, "the final closure on this whole thing," and says of her eating disorder, "It's behind me, I don't even have to think about it anymore, it's not even something I want to do."

I was so afraid of [pregnancy], and so I had all these horrible expectations. And then when it was such a joyful, beautiful thing, I think that really made a difference. Also that my body was really, I could trust it. It was doing something successfully. And every time I went to checkups, they would say, "Oh, a healthy baby. Good heart rate." I was doing something right, and my body was doing something right. Imagine that! Here I'd hated it, everything about it was wrong, and then I was doing something okay.

It was very physical. In every ounce of your cells you feel that you're part of this experience. And even nursing, too, when I had just nursed, my body said, "You're hungry, you need to rebuild and get ready to feed him again." So I guess it made me trust something that I had no faith in and had totally denied and didn't trust. And how I shifted from that, how I let myself trust, I really don't know. I think it was just almost I would say chemical 'cause your body all of a sudden is very strong, telling you what to do. There are these amazing feelings. So I guess I really didn't have a choice in some ways, I had to trust it.

Gita no longer tries to reshape her body or change her weight:

Right now, just running around, I do try to get exercise, but I'm not compulsive about it like I used to be. I used to feel awful and blame, be angry at myself if I didn't do what I had to do. Now, if it happens it happens, and if I get to go swimming or do aerobics or whatever, it's great, but I'm doing it 'cause it's fun, I'm not doing it 'cause I have to do it. I've just come to a new sort of feeling about things that I don't have to push myself, that just living is okay, just enjoying. And having a sandwich if I'm hungry is okay. I don't have to panic about it.

How has that change become possible?

I guess because I've sort of proved to myself that it's all right, that it will work, that it's not the end of the world, and that if you do trust and don't panic about it, you're actually doing better. I'm more healthy, I'm stronger, even though I'm not lifting weights, I'm stronger because I'm just being.

Jill was surprised to learn that if she listened closely to her body it would competently signal when she had eaten enough. She describes trying an exercise of Geneen Roth's:

I can remember one exercise where she talked about being blindfolded: "Blindfold yourself, take your favorite dish or whatever"—and for me, I had this big thing for cheesecake, so I took this big, huge cheesecake. And I blindfolded myself. And she said, "It's gonna be really hard, but try to take a bite, and you can't feel or see where it's going, but just keep eating until you feel full. Don't look at the food, don't look at the portion, just keep eating until you feel full." And so I did, I did it. And I was amazed at how little of the cheesecake I ate. Because I could probably have consumed the whole thing. And I ate—you know the little slivers in some restaurants? It was just a little, teeny sliver. And that was all I ate. And I could not believe that it just took that little bit to make me feel full 'cause I was legitimately hungry when I started.

Thinking of her body as part of the natural world and subject to natural cycles and rhythms helps Abigail tolerate normal variations in weight and appetite:

Maybe where I'm at now, that there are cycles to things, there are periods of time where I might need to eat more and where I might put on like five pounds, and there are periods of time, where the weight just kind of comes off and I'm not hungry anymore. But today might be one of those days where I'm hungry. And tomorrow, I might not be as hungry. And that comes somewhat from being, and looking at things not with judgment but just like, "It's raining today, and rain is needed for things to grow." And so it's okay to feel sad, 'cause I won't always feel sad, that later I'll feel okay.

She recalls eating more during a stressful time: "It could be that when I'm under that kind of stress, it might be something that I need to put on a couple of pounds for . . . My body was telling me something. It needed more nurturance or sustenance. It needed certain vitamins because I was under stress. And I was interpreting it, like panicking about it and going for the panic-soothing foods. And that if I could just say, 'Well, it's another stressful period.' And that I don't get fat. It's just a different weight."

All the women were surprised to discover that their body remained at its naturally maintainable weight if they ate and exercised normally— that their body did not require their constant manipulation and calculation. For instance, Jill found that throwing away her scale helped her trust her body. She still weighs herself, but only occasionally, at her gym:

> I don't think my weight has fluctuated more than three pounds in the last four years. I think I could afford to lose a few pounds, but at the same time, the fact that it hasn't fluctuated more than three pounds is just astounding . . . And some of it I think is just 'cause I'm pretty active. It's all gradual, like within the last couple of years, my dress size has gone down a size or sometimes two, but it's not from dieting, it's not from trying . . . I think in that book [Roth] talks about a weight that your body's pretty normal at, and I think my body's pretty normal at this weight. It stays at this weight without me trying to do anything.

Jill has noticed that when her basic bodily needs for fuel and sleep are met, she has the energy to do things that help build her confidence:

> Physically I feel better. I have more energy. I get my sleep that I need, I eat what I need, and so I think that just those simple behaviors, which probably come naturally for other people, which never came naturally for me.

Learning to be responsive—?

Yeah, to your physical needs and stuff. And I think that somehow that helped me to feel better about myself . . . I think it just carried over into a lot of things I do. I know that on a scale of one to ten, my self-esteem used to be one, very low, and it's certainly not ten, but those behaviors helped me to raise my level of self-esteem. I'd have the energy to do other things and the confidence in myself to do other things.

KNOWING ONE'S HEART AND SOUL

The women came to recognize and respect core aspects of self by sensing their emotional pain, their inherent adequacy, their authentic experience, and their capacity for pleasure, and by sensing themselves as separate beings.

SENSING PSYCHIC PAIN

The women report having been profoundly disconnected from their own emotional experience. Referring to a relationship she had with a young man, Beth says: "He'd ask me, 'How do you feel?' and sometimes I'd just start crying, 'cause no one ever asked me how I felt about something, or no one ever listened to me. So sometimes I didn't even know how I felt so I would just start crying. He'd be like, 'Why are you crying?' And I'd just be like, 'I don't know.' But it was like I couldn't say 'I'm mad' or 'I'm sad' or 'I'm anything,' 'cause I didn't know."

Jill found that Roth's book *Breaking Free from Compulsive Eating* helped her translate her bingeing behavior into words that described her experience: "Because I'd find myself suddenly consuming these volumes of food, and I had no idea why I was doing it. How did I get into this? How did this start again? And so [Roth's book] really made me look at that . . . I didn't, when I was bulimic, have that awareness. I had no idea why I was doing what I was doing. I had none, none at all."

Looking back, Jill can see that her purging was partly an effort to convert her psychic pain into physical pain to make it real and resolvable: "When I was first trying to stop purging, I can remember having feelings where I wanted to . . . I really wanted to jam my fingers down my throat and create pain, like make it hurt and make myself hurt and just purge myself of all these angry feelings I was holding inside and rage and stuff. And I think it served that purpose. 'Cause I could get into these fits of rage and stuff, but by throwing up, it took that energy away, or it released it in a different way."

Before Rebecca entered therapy, she had not felt connected to her psychic pain:

> I feel the bulimia was actually something that, unfortunately, needed to happen in one form or another. There were so many things going on in my life that I didn't have control over and that I just was very unhappy about. That I, at that time, I couldn't tell you that. It took me many, many years to get to the point that I, really, "How are you feeling?" "What are you feeling?" Most of the time you don't feel anything 'cause you don't know how to feel anything. The purging becomes your way of expressing whatever you feel.

As they developed ways of tolerating painful experience, the women began to experience rather than embody psychic pain, and to recognize that pain is a vital, essential aspect of self. Kate says: "I actually got my ability to feel things back, like to really feel things, whether it's painful or not. I had lost that for a long time. Like when my father died, I didn't have the ability to feel the intense sort of loss that you imagine somebody should feel who loses a parent. So I actually, I gained an.ability to feel anguish, if you want to put it that way, that I hadn't allowed for a long time . . . So I think it restored my emotions. It put them back in a place where they're useful to me."

For years Sarah was psychically numb. Even in therapy, she would feel, "Here I am again, totally stuck, sitting in therapy for an hour talking about all this stuff and not feeling a thing in the world." Through therapy, however, she learned to tolerate psychic pain. Her feelings are still powerful, but she is no longer swamped by them:

> In terms of just the actual bingeing and the purging, I think it was just protection from my feelings, from really having to look at what was going on with myself, because when I do start to feel, I have a tendency to get flooded, and flooding leads into anxiety and panic. That it was much easier to fend off, keep those things away and not feel and just kind of go through

my day not feeling . . . And today when I sit in therapy and am totally over-come by emotions, I can think at the same time . . . I can be reflecting on and thinking about what happened as well as feeling about it. So that it doesn't seem like it's just a flood of emotions and I can't think straight.

Sarah sees therapy as a process of discovery in which she continually works to unite her affective experience with her cognitive knowledge:

I still haven't put all the picture together in my head exactly, how growing up in my family affected me and affected the development of the eating disor-der. I guess, part of it is because I still feel kind of disconnected from feeling about what happened to me as a kid. I kind of can know, but I don't have that real knowing . . . It just takes a really long time and then—pfoom! That seems to be how I work, anyway, that things kind of go along, and you feel like "What's going on? Am I doing any work?" and then—pfoom! I have this connection, something clicks, and finally the affect comes together with my head, and then I feel like, "Okay, that's one." But it still feels like there's many of those ahead of me that need to happen.

Sensing psychic pain—and even sensing pleasure—required that Rebecca be able to tolerate her fear:

It served a lot of needs. Emotional needs. It gave me a focus. God, it was everything. It became all-consuming in a lot of ways for me. Any feeling that I felt that I couldn't validate, I could purge it. If I thought I did bad on an exam, or if I didn't study enough, I could find any reason in the world, any negative thing. It could even be a positive thing, too. If something good was going on in my life, "My God, maybe this isn't real. I'd better get back to my reality, which is bingeing and purging." It's a lot of fear, wondering if a rela-tionship is gonna work out. It was a companion. It gave me something to do and something to identify with without really feeling those feelings of the unknown.

Rebecca's account suggests that defending against positive feelings can be an effort to avoid shame: if you let yourself enjoy something or some-one, you run the risk that the experience will not last and that you will feel exposed and deflated.

Abigail discovered that although eating dampened feelings in the short run, it only delayed the point at which she had to reckon with them:

"I just think when you're angry and you're eating to stop that rather than because you're hungry, that you're still angry after you finish the meal. You haven't addressed what you're trying to address, and then you're eating way past hunger, and it's not helping, it doesn't really help anything. I guess it helps momentarily, it distracts you from the anger or the sadness or whatever it is that you're feeling." By contrast, she recalls a time when she let herself feel instead of numbing herself with food: "So he broke up with me, and I actually remember just being really sad one day and not eating, just allowing myself to feel the sadness."

SENSING ADEQUACY

For women who had felt deeply inadequate, sensing their own adequacy was a powerful experience. Feeling fundamentally accepted fostered a sense that they were inherently enough, that they did not need to do or be something extraordinary to be worthy of love and respect. Abigail derives self-acceptance from identifying with the natural world:

> I've always had a hard time just being with whatever is, with me or whatever's in the moment, because I've always been trained to worry about the next hoop. And I think instilled in that was a sense that I wasn't okay just in and of myself, that it relied on these hoops . . . I guess I felt like there was a list of criteria I had to meet in order to be valuable. But if you look at things in nature, they're not really meeting any criteria, they're just growing, and they're going through cycles, and they're not always looking beautiful or in bloom, but they're still beautiful, they're still valuable.

In Overeaters Anonymous, Beth found an accepting regard that helped her believe she was inherently okay: "People just caring about me in the meetings and caring about me unconditionally. I couldn't believe that I could talk about the things I did with food and that people wouldn't blink an eye." The anonymity in OA was helpful: "People don't even know my last name. They don't know where I went to school. They don't know what degree I have. They don't know what I majored in. And they accept me as I am . . . That's the basis for being there, is that you have an eating problem, and so people are just totally accepting of each other."

When Jill realized she could not be authentically herself and be accepted by her mother, she rebelled:

Up until I was about 15, I was the perfect child that never did anything wrong. Star athlete, star student, the whole bit. And I did pretty much everything my mother wanted in the way she wanted it. But my mother grew up with two sisters in a very prim and proper family, and they all took ballet and they all took piano, and they were all dressed alike and they did everything the same. And I was real tomboyish. I only had brothers, I had all male cousins, there were only boys in the neighborhood . . . And so from the beginning, my mother would try to mold me into being like she was or doing what she did, but I really didn't wanna be that way. And then when I started drinking, that's when I just totally rebelled . . . So I wasn't the daughter that she wanted.

Jill felt accepted and loved for herself in her relationship with Georgia, her sponsor in Alcoholics Anonymous: "I wanted unconditional love. I didn't feel like my mother's love was unconditional, so that's what I would look for. 'Cause nothin' I ever did really measured up for my mother, and so I wanted someone who didn't care. And Georgia, she didn't care how much I weighed or how I looked or what my problems were, what my issues were, what my job was."

SENSING AUTHENTICITY

The women had reached adolescence with an insubstantial sense of identity. They developed a sense of identity by learning to identify their authentic needs, feelings, limits, and desires. Rebecca, when asked whether she believes it's possible to fully recover, replies: "I was talking to my mother over the holidays, and she said, 'I finally feel like I have the Rebecca back that I used to have.' And I feel the same way because I'm—even though I don't remember clearly who I was prior to the eating disorder, I am myself. I am true. You know, a spiritual sense of trueness to who I am. You know, the True with a capital T. That's how I feel. And that's the way I want to feel, and that's who I am. I'm being true to myself." To recover, she had to be true to, among other things, her physi-

110

cal nature: "I'm not meant to be a skinny person . . . My body weight is not meant to even be 120."

Like Rebecca, Kate had to learn to be true to her body's identity: "I'm never gonna be sleek. I had to come to the conclusion that I'm never gonna be a thin person and be able to be healthy at the same time." What helped her accept her body's natural shape and size was feeling appreciated for more substantial aspects of herself that she had kept hidden: "I think that being in counseling and getting the emotional baggage out there made me a much more open person, with other people . . . being more able to be open to other people and not keep so much of myself hidden. The sales people that I'm working with for the last six years tell me that I'm a much different person now than I was when I first started. Much more relaxed, or whatever, there's just something different about it."

Throughout her life, Abigail had struggled to identify and voice her needs and preferences. During her medical training she became aware how difficult this was for her: "I had no idea what I wanted. What *I* wanted. I thought I had never done what I wanted. 'I don't even know what I want. I don't even know how I feel . . . How to identify what I want. How do I do that?' And I thought, 'Here I am, I'm a doctor, and I can't identify what I want' . . . There's something that people have that they take for granted in their ability to identify and speak what they want that I don't have . . . I think that everyone has it when they're born, but I think that when you lose the connection to that, it's a very valuable connection . . . to identifying what you want." Not knowing how to identify what she wanted had made her vulnerable to trying to be what she imagined other people—particularly her parents and her boyfriends—wanted her to be. It was partly her belief that if she lost weight she would win others' approval that led her to start dieting, then later bingeing and purging.

Abigail experienced a moment of authenticity when she switched from a residency in internal medicine to one in psychiatry: "Doing internal medicine, it wasn't me. There were parts of it that I enjoyed, but I was being a fraud . . . And when I finally declared it—'I am a fraud. This is what I need to do'—I felt a lot better about things . . . I didn't know anything about psychiatry, really, but I just felt like it was something I needed to do. I had, I think, an instinct. And I went with that. And that was a real good experience for me."

SENSING PLEASURE

If the soul reveals itself through its pleasures, then it is by sensing what brings her comfort, joy, and satisfaction that a woman experiences a sense of authenticity. Jill is still discovering her preferences:

> I'm more comfortable with myself, in who I am, and I started to learn what I like and what I don't like. Like I know what kind of books I like to read, what kind of books I don't like to read. It's still a never-ending process. Some people know all the things they like, but I'm still learning what I like, what I don't like to do. 'Cause I didn't know how to fill my time, so I would binge and purge all day long. So now I'm learning—I don't want to say it's really a question of filling my time, but I'm learning what I'd like to spend my time doing versus not, what are the things that make me happy, that I'm interested in.

By trying an approach to movement recommended by Geneen Roth, Jill found that physical activity was a source of pleasure and vitality:

> I was like the jockette growing up, and I always felt like exercise wasn't for fun or for enjoyment. It was to be the best at your sport. I was always kind of driven that way. And so for a long time I didn't do anything. It's like "Well, if I can't be the best, I'm not gonna do this. Then I'm not gonna do anything." And I think that [Roth] danced, she took dance lessons, and liked to dance, and she did it just to move. Just to move, just to feel herself move . . . I took a yoga class, and that was great. Talk about really feeling your body move . . . That's when I started to take skiing lessons. And I started to do some things like that for myself, not to go out and be the best, not to work at it ten hours a day, but just to move. I just remember her talking about moving versus strenuous exercise. Just walk, move, dance, do something you like to do.

When I ask Rebecca how her boyfriend helped her recover, she talks about his introducing her to sensual pleasure and playfulness:

He was just a wonderful person. He just would hold you and it just made you feel so cared for. And he did things with me that nobody else had done with me, sexually, and just timewise. Just things that I never—he kinda let me explore a lot of myself that I never knew was there to explore. And he was so comfortable with me, he was more comfortable with my body than I was with my body. And he was funny. He just, a lot of playful things, a lot of things that just kinda came out just 'cause of who he is, and he was, and it was so natural to him that it just made me be a little more at ease with myself. And that kinda just progressed. 'Cause I had never—there were just things that I never knew existed. I didn't know things could be like that.

After years of avoiding playing her cello because she was not good enough, Claire is playing again, for pleasure:

I was very perfectionist, how I had to play . . . And there was a while when I couldn't pick up the cello and play because it wasn't perfect. Because I had been out of practice when I was nursing 'cause I didn't practice very much. I hated the cello. And now, I practice about once every two weeks, but I can pick it up and like the sound that I make and feel good about it. And I know I can do it much better, I know I could perform the piece, but I can pick it up and still like it. And not doing something perfectly is all right. It's still my sound. And it still feels good for me.

Jessie has now discovered worlds of simple pleasure:

I have more interests, I do more things. I have time now to focus on other stuff. I have my job, my family, my dog, my boyfriend, my paint now. I got into continuing adult education classes. I took interior decorating. I'm taking gemology. Different things like that. You just become a more well-rounded person . . . Because when you have an eating disorder, that's your only concern in life. You have nothin' else, you don't care if you have a hobby, you don't care if you have interests, you don't care if you do anything or go anywhere. That's all you wanna focus on. And you can just expand so much when that's gone. All your time is free to do good things and enjoy life. And that's what I do. Even if I just hang around the house. Veg out with the dog. That's quality time to me, too.

Sarah had thought that when she recovered she "would be happy all the time." While discovering that this was not the case was disillusioning, she is learning to enjoy the dailiness of life:

113

If I thought about it from when I was still actively purging and thought, "What's life gonna be like when I'm not doing this?" I probably thought that I would be happy all the time. I think one thing that was a total sham is that no one ever told me that you weren't supposed to just grow up and not be happy all the time. That's what I thought happened. Like one day, you just suddenly were happy, and every day was happy, and you were happy. And no one ever told me about all these other things. And all these other emotions that were going to be part of what day in and day out life is. And that in order to feel happy that I'm gonna feel profoundly sad sometimes, too.

. . . Sometimes I tend to get in this mode where everything I'm doing is something I'm getting through to get to X. So I've gotta go grocery shopping and I've gotta do the laundry and I've gotta do this reading and I've gotta do, do, do, do, do, do, do, do, and I'm trying to think, "Why do I gotta do all these things?" But it just keeps seeming like there's just more and more and more to do. In terms of bigger things, like finish this school year, I've gotta find a job.

And I said to a friend of mine, "Did you ever think that doing the laundry and getting your car fixed and all that stuff is what life is?" [*Laughs.*] That we're not doing all these things to get on with life. That this is what life is. That's kind of not so exciting anymore. So I think that it's just, it's not as exciting and beautiful and wonderful and all happy as I thought.

I respond: "But you giggle about it. There's a sense that you're not really so distressed about that, like there's also a relief about it all?" And she replies: "Exactly. That I can just slow down and just enjoy it while I'm doing the grocery shopping and not rushing to get home to do the next thing. Yeah, I think that that's some kind of a relief in that sense."

SENSING SEPARATENESS

In sensing their authenticity, the women also sensed their capacity to claim their lives as their own rather than live in response to others' wishes and expectations. In particular, this involved separating from their parents.

Separating has been difficult for Kate, who, at age 32, has always lived in her family's home except during one brief period when she had an apartment. Living on her own, she binged and purged frequently, and her worsening symptoms led her to seek therapy. But she has begun the developmental task of separating, in part by taking the risk of letting her mother know how their views differ:

> She's very opinionated, and she's very critical, and she doesn't like you dis-agreeing with what she has to say. Which was really hard for a long time. It's not so hard anymore because I can sit and say to her, "I'm not saying that you're right or wrong. I'm just saying I don't agree with what you're saying." Because she feels that anytime we disagree with her that we're taking away her right to have an opinion. And you have to explain to her, "Nobody's say-ing you're not entitled to your opinion, but other people are entitled not to agree with you. And we are also entitled to an opinion."

Abigail, too, found it important to realize that separate people can have different takes on something without one person's experience trumping the other's. In her relationship with her therapist, she came to understand that she did not need another person's agreement to claim the legitimacy of her experience: "I've sort of learned that it doesn't really matter if he acknowledges that I'm right. I can still be right even if he's saying he disagrees with me." This understanding applies outside therapy as well: "I had a relationship recently with someone where I real-ized how insistent I was in wanting the person to agree with me . . . Like if I said, 'You're being defensive,' it wasn't enough that I could just know that the person was defensive. I wanted them to say to me, 'You're right, I'm being defensive.' But people don't do that. When people are really defensive, they don't say, 'Oh, yes, you're right.'"

While in residential treatment, Meg began to separate from her mother and take responsibility for her own feelings. A turning point came when she confronted her mother:

> The hardest thing to do in my recovery was to have this confrontation with my mother where I told her that I didn't think that she loved me. And that was just horrifying. My parents came down for family therapy. And I had been talking about it with my therapist, what we were gonna talk about and what I was gonna say, and we decided that I should tell her that. And I knew that I wasn't gonna be able to do it, and knew how upset she was gonna get, and how awful that was gonna feel for her, and—I start to get upset just thinking about it now. I can't imagine your child telling you that they don't

think that you love them. But I did it. And I had to do it . . . That was important both in my learning to be able to confront people but also in changing my relationship with my mom.

When I ask what enabled her to risk being that honest with her mother, Meg replies:

That was one thing that Jennifer, my therapist, was really good at, was helping me to do, was to understand that it was going to be really, really hard to do that, and that I really had to think of us as two different, really two adults who both had their own feelings. Before, I couldn't let my mom just be unhappy, and she couldn't let me be unhappy . . . So Jennifer just talked to me about what that was gonna be like, and that she knew it was gonna be hard. But I wanted my mother to know that that's how bad I felt about our relationship and that we had so far to go. That I was really just gonna show her how much need there was.

That confrontation marked the beginning of a more authentic relationship between Meg and her mother.

When Meg returned to college, she soon resumed bingeing and purging. In an effort to consolidate what she had learned at the treatment center, she arranged to complete her degree requirements at a college near her home. She lived in an apartment near her parents, worked part time, attended college part time, and was in therapy. In conversations with her mother, Meg came to appreciate her mother as a separate person:

She just wasn't very affectionate. She didn't ever say that she loved me. She didn't hug me and kiss me like my dad did. And so when I told her that, we talked about how she had been the disciplinarian, and she was always there, and Dad wasn't there, and that wasn't fair because she always had to be the bad guy, and how that felt to her, and how I had to try and understand her as a person. And she wasn't like my father, she wasn't affectionate really. And I saw that as a fault, I thought not being affectionate was bad, and I thought she was antisocial and introverted . . .

I learned a lot about her and learned that she had shown that she loved me in more ways than I was ever, ever able to see, that she would give up anything for me, and she still, like after I got out of [the treatment center], she would write me a letter almost every day. She sent me cards for support.

And still now, whatever I want, she'll sacrifice whatever, and that was always her way of showing me that she loved me, but I had never seen it before. I was always looking for more, for extra.

BEING HUMAN

Coming to sense that they were inherently enough involved the women's sensing their own fundamental humanity, including their legitimacy, their human limitations, and their capacity to contribute something of value.

SENSING ONE'S LEGITIMACY

Recovering involved experiencing, often in the context of treatment, interpersonal counters to the women's core sense of shame. Such counters were typically associated with feelings of legitimacy and validation. Meg recalls being in the residential treatment center, where she felt free from judgment: "Sometimes whenever I'm feeling bad, I just think of it as a place I would love to escape to sometimes . . . Just being able to say anything and not feel in any way that you're being judged. Either about your eating disorder or about yourself."

Similarly, Isabella describes a therapy group in which she could trust that she would be taken seriously: "You could say anything. I felt safe enough. Feeling safe, safe enough to open myself up. And I did, I forced myself to just say anything that was on my mind. And I think that really helped me. Just the acceptance that they gave me . . . Nothing you said was wrong, no one ever laughed, everyone took you seriously, and it was okay."

Kate attended group therapy for four months before she spoke in the group. It took her that long to trust that her experience was worthy of the group's time:

I think I needed to feel that I had a legitimate complaint with myself, that what I was experiencing was actually something that legitimately needed to be fixed, that I wasn't just being overdramatic about something. That I genuinely cannot deal with this on my own and I definitely need somebody's help to do this. Because for the sixteen years before that, it was something that I always had to deal with myself.

And what made that possible? To begin to feel that sense of legitimacy? . . .

I think even just from watching the group dynamics . . . There was never any feeling that if you said something you were gonna be criticized for saying it. Or that if I actually said that I had this problem somebody wasn't gonna say "You don't know what having a problem is like." I think that's what I was afraid of, I was afraid somebody was gonna say to me, "You think that's a problem? That's not a problem. Why can't you just deal with it yourself?" 'Cause that was always the thing in my family was that you can deal with these things yourself. You don't need to seek outside help . . . Once you reach a certain age, once you reach the age of reason, once you reach the age of you're an adult on your own, you should be able to handle things on your own. So I guess, the four months that I didn't say anything was making sure that nobody was gonna say to me, "You should be able to handle this on your own."

Reading about eating disorders helped Kate believe that people overeat for legitimate reasons and that she was not simply a weak person: "There was more and more information available about how psychologically it was linked, that it wasn't just a character flaw, basically. That there were actual, legitimate, emotional issues behind why people overeat, the issues of control and the issues of perfectionism, striving to be the perfect child or the perfect daughter . . . My siblings and I always were made to feel that not knowing how to control your eating is a character flaw, a weak link or something somewhere."

Sarah experienced a sense of legitimacy when her therapist made clear that whatever she wanted to talk about was worthy of their attention: "I remember in the first session asking her if I even needed to be there . . . But I remember anything I brought up she would say was important. Even just bringing up—she asked me what I wanted to do, and I said I wasn't sure. I was majoring in psychology but didn't know if I wanted to be a psychologist or not. She said, 'Well that alone is something we can talk about' . . . And that seemed like, 'Oh, okay. I belong, I can stay here.'"

SENSING ONE'S HUMAN LIMITATIONS AND HUMANITY

For many women, sensing that being human was good enough diminished their feelings of inadequacy. When Rebecca was in a treatment program, she let people know that she was not the invulnerable person she had appeared to be:

> It was a time that I told a lot of people in my life that didn't know about my bulimia. Because "I'm doing something about it, I can talk about it now" . . . Rebecca was kind of like, there was something about me that people couldn't read . . . And I think that's kinda the bulimia, I was never able to be vulnerable to anybody. And my coping mechanism was being very defensive. I could put up this wall around me, and I could save myself, and I could get people to stay away from me by making them think I was so put together and had everything and that they were the opposite. And it worked very well because I used it for many, many years. Even when I was in high school, everybody thought I was very snobby—and on the exterior, I was very snobby, but deep inside, I was just this poor, little, soft girl that needed to be vulnerable.

It was a relief to let herself be human in others' eyes: "Nobody, nobody, nobody that was in my life turned their back on me because of it. If anything, people understood me a lot more and were able to be supportive and were able to see that Rebecca isn't unconquerable, that she's just a human being. 'Cause I think I really put on this persona that I was kind of above being human."

Rebecca found it humanizing that her therapist occasionally shared her own experiences as an overeater and as a married woman:

> It makes much more sense to me to hear her say that she has similar problems, or similar experiences, or this is how she deals with it with her husband when the rug hasn't been vacuumed. It makes it just very real and makes it very, very concrete, and other people are going through this— other, normal people. So you don't feel like you're talking from left field, and

so I think even with the disclosure of being an overeater . . . She's not just an educated, going-by-the-book "This is what I'm supposed to say," "This is what I'm supposed to do" . . . She was talking from the heart and soul. I think that probably made a lot of difference . . . just breaking down that barrier and making them feel like a real person can make you feel that you can conquer the things that you're dealing with because some of the problems are the same, it just makes it more real.

Some of the most humanizing contexts were found in group therapy and support groups. Back at college after inpatient treatment, Beth attended campus OA meetings. The willingness of people there to talk about their darker experiences enabled her to feel she was part of the human race: "I think just hearin' people talk about hating themselves, and abusing themselves with food, it was just, it felt so good to have people just be really honest, just talkin' about themselves like nobody did on campus. Everybody [at school] was great, and looked great, and looked beautiful, and had it together."

Through her work as a psychiatrist, Abigail has become more accepting of her own humanity:

I think it's been a very slow process of valuing myself for whatever I am. And getting to know what people are really like, and that this goal that I have for myself doesn't exist. Just getting to know people, and seeing that there aren't hierarchies of like "This person's perfect, and then this person is less than perfect." That everyone has struggles. That this is my stuff that I have to deal with, but someone else who looks thin and perfect has some other worse thing or—

And how did you come to know that?

Probably being in psychiatry, 'cause I had this stuff day in and day out not only in my therapy but in my work and in my reading. So I began to learn what it is to be human.

It was also helpful for her to witness her therapist's fallibility, to see "that he has faults and that he's human":

Just silly things like, he screws up in his billing all the time, just accidental things where he'll screw up his schedule or something. And he's a little fat, too, which is kind of nice . . .

120

How is that important? Well, it's my fantasy that, he's not like the kind of man that I would, just by looking at him, think is perfect. But when you're in that kind of relationship with someone, the transference, you can imagine that they don't have any problems. But I can imagine all the reasons why he went into this field like, that he's in analysis—and he doesn't talk about how great he feels four or five days a week. And so I guess it makes me feel like I'm just like anyone else, that I'm not really better or worse.

Jessie finds that now that she has recovered she can attend more to the world around her and feel more human in the sense of feeling more humane:

It's almost like you gain a new outlook . . . Things look different. You experience things differently. When you like yourself, you can experience a walk down the street differently.

I've become more sensitive. I don't know if you've seen the newspaper today about that boy that was killed when he was helping the dog? . . . A dog got hit by a car, and this teenage boy stopped to help this dog. And he got run down by a car. And killed. And my heart just broke. And before, I didn't feel things like that. It was like, "Oh, too bad." I would feel bad, like "Oh, this poor kid got hit by a car, but woe is me. Woe is me, I'm ugly, I'm fat today. Sorry, kid." But you can say, "Oh, God, I'm lucky. I'm healthy now. And this poor kid, his whole life ahead of him." And I cried. It was very sad.

Things like that. You just view things very differently, if that makes sense. You become more focused on what's around you than you. Because when you is good, you can enjoy everything else. When the you is bad, you seem to just focus on the bad, and the good gets pushed away. So you see more, you enjoy more.

SENSING ONE'S CAPACITY TO CONTRIBUTE

Many of the women say it was helpful to feel they were valued not for their appearance or accomplishments but for their spirit and their ability to make meaningful contributions in the world.

Gita felt this way after she had a child: "I think having a baby gave my life a meaning that I've always been searching for, too, in that I've always loved children and loved caring for things . . . And I do love my job, but it was just the sort of personal fulfillment and the love with Paul that I think gave me something that maybe was lacking . . . Something was missing for me starting, particularly in puberty and moving forward. I don't know why that is, but there was a hole and now it's not there anymore."

In our second interview, I ask more about how having a child filled the hole in her life. Gita replies:

> I think it was more actually having a worth. Having a value that meant something to me. Not just being someone's little daughter, little girl, or not just being a student. All these things I think are important, but I wanted to have a worth that meant something to me. And being a mom and caring for a child is I guess what I thought was worthy. I think at that point certainly, it gave me a self-worth that I never had . . .
>
> I think the majority of time from maybe 7, or 11, somewhere in there, I really didn't like myself, and I was very concerned about what the outside world thought, what my parents thought and my friends thought, and how I appeared to people . . . So my self-worth became very outward, and I judged it by the outward things. And I think somehow pregnancy, and becoming a mom, there's so much of it that's private and intimate and personal and between few individuals. I guess that made me realize that my days are filled with *my* worth and my giving it meaning. That I can't live what other people think, I don't have time anymore. I have to survive and meet essential needs of my child and myself. They're more important.

Several women found it helpful to feel competent and able to contribute something worthwhile in their work. Sarah derived a sense of competence and value from her job on an eating-disorders unit of a hospital:

> I don't remember anything significant about that summer except loving working at the hospital, just finally feeling like I had something other than school. That I could see myself one day really loving this profession. I knew that's what I wanted to do.
>
> *Was that a new experience for you?*
>
> Yeah, because I was afraid that, "Yeah, I'm great at school, but who knows if I could actually do this? Or what if I'm totally bad at it? Or what if I'm so screwed up that I couldn't help anybody else?" So, yeah, that was definitely new. And it felt good.

She remembers feeling "I'm good at this" and "I can be helpful" not only because others told her she did a good job but because she herself sensed that her interactions with patients were healing for them. When one anorexic woman was discharged from the hospital, she told Sarah, "I feel like Dorothy in *The Wizard of Oz* when she said to the scarecrow, 'I'll miss you most of all.'" Sarah took pride in that acknowledgment and attributed it to her ability to "see the uniqueness in each person and to have the patience and energy to discover that."

Claire drew upon her own knowledge of the pain of sexual abuse to make a powerful response to a girl in a group at the psychiatric hospital where she works:

> There was just this one therapy session we had where the kids, they can talk about whatever they want, and there's a psychologist and myself, and one girl was talking about sexual abuse, and she was being very graphic. And a group of them was discussing it, and it was very emotional, and the session was supposed to be an hour, and it was getting on to two hours. And she was saying what happened when she told a relative, and she was very angry at the relative's reaction, they said that she shouldn't have said anything.
>
> And I said to her, "When you tell a loved one or a relative, they feel very frightened or very useless, and very embarrassed. And they're often not the best person to help you. Sometimes they have a lot to sort out themselves. Sometimes you need to go to somebody, a third party, a psychologist like David or myself that can be there for you." And it was great, and the psychologist said, "That's the best thing you could have said." And of course, how else would I have known? And suddenly my own experience felt very useful. And after that I would see this girl, and I was "great" and I was "awesome."

Beauty and the Beast

It is difficult to describe one's experience of recovering from an eating disorder in a way that means anything to anyone else. After a talk or a panel presentation on the personal experience of recovery, someone from the audience invariably asks, "But I still don't understand—what did you do to get better?" And the recovered person says something like, "Well, I had to learn to like myself. And to know myself. I had been so busy trying to be what I thought others wanted me to be that I had no idea who I really was." Or, "I realized that there were a lot of things my family couldn't find a way to talk about and that my eating disorder was my way of communicating that something was very wrong."

The person who asked the question looks bewildered, as if this response seems vague and mysterious to her. Then, invariably, someone else asks the question a little differently: "What *exactly* did you do to get better? What did you do *instead* of bingeing and purging, or *instead* of trying to control your weight?" This time the recovered person says something like, "I tried individual therapy (and/or group therapy, family therapy, a self-help group, hospitalization, medication, meditation), but what really happened is that I learned that my eating disorder was an expression of a lot of feelings that I didn't know I had. And once I learned that I could feel—that I could be sad and scared and lonely and even angry—I discovered who I was, and that I was okay, and then I didn't need my eating disorder anymore."

I suspect that this response sounds just as vague and mysterious to the questioner, because while the person in the audience is asking one question—"What did you do to stop?"—the recovered person is responding to a different question—"How did I come to be more fully myself and more accepting of myself as a whole person?"

What did you *do?* How did I come to *be?* Both are valid questions: recovering requires both doing and being. But stating what one did does not convey the hidden, private process by which one came to be more fully oneself. As Abigail Lipson observes, metaphor helps us communicate such interior experience: "I describe one thing—my private experience which can be known only by me—in terms of another, different thing—an image that I hope you, too, can imagine" (1989, 11).

As I listen to people's stories of recovering from bulimia nervosa, I hear many metaphors, but one that is especially salient is that of Beauty and the Beast. If we read that fairy tale not as the story of a fair maiden finding her Prince Charming but as a tale about a drama that happens within the self, it is a metaphor of coming to accept aspects of oneself that one has considered ugly, unacceptable, and unlovable. It is the story of a young woman's quest to become whole. Although the tale of Beauty and the Beast has traditionally been interpreted as an oedipal drama of a relational triangle in which love is transferred from one object to another (Bettelheim, 1975/1977), it can also be understood as a preoedipal story about the integration of affiliative and aggressive strivings which takes place within the self in the context of a dyadic relationship.

I draw heavily upon Marianna Mayer's book *Beauty and the Beast* (1978); all quotations in this section are from her retelling of the story. As Mayer tells it, Beauty was the youngest daughter of a wealthy merchant who had three daughters and three sons. His wife had died many years before, but "his children filled his life and his business gave him little time to be lonely." One day the merchant lost all his wealth when a storm destroyed his ships. He and his children were forced to leave their house in the city, move to the country, and work the land there. All the merchant's children complained about their plight except Beauty, who reassured her father that the move would bring its own rewards. Of the three daughters, Beauty "was the most like her mother" and, like her mother, she loved the country. Beauty did the difficult field work with a smile and grace and "never thought to complain," for "the look of pride in her father's eyes was reward enough for her."

When the merchant received word that his ships had been found washed ashore, Beauty's sisters were excited at the thought that he might recover his wealth after all. They asked their father to bring them back fine dresses and shoes and a carriage. When he asked Beauty what she wanted him to bring for her, she insisted that there was nothing she needed. When he persisted, she felt obliged to ask for something and said she would like a rose.

But the merchant discovered that the ships' cargo had been either damaged or seized by bill collectors. Defeated, he set out for home. On the way back he got lost. Seeking shelter for the night, he happened upon a palace with open gates and open doors. There he ate a meal that was waiting on the table, slept deeply in a luxurious bed, and woke to find a delicious breakfast on a tray next to the bed. He walked around the grounds hoping to find someone to thank for such hospitality, but he saw no one.

He did see some beautiful roses, and, remembering Beauty's request, he picked one. Then he heard a roar that "shook the entire garden." "Stricken with fear," he "fell to his knees and covered his head with his arms." He looked up and saw "a most hideous beast," who was furious that the merchant had taken one of his roses. The merchant told the beast about his ships and his journey and Beauty's request for the rose, but the beast threatened to kill him. The merchant begged for his life on behalf of his children. The beast eventually said, "If your daughter loves you enough to come in your place I will take her instead. If she refuses, you will return to me to take your punishment." The merchant refused this offer, but the beast insisted that Beauty be the one to make the choice.

The merchant went home and told his children about the bargain. Beauty's sisters would not have been at all sad to see her go, but her brothers felt protective and threatened to go to the beast's palace and kill him. Despite her father's and brothers' protests, Beauty insisted that she would go. She felt the whole incident was her fault because she had asked for the rose.

A few days later Beauty and her father set out for the palace, with Beauty riding a black horse which the beast had sent with her father. When Beauty met the beast, she found him frightening, but she also noticed that his eyes were sad and lonely. When she agreed to stay, he said, "You may refer to me as Beast, for that is what I am and I ask only that we speak the truth here." The next day the merchant left for home, his horse laden with gold the beast had given him. Beauty was alone with the beast.

She spent her days exploring the palace, which was filled with wonderful things, including fine clothes and jewelry and books which the beast had provided for her. Every evening the beast joined Beauty while she ate her dinner. That was the only time of the day when she saw him. Beauty asked him where he spent his days. He said, "Do not ask me, Beauty." She pressed him: "Please tell me what you do." At her words, "The beast looked at her and a great sorrow filled his face. But just as quickly his expression changed to anger. He raised his rough fur-covered claws and answered, 'I hunt. I prowl the woods for prey. I am an animal after all, my lady! I must kill for my meat. Unlike you I cannot eat gracefully.'" Although Beauty "was horrified," she also heard that the beast was ashamed and sad. The beast left her "with an abrupt good night," and "Beauty ceased to ask questions that might hurt or embarrass the beast."

Over time, as Beauty came to know the beast, he became less frightening to her. She even began to enjoy his company. Each evening the beast would tell her stories, and they would laugh together. As he prepared to leave for the night, the beast always asked the same question: "Beauty, will you be my wife?" And Beauty always gave the same reply: "No, Beast. I am sorry, but though you are kind to me and have treated me fairly, I can never be your wife because I do not love you."

Although Beauty enjoyed the beast's company, she longed for a prince who appeared in her dreams, where, night after night, he "would come and sit by her side" and say, "Someday, Beauty, we will be together always." "But then the dream would change and he would be gone. In his place she would hear a woman's voice speaking to her, 'Look deep into others' beauty to find your own happiness.'" Beauty was frustrated that her prince could not be with her then and there. During the day she looked for him in the garden and by the pond but did not find him.

In her dreams the prince said that as a boy he had been "very vain and quite proud," and he told her how he had come to live alone in the castle: "One day an old hag came begging at my palace gate. I showed her no pity, she was so ugly. The sight of her did not move me and I sent her away without food or money. As she left she warned that I would spend the rest of my life wandering in my fine palace without a friend till some- one could find beauty in me. I laughed at her, but when I returned to my palace, I found it empty. I have been alone ever since."

One night, having declined yet again the beast's proposal of marriage, Beauty went to bed hoping to dream about the prince, but instead an old woman appeared in her dream and said, "Your prince cannot return to you, Beauty. Since he has failed to make you his wife, you must not really love him." The old woman disappeared. And Beauty said, "But I do."

The next day Beauty found a mirror, and, looking into it, saw that her father was ill. The beast told her it was a magic mirror: "If one is pure of heart, one can see into it. If you have seen your father there, then he must truly be ill." The beast granted her request to visit her father, but he asked her to return in three weeks. That night the prince did not appear in Beauty's dream. But the old woman did, and she admonished Beauty, "How blind you are! I had hoped you would know that happiness comes from seeing what does not always lie on the surface. Some things are not on the surface at all."

The next morning Beauty looked into the magic mirror and wished she were at her father's home. The black horse carried her swiftly home. No sooner had she arrived than her father began to recover. Although Beauty remembered the beast's stipulation that she return in three weeks, she was reluctant to leave her father. Her sisters, aware of the beast's terms, deviously urged her to stay longer, and Beauty stayed.

But then she had a dream in which she saw the beast lying on the ground near the palace looking very ill, perhaps dead. She "woke chilled, and filled with dread." She held up the magic mirror and wished to be back at the palace, and once again, the black horse appeared and her wish was granted. She found the beast looking just as he had in her dream. She "knelt beside him, cradling his head in her arms" and said, "My poor beast, this is my fault for being so heartless. I have repaid your love with my own blindness and selfishness. Please recover. If you do, I swear to be your wife. I do love you."

As she held him, "he began to grow stronger. With each breath he took, his beastly appearance began to fade." The beast became—and had always been—the prince. The prince told her that the old woman he had once turned away from the palace gate had put him and his palace under a spell until he could find someone who would love him. "At last Beauty understood the mystery of her dreams. The prince and the beast were one, and her love had saved them both from their enchantment." Beauty and the prince married "and lived with love and happiness."

THE NATURE AND ORIGIN OF THE BEAST

THE BEHAVIOR OF THE BEAST

The beast has much in common with bulimic behavior. He is in hiding most of the time but appears when Beauty eats. He joins her in the evening, an unstructured time of day when a bulimic woman is apt to binge and purge. He does not want anyone to see him eat because he is ashamed that he prowls, attacks, and eats voraciously. Bulimic women say that when they binge and purge they feel overtaken by something beastlike and out of control. Some call this something "the monster," "the other me," "the wild me." Rebecca felt seized by something fierce that would not let her go until she had binged and purged: "It's kinda like it's not even a part of you, it's like something else is grabbing you and saying 'You gotta do this *now.*'"

Beauty, identified only with goodness and virtue, is not unlike a bulimic woman, who aims to present only the ostensibly positive aspects of herself. Painful experience, base feelings, and aggression are attributable to the beast (and to Beauty's sisters). A bulimic woman feels she should be entirely "good," yet she has to contend with the "bad" in her, the fierce and willful part that binges and purges. Like all human beings, she has within her a Beauty and a beast, but she is unable to marry the loving and hating aspects of herself, to let herself be the complex, whole being that she is. She tries to hide her bulimic behavior and all her other beastly aggression.

Although a bulimic woman cannot accept the beast in herself, if anyone else tries to evict or reform it, she fiercely protects it. Like Beauty, who comes to enjoy the beast's company, a bulimic woman comes to experience her bulimic behavior as a companion. Rebecca says she relied upon her bulimia as if it were a friend:

> Because the eating disorder was so familiar to me, too, by that time—I had it for two years before I got into college, and then I had it all through college, so it was just, it was basically, sickly, my best friend. So to give that up—I didn't wanna give that up. I hated it, I hated it with a passion, but I didn't wanna give it up . . .
>
> There are so many things in your life that—or at least I had—some familiar things that you can identify with and maybe feel secure with, if it's a blanket, or if it's a book, or if it's your mother, or whatever. But that's what the bulimia was for me, it was something that was very familiar and very safe because whatever I did, I still had it with me, and it wasn't gonna go away on me, and even though it seems really perverse, it wasn't gonna treat me badly, even though obviously it was. But it wasn't, it was always there, it was—

Dependable.

> Yeah, very dependable. It wasn't like my father, it wasn't like men in my life, be it male acquaintances or boyfriends, it was just, it was very, very secure and familiar.

Yet, as familiar and dependable as the bulimic self is to her, as much as she will defend it if anyone tries to defeat it, like Beauty, a bulimic woman does not fully embrace that part of herself because she regards it as too unlike the person she wants to be. She refuses to marry it. But the more unwelcome and unappreciated the beast feels, the more it demands recognition. In response to her efforts to banish it, the beast only gets more voracious, more insistent. It does everything in its power to get her attention. She finds herself bingeing more, purging more. The beast will not let her be only and always good.

THE BIRTH OF THE BEAST

The object relational and self-psychological theories of Ana-Maria Rizzuto, D. W. Winnicott, and Susan Sands explain how the beast originates in normal development; how it grows disproportionately powerful in the lives of bulimic women; how it expresses itself through bulimic symptoms; how it becomes dissociated from other aspects of self; and how, in the process of recovering, it becomes integrated with the whole self and brought back down to size.

Rizzuto seeks the developmental origins of bulimia by looking at normal development in the second year of life, the time when the child is separating from the mother. This is the beginning of a time during which children manifest what Rizzuto calls "the intense libidinal and aggressive wishes typical of the anal period" (1985, 209). This period is commonly known as "the terrible twos" (and, as many parents know, can become the terrible threes). At this age, "the child's ability to fantasize begins to reach a high moment" and "the child progressively creates a universe of nonexistent creatures ready to take any of the projections the young individual bestows on them" (203). As Rizzuto notes, "the child does not know how to talk about these beings until the adult world, usually through stories, provides the name of monsters" (203). A young child typically loves to be read stories about monsters and will talk about her fears of monsters.

In normal, healthy development, caregivers acknowledge and appreciate a child's aggressive wishes and impulses even as they contain her aggression by setting limits on her behavior in the service of her safety and socialization. In learning that her experience can be appreciated and known, even if not all of her behavior will be welcomed and tolerated, a child learns to integrate the affiliative and aggressive aspects of her self. As a result, her monstrous aspects do not feel out of proportion but are known and held in relation to the whole of her.

But Rizzuto traces a different path for children whose "natural aggressiveness is severely curtailed" (209), including children who go on to become bulimic. If a child's caregivers respond to her aggression with hostility, criticism of her core self, or withdrawal, the aggression is amplified rather than modulated. Consequently, her aggression feels exaggerated and out of proportion to her, and she experiences her aggressive aspects as so monstrously bad that they must be banished altogether.

For instance, Beth remembers that she always felt "too big." From this memory she associates to having broad shoulders, a temper, "a lot of anger," and "too much inside of me":

> 'Cause I'd look at pictures of myself, and I was not fat at all. Though I always felt like I was too big, I have broad shoulders and stuff, and I always felt too big. I had a temper and stuff, and I don't know if this connects, but I felt like I had a lot of anger inside me. It sounds funny saying this, but I always felt like I couldn't control it. My father was very authoritarian, and I always felt like I couldn't do anything, as though I had a really bad temper. I think part of it was I just felt like there was too much inside of me.

In associating to her father's authoritarian nature, she suggests that her anger and willfulness were not allowed and contained in her relationship with her father. He, and consequently she, did not hold them in relation to the whole of her, and so she felt she was too much and unacceptably bad.

Feeling unacceptably bad, according to Rizzuto, leads to the development of a hidden self. The child does not want anyone to see her badness, so she hides the monstrous aspects of herself behind compliant behavior. Her parents may actually reinforce her hiding because their life is easier without a monster in the house. Their failure to help their child integrate her aggression may be due to their not having been able to tolerate, regulate, and integrate their own aggression. Most typically, the mother dissociates her aggression (like Beauty), while the father does not modulate his aggression (like the beast).

As a result, the child's aggressive aspects of self remain out of relationship—either to the parent or to other aspects of the child: "The voracious, angry monster, hidden behind good conduct, never meets the parental eye. The absence of this event does not permit the internalization of the parental eye in relation to the monster, leaving this aspect of the child isolated from a meaningful contact with the parent" (209).

Such a child comes to feel isolated and unknown:

> The child whose parents do not accept and do not help her to accept some of her own badness grows into a progressive sense of psychic isolation. The child now develops a compelling need not to be seen, psychologically, in real life. Many of these children find favorite hiding places. However, even when they are not in hiding, they learn to hide psychically by complying with and obeying their parents without the subjective satisfaction of self-approval or the ability to accept some parental compliments; they are now convinced of their secret but unquestionable badness and feel constantly that they are fooling their parents. (207)

That is, the child develops a false self. While her parents and others appreciate and praise the falsely compliant self, she feels she is fundamentally bad. So she perpetually works to hide the bad parts of her and to behave as if she were only good. She may hope that if she tries hard enough to act as if she is good, she will become good. She is intent on seeking others' approval. She makes choices guided by others' expectations and desires and does not assert her own will, desire, and zest. Although she may be a source of pride for her parents, such a child leads a joyless, exhausting, burdensome existence, without a true sense of pride in her activities.

Rizzuto compares the experience of a bulimic-to-be with that of an anorexic-to-be.* As Rizzuto sees it, a child who goes on to develop bulimia is someone who does "feel seen as an individual" (209) by her parents but who, as she develops more independence, learns that her developmentally normal voraciousness and anger are not acceptable.

---

*This differentiation between people with anorexia nervosa and those with bulimia nervosa is not a clean distinction: some people with one diagnosis cross over to the other.

The child who goes on to become anorexic, however, does not feel that her internal, subjective world is known at all by others. She may try to be seen and appreciated for her external, objective aspects of self, namely her appearance, activities, accomplishments, and accommodating behavior. But even that effort fails since she is never really seen or appreciated as an other and remains only a narcissistic projection of what her parents need her to be (Miller, 1981/1994). She does not feel seen or known as a real person. She develops an "as if" personality, feeling unreal, wooden, and mechanical rather than real, spontaneous, and alive. The bulimic, by contrast, has some sense of her authentic self but feels she must hide the most intense aspects of herself because they will be too much for people.

The bulimic-to-be, according to Rizzuto, gets the message that some aspects of her are unacceptable "not so much through punishment but through lack of acknowledgment" of her neediness and her aggressive impulses and wishes (209). That is, she learns to conceal the beast through passive, covert shaming. Lack of acknowledgment arouses more hurt and anger, leaving her with an even bigger beast to hide.

If we regard Beauty and the beast as aspects of the same person, Rizzuto's conceptions about monsters are congruent with the fairy tale. The beast was once a beautiful and privileged prince, but because he could not accept the needy, ugly, undesirable aspects of his humanity (he turned away the old woman who came begging at the palace gate), he fell from grace. His baseness was exaggerated, and he was exiled to live alone in his palace, out of relationship to others and to nobler aspects of himself. He is ashamed to lead the life of a beast, so much so that he begs Beauty not to ask him how he spends his days.

Beauty, meanwhile, is too good to be true. She is a devoted daughter who, despite hardship and hard work, never complains. She acts as if she has no needs. She speaks only of positive, noble feelings. Any painful feelings—of disappointment, loss, or anger—and any desires, strivings, or other expressions of self-definition and self-determination are expressed only by others, in particular by her sisters, who are portrayed as selfish and ignoble.

Beauty and the beast are both incomplete. One is too good to be true, the other too bad to be true. To be whole, one needs to claim her badness, the other his goodness.

Although D. W. Winnicott did not write about people with bulimia nervosa in particular, his object relational approach resonates with Rizzuto's formulation. (Here I rely largely on Eugene Beresin's understanding of Winnicott's work.) Winnicott, following Melanie Klein, regards the integration of love and hate as one of the basic developmental tasks for all human beings. That is, in normal development, a child faces the task of integrating the libidinal, affiliative drives and the aggressive, destructive drives that coexist within her, even toward one and the same person: she can and does hate the very parent she loves.

While a child's aggression may be activated in response to an environmental frustration or failure, that is, when her needs are not met, to Winnicott's mind, environmental disappointment is not the ultimate source of aggression or hate. He regards aggressive drives as innate in human beings. An infant, he notes, has very different experiences of the mother depending on "whether the baby is quiet or excited," and the infant links libidinal instincts toward the mother with the quiet phase and destructive impulses toward her with the excited phase: "The human infant cannot accept the fact that this mother who is so valued in the quiet phases is the person who has been and will be ruthlessly attacked in the excited phases" (1958/1975, 266). The infant has not yet integrated her feelings of love and hate for the same parent.

In normal development, a child comes to realize that if she destroys the mother she hates she will also lose the mother she loves, the one who fulfills her needs. Her fear that her hate could destroy what she loves leaves her with anxiety that becomes a source of primitive, preoedipal guilt. To deal with the guilt, a child tries to make reparations to her mother in the form of hugs, kisses, artistic creations, or tokens (a flower, a toy). If her mother can accept the reparations and respond without betrayal, abandonment, smothering, or retaliation, the child is able to experience concern for her mother and to take responsibility for her own instinctual, destructive impulses. To accept a gift, the mother has to feel good enough and whole enough herself. If the mother accepts the reparations, the child learns that she can make things right, and she is therefore able to tolerate the ambivalence inherent in experiencing both her love and her hate. When she realizes that her mother both accepts her reparations and survives her rage, she learns that her rage cannot destroy the object of her love. Winnicott sees a child's learning that she can do something about her guilt as the origin of empathy and concern.

Beresin, applying Winnicott's theory of development, proposes that for a child who eventually becomes bulimic, it is likely that the child's aggressive impulses were not accepted, that reparations were not received and were instead met with retaliation or abandonment, with the result that the child did not learn to integrate love and hate toward objects of love or within herself. Beresin refers to Laura Humphrey (1988), who found that relative to normal families, families of bulimic women tend to demonstrate "greater mutual neglect, rejection, and blame" and "less understanding, nurturance, and support." Humphrey observes: "Just as the bulimic craves food during a binge, so do she and her family 'crave' nurturance, soothing, and empathy in their relation-ships with one another. Similarly, family members are thought to 'purge' themselves by projecting the hostility and frustration toward each other, without structure, focus, or resolution" (544).

Beresin argues that in bulimic families, where criticism, hostility, and emotional neglect are typical, a child experiences a chaotic emotional en-vironment. Adults in bulimic families do not help modulate the aggres-sion in the family. A child's aggression is not contained and tempered but rather is reflected back at her, or even magnified, giving her the message that her badness is enormous and dangerous. To make matters worse, in such a family there is no way to kiss and make up. Any reparations she offers are likely to be met with retaliation or rejection rather than with acceptance and forgiveness. Given that her parent cannot help her inte-grate her love and hate, she has to split off her aggression from her love. That is, because she cannot tolerate the ambivalence of hating the parent she loves, she must choose to only love or only hate her parent. She must choose love so as not to destroy the parent, who is essential to her sur-vival, and so as to preserve her own sense of being good.

But although publicly she tries to be good and loving, privately she feels deeply, if unconsciously, guilty for her badness and hate. The beast is a projection of the split-off, aggressive aspects of herself. When she behaves aggressively, her aggression becomes a source not only of guilt but of shame, both shame by her own internal standards and shame in others' eyes. To avoid the shame of exposure, she works even harder to hide her badness.

Beth describes such a split in herself:

> I always felt like I was a bad person, and even if I thought bad things that I was bad . . . And also with sexuality, I went through Catholic schools, K through 9, and they never, ever, ever taught one class on sex ed. They didn't even show us a movie. And I just felt that kind of non-acceptance of people's bodies, of sexuality as a healthy part of being human . . . And I always felt God was punishing, that if I did something bad that that was it, I was going to hell. That there was no kind of acceptance of, that if you're human, you're gonna have these things happen to you, you're gonna have bad emotions, you're gonna have selfishness, but it's your actions that count . . . I always felt like waiting for myself to do something bad.

Just as in families of bulimic women it is hard to find consistent emotional sustenance, in Beauty's family there is no mother. Other than Beauty, no one attends to the family members' need for nurturance. Beauty is attentive to others' needs, in particular to her father's. But her attunement to others comes at the expense of self-attunement. This is also true of women with bulimia nervosa. For Winnicott, over-attunement to others and under-attunement to self results from "impingements" (1965/1994, 86), that is, from the repeated interruptions of being that one experiences in the chaotic emotional environment of a family where criticism and hostility are unmodulated. In the face of chronic environmental disruption, one learns to be highly aware of changes in the environment—keenly attuned to others' emotional states—in an effort to have some sense of predictability and control.

In such a situation a woman comes to regard her own needs, desires, and preferences as unworthy of attention. Beauty is portrayed as gracious and good for seeming to have no desires or strivings at all. She feels blameworthy for expressing even the simplest desire. Being guilty of asking for a rose, and having a father who cannot modulate the beast's aggression, she believes she is the bad one, the cause of all the trouble, and she leaves to live with the beast. Her openly hostile, critical sisters are pleased to see her go. Beauty's experience resembles that of bulimic women in that within the family she endures chronic emotional neglect and overt hostility.

Just as bulimic women work to keep their bingeing and purging hidden from family and friends, the beast is entirely separate from Beauty's familial world. Beauty and the beast become intimate friends only outside the context of her family. No one in Beauty's family demonstrates the ability to integrate love and hate. Beauty's siblings hold the aggression in the family—her sisters' aggression taking the form of envy and greed and her brothers' the form of protective rage—while Beauty's father is sweet but powerless and Beauty herself embodies only generosity, grace, and devotion.

THE BANISHING OF THE BEAST

Women with bulimia nervosa wish they could get rid of, or at least contain and control, the beast within. A bulimic's contempt for the beast leads her to want to silence it, as if it were a demanding nuisance; to evict it, as if it were a troublesome tenant; to overpower it, even kill it, as if it were an enemy; or to cleanse herself of it, as if it were a stain on her otherwise spotless life. At the very least, she tries to hide it.

But given the beast's power, hiding it requires great energy, as Jill recalls: "I don't know how I was so successful, if I was, in hiding it. All the work and the effort that went into it. And I just, I feel very free that I'm not engaged in that anymore. Which is always like this big revelation to me if I sit down and think about it. I feel a huge freedom."

As discussed in Chapter 1, we can understand bulimia nervosa in terms of the dissociation of language and affect and the dissociation of archaic needs, feelings, and other rejected aspects of self. Susan Sands (1991), drawing on self-psychological theory, describes a hidden "bulimic self," a dissociated self-state formed from the banished aspects of self. When a child's basic narcissistic needs and primitive aggressive strivings are not met with attuned responses by her parents, she learns that those aspects of her are unacceptable, and she dissociates them into a separate, hidden sector of the self. Many bulimic women experience the hidden self as "other": "When the therapist talks more directly to the 'bulimic self,' he or she will often find that the patient has already given it her own personal label—for example, 'the body,' 'the monster,' 'the little girl,' the 'dark side'" (37).

Bulimic behavior, Sands notes, allows the bulimic to make contact with the hidden self:

> On the one hand, the patient experiences the bulimic self as negative and "not me" because it is self-destructive and out-of-control, almost involuntary. It expresses the rage that usually follows when needs are unmet . . . On the other hand, the bulimic self is unconsciously regarded by the patient as intensely positive, the only "true" part of her, because its actions are for her, not for her parents or anyone else. Because the bulimic self represents her urgent demand for selfhood, it is unspeakably precious to her. The bulimic behavior is thus both an assertion of self *and* a punishment for it. (38–39)

Because bulimic behavior and dissociation so successfully exile a woman's basic emotional needs into a separate self-state, it is hard to do the psychological work of integrating her needs with her whole personality. A bulimic, Sands argues, "will not begin to reveal her hidden self until its paradoxical and multidimensional nature is fully acknowledged and accepted. The therapist must let the patient know that he or she can appreciate the self-affirming as well as the self-destructive intentions of the bulimic self, and must also communicate a kind of reverence for this secret, sacred part" (39).

THE BADNESS OF THE BEAST

These theoretical understandings shed light on bulimics' experience of stealing and of destructiveness. Shoplifting is common among bulimic women. Several of the women I interviewed say they stole while they were bulimic. Like the beast, who felt bad about hunting, prowling, and killing his prey and yet felt compelled to do so, these women feel guilty and ashamed about stealing and yet driven and even entitled to do it. Some of the women who did not shoplift stole food from friends or from their families. And of course purging is, among other things, an act of destruction.

Claire felt deeply guilty and ashamed when she stole her fellow nursing students' food:

> This sounds really sick I'm afraid. It's very bizarre. But in the night I would be up and I would steal from the fridges. And I am not a thief, I am not someone who can do that. But in the fridges there would be stuff like bread and cheese and spread. And so a sliver here, a sliver there, nobody would miss it. A slice of bread from a bag of sliced bread, nobody would miss. And then it got to be taking a bag. And then, in that particular kitchen, nobody would put food because it got to be eaten. And so I left money from time to time. But then eventually, nobody would put their food in the fridge. So I would eat out of the dustbins. This was the next best source, the dustbins in the kitchen there. Which meant anything that had been thrown away half eaten or had mold on it, I would eat. And when in my friends' rooms having coffee after a shift, when they would go to the toilet, I would steal from their food cupboards. I would shove food into my pockets. And my dearest friends, people that you love the most.

Abigail associates her stealing with the sense that there was something "exciting and kind of wild" in her that she felt she had to hold back:

> I've had a lot of dreams about stealing in my life . . . I used to steal when I was little, and I think they say that the kleptomania and bulimia are sometimes related. And I think for me, what I've come up with about the stealing is that it was my way of expressing myself as a kid. I was gonna do mischief. I didn't do it to have things, I did it for the real doing it. I think if I could've expressed myself freely in front of everyone, I wouldn't need to do these covert behaviors to get some sort of satisfaction. But when I brought this up to one of my supervisors in residency, he said, "Hmm, stealing, you could think of it as s-t-e-a-l or s-t-e-e-l, like holding yourself back, steeling." And when he said that . . . I've wondered, "What's held back? What is underneath

that's being held back?" And then I had this dream with the mountains on fire. This sense of something being inside me that's really exciting and kind of wild. People have commented about that to me, friends or lovers. But I think that all along those years there was developing this need to be free.

Stealing is one of many impulsive and compulsive behaviors in which some bulimic women engage—including bingeing and purging as well as substance abuse, excessive shopping, sexual risk-taking and/or promiscuity, and self-mutilation. Impulsive and compulsive behaviors are thought to result from deficits in self-regulatory capacities and to serve, among other functions, to generate a rush or high that temporarily counters depression or enables one to escape from painful emotional experience.

But as I listen to my clients and the women I interviewed, it strikes me that when they steal, they typically steal basic necessities or simple treats: food, a piece of clothing, a lipstick. It is as if what they take is so basic that they feel entitled to it. I believe stealing expresses their sense that they are rightfully entitled to have not the item they steal but something else very basic—namely nurturance, particularly attunement to their emotional needs by a person who matters to them.

Winnicott refers to stealing and destructive acts (such as vandalism or breaking something) as "two trends in the antisocial tendency" which tend to go hand in hand, "although the accent is sometimes more on one than on the other" (1958/1975, 310). He notes that stealing and destructive acts "may be found in a normal individual" and are not necessarily signs of a personality disorder (308). He understands stealing and destructiveness as efforts to lay claim to love of which one feels one was deprived. Antisocial acts arise when a child feels "deprived of certain essential features of home life" (308), in particular, when there has been "a de-privation" of nurturance and affection: "a loss of something good that has been positive in the child's experience up to a certain date, and that has been withdrawn; the withdrawal has extended over a period of time longer than that over which the child can keep the memory of the experience alive" (309). This construction—having a positive connection with someone, experiencing a break in the connection and a desire for reconnection but no restoration of the connection—is the same construction Kaufman and Tomkins use to trace the interpersonal origins of shame (see Chapter 1). Thus de-privation and shame appear to be intrinsically linked. Referring to the work of John Bowlby, Winnicott says, "There is now a widespread recognition of the relationship that exists between the antisocial tendency in individuals and emotional deprivation, typically in the period of late infancy and the early toddler stage, round about the age of one and two years" (309). This is near the age Rizzuto identifies as crucial in the development of the hidden, aggressive self.

Winnicott sees stealing and destructiveness as serving different functions. When someone steals, she is "looking for something, somewhere, and failing to find it, seeks it elsewhere, when hopeful" (310). She typically steals in such a way that she will be caught. In so doing, she is trying to bring back into her life someone whose loving regard she has lost or to recruit the involvement and loving regard of someone new. That is, stealing is a manifestation of a libidinal, affiliative instinct. The child "is not looking for *the object stolen but seeks the mother over whom he or she has rights*" (311).

By contrast, when someone is destructive, her effort is not to find a lost connection to someone but to experience someone's steadiness, "that amount of environmental stability which will stand the strain resulting from impulsive behavior" (310). She seeks a reliable relational environment on which she can depend no matter what she does, no matter how bad she is. Winnicott describes this effort as "a search for an environmental provision that has been lost, a human attitude, which, because it can be relied on, gives freedom to the individual to move and to act and to get excited" (310).

For Winnicott, the observation that the antisocial tendency comprises two trends, one libidinal in nature (object-seeking), the other aggressive (object-destroying), indicates that the antisocial tendency is an effort to integrate love and hate. If someone who steals or destroys lets herself get caught, she creates a new chance for reparation. The new chance is needed because she has not resolved primitive guilt, the unconscious guilt that derives from the failure to integrate love and hate. Because the guilt arises from a destructive impulse which is often unconscious, she cannot make sense of the guilt. Winnicott, drawing on Freud's notion that unconscious guilt is the source rather than the result of crime, notes that being unable to understand why one feels guilty is so unsettling that it can lead a person to do something bad so that she can at last attribute her guilt to a specific behavior. Once she has committed a crime, her guilt makes sense to her.

"The antisocial tendency implies hope," Winnicott says, because it is while a child is experiencing a "period of hope" that she steals or commits a destructive act (309). The child hopes that despite her previous failed attempts to recruit involvement from her environment and establish its stability, this time people will be as responsive and reliable as she has always wanted them to be. Winnicott notes the importance of responding in a way that affirms the hope. He also implies that the responsive act must be timed to "the moment of hope": "The understanding that the antisocial act is an expression of hope is vital in the treatment of children who show the antisocial tendency. Over and over again one sees the moment of hope wasted, or withered, because of mismanagement or intolerance" (309). The response must be active and practical: "The antisocial tendency is characterized by an *element in it which compels the environment to be important*. The patient through unconscious drives compels someone to attend to management" (309). *Management,* from a word meaning "hand," implies that the person needs someone to lend a hand.

A brief moment of hope and the need for active management are consistent with my observations about the importance of a felt sense of enough, a timely and attuned response (see Chapter 2), and authentic, attuned acts of care (see Chapter 6). If stealing and destructiveness are expressions of hope that one's need for love and reliability will at last be acknowledged, it is important to affirm the validity of that hope through a timely, attuned act rather than to let the hope be dashed.

This understanding of stealing and destruction finds empirical support in the women's interviews. When asked how she understands why she stole, Rebecca says: "I think for me, I wanted to get caught so I could tell somebody I had this problem and make them fix it." In our second interview she gives another reason for stealing:

> I think also it was just a way to have things, kinda like being a klepto, I guess. I went to a college that had many girls that Daddy wrote out the check. I didn't have . . . I wasn't at poverty level—we were lower middle class—but I still kind of felt like it was, you hear people say that all the time, "I deserved it," or "I can justify it" by "I don't have what this other person has, there-fore."

And you remember feeling some of that kind of resentment?

> Oh, yeah, I couldn't. They could fly to the Caribbean during Christmas break, or Daddy would take them shopping at Neiman Marcus.

Rebecca's associations suggest that her sense of not having enough is linked with her sense of lacking an attentive father and, most fundamen-tally, of lacking the ability to hold a man's attention. A sense of lacking is ultimately a sense of shame, of not being enough, not mattering enough. Her stealing may have been an expression of rage in response to feeling that she did not matter enough to her father. He had once loved her enough to buy her a horse and help her care for it. But he became inat-tentive toward the entire family and neglected Rebecca and her horse. Rebecca experienced Winnicott's "de-privation": she once had her father's love and attention, but then she lost it. To her mind, the love she had once had and the emblems of that love were her due and ought to be granted to her.

I ask whether attending college was her first intense exposure to class differences. Rebecca replies: "Oh, definitely. I never, I never—where I grew up, everybody was basically middle class. Some people had nicer homes than others. But I never knew anybody that had a Mercedes or a Porsche." She then associates to a relationship in college with a man who was of a different religion than she. As she had done with her father, she took this man's lack of attention as evidence that she herself was lacking:

> And also racial-wise, and religious-wise, I never knew that Jews weren't sup-posed to be hanging out with Christians. Because I had a boyfriend who was

Jewish, and I didn't understand until I was probably 22 that the whole reason he never told me the first six months that he was Jewish was because it was obviously embarrassing to him and embarrassing to his mother that he was with me. And I never understood any of this. I just kinda thought deep down it was me, there must be something wrong with me, and I must not be good enough to take home.

Gita describes a destructive act—an accident with her stepmother's car—which seems to have been an effort to recruit her parents' emotional and practical involvement and to establish their relational steadiness. She took the car without her stepmother's permission and drove it after having two glasses of wine and without wearing her glasses. She describes her parents' reactions:

> I think when I smashed my mom's car—oh, she was totally irate, didn't trust me, didn't speak to me for three months—nodded her head if I asked a question, but I think she didn't wanna have to deal with those things. I had a problem, but I had to solve it myself, and she didn't want anything to do with it, and I was awful, and I'd fallen from grace. I'd always been her little angel. At home I was the goody-goody, I did all the dishes and cleaned the house and so now I'd done a big mistake, and I think it was my cry for help. I certainly didn't purposely smash the car, but getting to that point, it seemed to me a climax . . . But my dad was, in that case, he yelled at me for two days and was mad as hell. "How could you do this? Why didn't you go on the right side of the car? You could have smashed into, you could've hit oncoming traffic," and he went through all the physics of the accident and was mad at me. And I offered to pay right away. And that sort of got it out, and I was sad about that, and mad, or not mad, but upset. But she didn't say a word.

Gita succeeded in recruiting her father's involvement and steadiness: he expressed his anger directly and did not withdraw from her. But her stepmother refused to accept Gita's reparations and withdrew entirely. Beresin suggests that it would have been ideal if her stepmother had expressed her anger but remained involved, in effect saying: "You did a really bad thing. You're gonna pay for this. But I still love you. I'm not going to let you get away with this, but I'm not going to let you get away." Her acceptance of Gita's reparations would have helped Gita tolerate her guilt, take responsibility for her aggression, and feel empathy for the one she had hurt. If Gita had discovered that her aggressive impulses could not destroy a person or a relationship, she would have been equipped to integrate her destructive and loving capacities.

BEFRIENDING THE BEAST

Like a bulimic woman who regards the bulimic self as both alien and essential to her true nature, Beauty regards the beast as too foreign to marry and yet is deeply fond and highly protective of him. In his more-than-meets-the-eye complexity, the beast is akin to the bulimic self. Although he appears ugly, rageful, and frightening, he holds Beauty's best interests at heart. Like the bulimic self, he is committed to speaking the truth ("I ask only that we speak the truth here"), and he insists on acknowledging the whole of what is true, including both his nobler capacities and his baser aspects. Beauty, too, manifests increasing complexity as the story progresses. At first her capacity to love is limited: she repeatedly refuses to marry the beast because she does not love him. Later on, she demonstrates the extent of her capacity to love when she chooses to marry one who seems so radically other. The beast insists that Beauty come to live with him because he knows that his only hope of transformation is to be known for the whole of who he is. When Beauty comes to appreciate the whole of him, she realizes that she cannot bear to lose him. A bulimic woman is moved to acknowledge and accept the bulimic self when she recognizes that its depth of feeling and truth-telling, its loyalty and vitality, its capacity for abandon and glee, and its sheer zest are essential to her sense of wholeness.

Women who have recovered say that it was only when they acknowledged and appreciated their aggression that the beast in them became less destructive. As they came to know the seemingly hideous aspects of themselves, those parts became less threatening and more enlivening, and the women began to feel more whole and alive. Claire, whose experiences of recovering from gynecological surgery and bulimia were interwoven, uses the story of Frankenstein's monster to convey how she came to accept seemingly ugly aspects of herself:

I had these horrible staples, they use staples instead of stitches. And it felt unfeminine, so you kind of felt like Frankenstein. I didn't know who I was or what I was supposed to be. Have you ever read *Frankenstein,* Mary Shelley's *Frankenstein?* . . . Oh, it is a beautiful, beautiful book. It is extremely sad. It's not frightening, it's not gory. It's about somebody, a monster that's made, and then its maker denies it. Ignores it because it looks ugly and it doesn't want to know it. And it's trying to survive. And it means to do well, it wants to understand people. But it's this big, clumsy, ugly-looking monster. And everyone's really mean to this monster. He doesn't mean to upset everybody. And in the end, of course, the climax is, Frankenstein is trying to kill the monster, but really he just wants the maker to love him. It's just, it's a beautiful book.

Once bulimic women accept their beastlike aspects as self, not other, they see those parts in relation to the whole of them, in proper perspective, no longer looming larger than life. As the women integrate darker aspects of themselves with lighter ones, they experience a sense of wholeness. Feeling more complex and more complete is accompanied by a sense of liberation, a sense that it is okay to be human. They are surprised and relieved to realize that the bulimic self had all along known and expressed something essential. A woman who was a member of a panel on recovery said: "I stopped seeing the disorder as the enemy and saw that it was a message from a part of myself—a part of myself I ultimately need to recognize and include. It's the part of me that feels deeply. When I recognized that and focused on that, my bingeing and purging stopped."

Meg conveys how freeing it is to assert her needs, preferences, and limits:

With interpersonal relationships, I don't feel the need anymore to please everyone. I feel like I have a self, that I project a certain image on people with my personality and that they can like it or they can dislike it. I am much more assertive than I ever was before. I have definite opinions, and I express them. And I know I have a bitchy side, which is fine, and I can be aggressive and overbearing, things that I never would've ever thought that I could be before or even thought about being. I was just basically a doormat [*laughs*], could never say no to anything, anyone.

147

It is difficult to meet, much less befriend, the monster within a bulimic woman given how well she keeps it hidden. In clinical work with most people with disorders of self, therapists find that archaic needs naturally manifest in the transference "if one provides an empathic environment and analyzes the resistances to developing such a transference" (Sands 1991, 37). But for people with eating disorders, empathy and analysis are not enough. Because the bulimic's basic needs and yearnings "are not only repressed or split off" but "have been detoured into eating-disorder pathology," they "are less available to fuel a self-object transference" (37), and usual therapeutic methods fail.

Therapists cannot simply wait patiently for the beast to make its presence known but rather must "actively search for and rekindle the needs by empathizing directly with the bulimic self" (37) "in order to uncover the archaic needs embedded within it" (34). This searching can take the form of being alert to rumblings of the beast that might go unnoticed. For example, when a client who rarely phones her therapist between sessions calls in a panicked or distraught state, she may be trying to let her therapist meet the beast. When a woman whose presentation is typically polished shows up for a session dressed in sweats and wearing no make-up, we might also suspect that we are being allowed to meet a more archaic aspect of her. In such states, she is asking, "Can you love and respect me even at my worst?"

To welcome the bulimic self, the therapist must be open to knowing the patient's experience of how bad that self can be and must appreciate that the aggression of the bulimic self is essential to the patient's vitality and wholeness: "Since the bulimic self came into existence to protect the survival of the patient, its greatest fear (and hence source of resistance) lies in the conviction that the therapist is out to eliminate it. If the bulimic self is threatened with extinction, therefore, it will fight for its life—if need be, sacrificing other parts of the patient" (39).

Sands cautions therapists to avoid talking only *about* the bulimic self. Rather, they need to talk directly *with* it: "To try to talk the bulimic self out of bingeing or purging is like telling a cat stalking a bird to stop its carnivorous pursuit. What the bulimic self is able to hear is, first, an acknowledgment of its deeper needs in the present, and then, later on, an explanation of its genetic roots" (40). Talking directly with the bulimic self can mean asking a patient what her body has to say, recognizing a young part of her and acknowledging that it needs a chance to develop, asking how she feels "underneath," and recognizing that even her self-destructive behavior may be an effort "to make herself feel better in the only way she [knows] how" (45).

While it is important to listen for the bulimic self, Sands wisely notes that it would be intrusive to "suggest to the patient that she has a hidden self" (42). Instead, the therapist needs to be alert to moments when the bulimic self naturally enters into the therapeutic relationship. I would argue, however, that once the bulimic self has been experienced in the therapeutic relationship and once the therapist has responded in a way that lets the client know that all aspects of her experience will be respected, it can be helpful to offer the metaphor, always with a light touch and ever open to revision based upon the client's experience.

In one therapy group for bulimic women, as I listened to members recount their binges, I heard, alongside their shame and discouragement, a wild, untamed glee. I told them it was as if they had a Cookie Monster inside of them, a creature of appetite and abandon that barked "COOK-IE!" and "MINE!" and that would not let anyone get in the way of its fundamental right to binge. Group members delighted in this analogy and in my recognition that their binges and purges were not only manifestations of their self-hatred and shame but also expressions of their self-determination and might.

In my clinical experience, when a client and I allow the beast to be present with us, the client often says something like "I feel more whole" or "I feel more me," sometimes even wrapping her arms around herself as if to embrace her whole self. The metaphor of Beauty and the Beast is a metaphor of a young woman's bid for wholeness. It clarifies the limitations of other metaphors a client may hold about recovering. Clients rarely, if ever, come to therapy talking about wanting to appreciate and comfort a banished part of themselves. More often, someone comes in with metaphors based on wanting to silence or eliminate a part of herself that she cannot abide. A member of a recovery panel said, "I was afraid I would not be lovable if I were angry or needy, so I stuffed those feelings" (an apt metaphor for bulimia nervosa). As a therapist, I need to explore with a bulimic woman both the hopes and the hostility implicit in her metaphors. I also need to recognize the limitations of her metaphors lest I be recruited to the cause of lopping off parts of herself, like the step-mother in the Grimms' version of "Cinderella," who hands her step-daughters a knife and tells them to chop off pieces of their heels and toes to fit into the golden slipper. I risk being as cruel to the beast as the bulimic woman is when what the beast really needs is someone who wants to hear its deepest yearnings, rage, shame, envy, and sorrow.

The metaphor of Beauty and the Beast informs our understanding of clinical impasses. If a client is trying to silence or kill the beast, and I am hoping that she can appreciate and comfort it, we will have trouble hearing each other. I need to bridge our metaphors by acknowledging that her eating disorder is inevitably both foe and friend. While we will work to help her feel less controlled by untamed forces, we will also aim to appreciate what the beast in her is expressing. Even if she uses a metaphor that I am prepared to join in—for instance, the metaphor of recovering as a journey—I need to attune to what that metaphor suggests her effort will be and what it implies mine will be. If recovering is a journey, does she consider me a travel agent? A pilot? A guide? Company on the road? Which of these roles am I prepared to play? Can she recognize that her journey, her body, and her life are inevitably hers and that I cannot take responsibility for them?

The metaphor of Beauty and the Beast fosters a belief that one can and will recover. It enables a woman to imagine the mysterious process of becoming whole. If she can imagine that process at all, she can begin to imagine it for herself. If she can imagine it for herself, she can begin to believe—not only hope, but *believe*—that it is possible for her. The metaphor enables her to sense what change might be, to see it in her mind's eye, and to desire it enough.

BEING WITH THE BEAST

SENSING RESPECT

To know and accept the hidden, hungry self, with all its aggression and voraciousness, the women needed to learn that someone could know the worst about them and still respect them and care about them. Sarah conveys how transforming such an experience can be when she describes being confronted by a friend about their one-sided relationship:

> And I'm the kind of person who a lot of times feels like I need the other person to be strong and be there for me, and I don't really wanna, or don't really know if there's room for two people in the relationship. Because now that she's starting to have problems, I'm like, "Well, this is weird, we never did this before, it's always been me coming to you with my stuff." And I've always been there for little stuff for her, but she's never come to me in crisis the way that I've gone to her in crisis. And so she really started realizing how alone she felt. And kind of came to me with, "Sometimes I think you don't wanna hear what I have to say." And the problem was that she was right. And it was just incredibly hard to see that about myself. I got incredibly anxious over that just because I was so full of all kinds of emotions and felt like I had just seen myself in a way that nobody likes to see themselves, the part of me that isn't so great . . . But it also feels very relieving.

When I ask Sarah what helped her face her limited willingness to attend to her friend, she mentions that her therapist, Annie, already knows the worst about her and still respects her. Sarah's ability to evoke a sense of her therapist's respectful regard when the therapist was not physically present enabled her to acknowledge her behavior and to bear the shame of realizing that she needed to change:

> I knew my therapist had known this all along. That she saw what was going on with this relationship, and she knew. As Jane was saying all this, I was thinking, "This is what Annie has been trying to gently make me see." And so I felt like I wasn't alone. I felt like, yes, this was my behavior, and I was totally alone in that, but that somehow Annie was right next to me saying, that I knew that I could go right to her and tell her all this stuff, and she wasn't gonna say, "Yes, you're a rotten person," that she was gonna

151

empathize. Which is exactly what she did. And she asked me what I wanted to change about myself. And then she said, "I know that your capacity to be this way only hurts you more than it hurts other people" . . . But then I knew that she knew, that Annie knew and understood it. That I wasn't this horrible, bad person just because of this. So even though this feels like pain, it also feels like health.

In realizing that her friend and her therapist survived her neediness and accepted her regret for not giving as much as she took, Sarah, in Winnicott's terms, learned that she could make reparations and thereby do something about her guilt, and knowing this allowed her to take responsibility for her aggression:

One thing I think I didn't think about recovering was that I was gonna have to face so much the ugly or the yukky parts of myself. I thought recovery was gonna be finding out what everybody else did to me. And that yes, people have a part in who I became and that I can look at that and understand why I became the person I am, but that there are parts of me that are completely under my control to change. And then still coming to some kind of balance of what's internal responsibility and what I can change and what I can't.

She underscores the importance of her therapist's confrontations:

Any behaviors, she just confronted me on anything and everything that she saw, that if I was being passive-aggressive with my friends, or anything, she just calls it right on the line. And my first reactions to a lot of the stuff that she did was—it depended on her timing—but a lot of times I was ashamed, and I would get defensive, or wouldn't acknowledge it. Most of the time, because her timing is so incredible, I would just feel relieved, like, "Oh, my God, I didn't even know that I knew this. And now I realize that you know that this is what I do, and you don't think I'm horrible because I do this."

Sarah tolerated Annie's challenges, despite some shame, because Annie's timing and attunement enabled her to feel known and accepted. Annie's challenges demonstrated fundamental respect, as if to say, "I respect you too much not to call you on this behavior."

During Rebecca's hospitalization, the hospital staff challenged her defensive interpersonal behavior. One confrontation occurred when she returned to the hospital after having been out on a pass and was asked to give a urine sample. She felt humiliated by the request and was testy with the nurse who asked her for the sample:

> And part of me was gonna refuse to do this test, but then that leads people to think that you're guilty, so therefore—. But I had also run into a new nurse there, and I guess I really had challenged her. I was really angry, and I don't remember the exact circumstances. But I remember Monday came, and the therapist—Dr. Roberts, I think his name was—asked me how the weekend went. And I said, "Oh, it was fine." And this had happened Friday night, so to me it wasn't the weekend. And he said, "Well, what about the incident with Nurse such-and-such?" . . . And I just didn't acknowledge it for what it was worth, or the value that they put on it. Because he really made this big deal about it and said I wasn't being truthful. That I was really being deceitful about what happened.
>
> In a lot of ways, I guess, I had a problem with kinda twisting things a little bit. Which really brought—I remember it clearly now, so it obviously made quite an impact on me. Not always telling the complete truth and making that sound like it was okay, like it was acceptable when it really is not acceptable. That you can't do that, that's not how this world functions, and that it's not acceptable in society, and that it had much broader implications. It was kind of being manipulative.

Rebecca appreciated that Dr. Roberts respected her enough to call her on her behavior. When I ask, "What enabled you to hear it from him?" she says he "took his job very seriously," implying that she felt taken seriously:

> I guess 'cause I ultimately chose to be there, I wanted to get better, I didn't want to be doing this. You don't want to hear these terrible things about yourself, but if you don't, you really can't work on the areas that you need to work on to get yourself healthy again . . . And obviously, he was a very perceptive person and took his job very seriously. It wasn't any light-hearted chitchat when you went in to see him. It was heavy-duty business that you were working on . . . But I think they knew the individuals well enough to know how far they could push without going overboard. 'Cause I definitely needed it.

Knowing that someone could know the worst about them and still regard them with respect and concern is what Winnicott talks about when he refers to "that amount of environmental stability which will stand the strain resulting from impulsive behavior" and "a human attitude, which, because it can be relied on, gives freedom to the individual to move and to act and to get excited." That stable, accepting environment eventually is transmuted to an internalized self-respecting regard. Because of the guilt, shame, and contempt with which bulimic women regard the beast within, they speak to themselves in unimaginably brutal terms. Suzanne Repetto Renna and I have found that when we ask clients who have recovered from an eating disorder what helped them recover, they speak about their struggle to internalize new voices: "Many say that they had heard from a long line of people, over many years, that they needed to take their pain seriously, to get help, and to treat themselves with care and respect. And for years, it seemed as if none of those loving voices got through. In fact, those voices may have been . . . drowned out by the harsh and judgmental inner voices with which the person spoke to herself" (1991/2000, 5).

But one day, one of the respectful, compassionate voices began to resonate and reside somewhere inside them. And even one respectful internal voice makes a big difference. Recovering bulimics report that they took in such voices from many people—therapists, friends, lovers, teachers, authors. Even their sense of God may have shifted as they began to allow for grace, not merely judgment. This process takes a long time. Those who have recovered suggest that all of the harsh and judgmental voices that have ever found their way into their psyches tend to stay there, as if they have tenure. The women seem unable to get rid of well-established harsh voices, although some of them do quiet down over the years. As Renna has pointed out, it is *impossible* to banish internalized voices: attempts to do so only lead to further dissociation and splitting off of aspects of the self.

While they are not able to get rid of cruel voices, the women are able to grant tenure to kinder ones and to cultivate a new generation of voices. Over time, those voices take root and grow, becoming internal sources of support. Keeping oneself company in the face of pain does not make the pain go away, but it does make it tolerable. One recovered bulimic puts it this way: "I didn't recover from pain. I didn't recover from sadness or loneliness or anger or the way this society regards women. But I did find a kinder, more respectful way of treating myself."

Beauty came to appreciate the beast in part because of the voice in her dream, the woman's voice that kept challenging her to look beyond the surface. It took a long time for Beauty to understand and accept the woman's coaching. She had to hear the same message many times before it sunk in. Renna and I have heard many people who have recovered say it was important that people kept trying to reach them and kept repeating the same messages over and over, because one day they finally could hear and act upon those messages. They needed to hear voices of respect and compassion, even when—and especially when—those voices seemed to have no effect. Hearing such voices repeatedly was part of the process by which they internalized a more respectful self-regard.

Renna and I liken those voices to beans on the tray of a balance scale: eventually one voice tips the scales in the direction of self-respect. But it is not just the sheer number or weight of respectful voices that makes a difference. It is also the timing of any one voice with respect to the person's readiness to change. The state of readiness may be made possible by many things, including a felt sense of enough. As was true in Beauty's case, unless a person is experiencing a felt sense of enough, a voice of respect—no matter how clear or how compelling—exerts little force on her motivation to change. What ultimately made Beauty ready to let in the woman's voice was the threat of losing a relationship that mattered to her. Only when she feared the beast was dying or dead did Beauty realize that she cherished the beast and wanted to spend her life with him. Like Beauty, many bulimic women feel the imperative to change when they realize that their eating disorder threatens them with an irrecoverable loss, typically the loss of a relationship or of their health or life. Relationships and young bodies, as Margaret McKenna has pointed out, can take a lot of abuse before they give out, but when they do give out, the damage may be swift, devastating, and irreparable. Beauty was lucky.

Group therapy is one means by which bulimic women begin to take in voices of compassion and respect. They can hear, and eventually allow in, the grace and generosity that others in the group offer them—and that they offer others. As they sit in the group and listen to other members who feel just as rotten at the core as they do, they find themselves wanting to be compassionate and respectful toward the beast in others. And then they begin to wonder if they could accord themselves that same sort of regard. They begin to speak to themselves with a different voice.

SEEKING WHOLENESS AND COMPLEXITY

As noted in Chapter 1, Gershen Kaufman says that when we believe we are fundamentally defective, we regard differences between self and other as evidence that we are less than the other. We interpret difference as confirmation of our inadequacy. To defend against our shame, we try to become perfect. Perfection derives from a word meaning "done, finished, complete." The assumption that there is such a thing as a perfect person allows us to hope that if we could achieve perfection, then we could be done once and for all. We could at last rest and breathe easy, forever immune to competition, envy, and shame.

Striving for perfection becomes unnecessary when we appreciate that our job in life is not to be a perfect person but to be the unique person we are as fully as we can be. As the women came to accept the aggressive aspects of themselves, they began to relinquish their pursuit of perfection and to value their unique wholeness. Gita had regarded the darker aspects of her experience as illegitimate, believing that, by any objective standards, she should feel lucky. Even so, she had kept hoping that her parents "would notice or would hear me." When I ask, "Notice what?" she says:

> That I was sad. That there was something wrong with me. And that I felt badly about that. I mean, there isn't really anything wrong with me. I mean, I'm fine. But there was—

. . . So what does one do with that when something feels really wrong, and yet when you look at your life from some objective standpoint, it seems like you should count yourself among the lucky?

It was exactly that conflict. I've always been one of these people that sees the world and feels lucky. You know, "There are starving people and they don't have any food. Here I'm throwing up food? My God." And then I would get to this point where, "I'll recycle it, I'll go throw up outside, and at least the animals can eat it" [*laughs*]. That was just so weird, but yet it was this huge conflict. There's nothing, but there was something. I didn't know what it was, I couldn't tap into it . . . But there was something in there that was sad and sore, even when I was a happy person.

She now manages that conflict by letting the sadness, which she still does not fully understand, have a legitimate place alongside other experiences. She says her pregnancy helped make it legitimate to "have sad times": "I can talk about that sadness a little bit more now, that it has a place. It doesn't have to interfere with, it's not in a conflict with it anymore, it sits beside. I guess part of the pregnancy was you're allowed to have sad times, and I thought, 'Oh, okay then, well.' And I never really was sad in that case, but there have been times lately that I just get that little sad thing again, but it's okay."

She has found it helpful that her husband reframes sadness as "a sensitivity":

I think it makes me a stronger person. I think it's part of me that I like now. I don't hate it anymore. And I think in some ways Paul has that same part. We call it, he doesn't call it a sadness, he calls it a sensitivity. We're moved by things, or attuned to things that to others are not important or are meaningless or irrelevant. And we seem to—though ours may not be the same, he and I may not have the same sensitivities—but there are subtle things in the world that we pick up that aren't meaningful to other people, but that they have value just because we—or I've decided this now, I didn't think this before—have value because I noticed them. I don't have to deny them because just I see them . . . So I guess it's a confidence in my feeling. It's okay, I can believe in what I feel and it's not wrong because I'm the only one that feels that way.

I ask about the sadness: "Is it like grief, or is it some other kind of sadness?"

No, it's not grief, it's just sort of, my first images of it are black, dark, kind of things. Those are the words, but those aren't quite right either, but that's close to it. More lack of sort of real humanness in that we wanna be wonderful and we want to have peace, but we don't. There is a part of living that isn't the glory and the charmingness. It's the basic parts of life and death that arc black. Or we've called them that, they're not black. The heavy things. But they're not, it's not a good and bad, and they're not really on one side or the other, it's just sort of part of it all.

I remind her that no longer hating part of herself seems similar to her earlier description of needing to regrow her "center of self," which she had killed off (see Chapter 1). When I ask whether there might be some connection between her capacity to feel deeply and her center of self, she elaborates on her newfound commitment to accepting the whole of her experience:

I'm thinking of this as like some *Star Trek* episode I saw about looking at the human being as a whole, not that there's a good part and bad part, we are these whole things. And you can't always be the perfect, good, glowing, lovely, thin, or whatever. I can't be the ideal. There's a whole person, and that makes you wonderful even though it's maybe not what you want to focus on . . . there's the outward and the inward, but it's not the outward, it's your whole thing, and I don't like calling them bad, they're not bad, but all the things that aren't perfect that make you who you are aren't bad, they should be included.

And I think that when I was that self, I thought I could only be all the things that everyone admired—thin, smart, outgoing, light, da, da, da, da— and all the other things, maybe too loud, or snores, and all the things that aren't as admired had to be gotten rid of and just controlled in a way that you didn't show them or that they weren't part of you anymore at some level. And now I have to be the whole, and take them all in interwovenly. I hear some of the echoes of what my father said to me when I was little that sort of led me to this process . . . But there's this sense, when my parents said things to me, I misconstrued it and thought that I had to be all these wonderful things and never make a mistake and never fail.

The beast tells Beauty that if one is pure of heart one can see into the magic mirror, which allows one to see what is true, what is real. Recovering from bulimia requires that a woman face what is real, both for herself and for others. When she is honest, she knows, in the words of the old woman in Beauty's dreams, that "some things are not on the surface at all." Looking beyond the surface of the mirror, she can see the beast in herself. She can see that the beast is in pain. And she can see the beast without losing sight of her beauty.

Being honest also means acknowledging the reality of others' limitations. Just as Beauty looks into the mirror and sees that her father is fragile, a bulimic woman can understand that some of the people whose concern she most dearly wants are not able to recognize and respond to her needs.

Acknowledging the reality of what is means loss. A woman has to lose her conception of who she thought she was or thought she should be. For her to live an authentic life, something has to die. But that something is not her badness, which she had aimed to destroy lest it destroy her. What has to die is her old beliefs and feelings about herself and her family. She has to give up her belief that she could evict or vanquish the beast if only she tried hard enough. She has to accept that to be human is to feel both love and aggression. She has to relinquish her effort to craft a constructed self and instead must let herself be who she is. She has to grieve her idealized view of her family and forgo her conviction that if only she were good enough they would appreciate her. To live fully and to experience what Winnicott calls the True Self, she has to claim herself in all of her complexity. When she gets to know the seemingly ugly parts of herself, she discovers that she cares about those parts, that she is destined to spend her life with them, and that they are vital to her sense of wholeness.

A woman who claims her wholeness knows that she cannot be all good or all bad, only Beauty or only beast. Aggression is an inescapable, real aspect of our humanity. But the beast is a source not only of "badness" but of zest. In expressing our strivings for self-assertion and self-determination, the beast manifests our creative vitality. To deny the reality of the beast is to live a joyless life of obedience and compliance, to be what Winnicott calls a False Self.

To acknowledge and accept one's psychic complexity is arguably an essential aim of psychotherapy. Charles Ducey, who translates Freud's "Wo Es war, da soll Ich werden" (Lecture 31 of *New Introductory Lectures on Psychoanalysis*) to mean "Where It was, there shall I come to be," understands Freud to be talking about the psychological effort to experience and embrace even seemingly foreign aspects of oneself: "In other words, the areas of myself I experience as alien to me I should come to accept as aspects of who I am: in fact, aspects that define me most deeply."

The need to be true to one's complexity is so great that women will risk their lives to claim the True Self rather than lead a False Self's life of duty and compliance. For instance, in driving her mother's car without permission, without glasses, and after she had been drinking, Gita risked her life and her relationship with her stepmother to bring her beast to life. It was as if she had to do something outrageously bad to kill off the false, "goody-goody" Gita.

To recover, a bulimic woman needs to assert herself in ways that others may experience as hurtful, or at least uncomfortable, not because she is reckless but because when we claim our lives, others experience a change that may unsettle their conception of us and of themselves. Like Beauty, who must leave her family to know the beast and leave again to marry him, women with bulimia nervosa find that to recover they need to separate psychically and sometimes physically from their families.

Every metaphor has its limits, and Beauty and the Beast as a metaphor for recovering from bulimia nervosa is no exception. Unlike Beauty, a woman recovering from bulimia nervosa does not need to like the beast. She does, however, need to acknowledge, appreciate, and embrace it. And, as Beresin notes, she cannot just embrace the beast in the safety of fantasy or thought. She has to let the beast come to life, not necessarily by acting on her aggression but by experiencing her aggressive feelings, needs, appetites, and drives. Only when she can experience her aggressive strivings and know that she can bear them can she integrate her aggression. In so doing, she discovers that she does in fact love the zest that her aggressive strivings bring to her life.

Reality also diverges from the metaphor in that the monster within is not transformed into an impeccable, noble self. In real life, the beast remains a beast. Even in the fairy tale, we might imagine that the beast is not transformed back into the original prince but into a more complex and integrated human being. Beauty, too, is more complex and integrated after her marriage to the beast. As Beresin has observed, "The point is not to be really, really good." The point is to be real and to be whole.

5

Learning to Sense Self-Experience

Sensing self-experience is a capacity the women learned and developed both in formal treatment contexts, such as psychotherapy or clinical eating-disorders programs, and in informally therapeutic contexts in the rest of life. Their accounts reveal nine components of the process of learning to sense self.

COMPONENT PROCESSES OF CHANGE

SHIFTING SENSES

The women shifted from seeing themselves through their own or others' eyes to perceiving themselves through senses other than sight. They had to learn how to listen to themselves and to be in touch with their experience. Given their core sense of shame and their vulnerability to new experiences of shame, they had tended to live life from the outside in, painfully conscious of appearance and performance. These women who had been so highly attuned to other people had to learn how to tune in to their own senses, to hear their own song of self. Doing so was a move toward living life from the inside out.

The women learned to listen to their bodies. Rebecca, a graduate student planning to become a registered dietitian, emphasizes, "I do definitely believe in listening to your body." But it took her a lot of practice to learn how to attune to her subjective gauges of hunger and satiety:

I didn't even know how much I was supposed to eat. Yeah, I had all my nutritional knowledge: Have a half a cup of rice, two ounces of meat, and then a half a cup of cooked vegetables and a four-ounce glass of skim milk and one dinner roll. And I could tell you that, but I couldn't tell you what my body was being satisfied with and being comfortable with. So I usually would overeat, and then I had to sit with that fullness feeling unless I purged . . . I'm still to a certain degree learning how to eat . . . I try to use the knowledge I have, but I still try to feed my body what I feel that I'm hungry for.

Jessie, too, talks about learning to listen to her body's hunger signals:

Now, when I gain a pound, I don't freak out. That was hard at first because when you are eating whatever you want and not bingeing [and purging], there are days when you go past your satisfaction level, and you might gain a pound or two. But you learn to say, "This is not a problem. This is a temporary thing. I'm not reading my body. I'm not paying attention to what my body wants. I'm distracted. I have to give myself some time for me and let my body tell me what it wants. And I will be back to the way I was. The pound will go away."

Abigail, on the day of our interview, is tolerating a slight weight gain, feeling in touch with her body and accepting of it: "Right now, I feel, I weigh three or four pounds more than I'd like to. And what I can do though, is I can feel how my pants feel different, and I'll just notice that and not judge it. It's interesting, the way I can feel the limits of my body, and without saying, 'Oh, this is terrible, everyone's going to be able to tell, and they're going to hate me.' I know goddamn well no one's gonna be able to tell. And just like, 'But how does it feel?' And it feels okay."

Isabella had kept herself compulsively busy in an effort to avoid being in touch with her experience. In the hospital, the staff and structure helped her tolerate making contact with her feelings: "I was always on the go, running, running, running, running. Never let myself stop and think. And in the hospital they made us just sit and be alone with our thoughts and write and meditate. They controlled the rest of our day and our eating and our daily functioning. All we had to deal with was our thoughts and our feelings. And it was a matter of breaking through to let yourself feel something. I had turned myself off."

A ten-week course on meditation and yoga helped her focus on her subjective experience without being overwhelmed by anxiety:

> And so I learned to sit for longer periods of time with myself, to just be with myself. And at first it was very difficult. I literally couldn't sit there, I was aggravated. But it's gotten to the point where I really enjoy it. Sometimes I just sit and focus on my breathing. Other times, I have some tapes, specifically healing tapes, where I might imagine an atom going through my body healing me. It just helps me to focus myself, center myself. Because now I can find myself at times, if things are getting too crazy, getting the anxiety back again. So that helps me to just slow down and center.

Many women used specific strategies to help them listen to their bodies and psyches: writing in a journal; rereading journal entries; observing their thoughts, feelings, physical sensations, and behaviors; learning to distinguish among those types of self-experience; identifying self-defeating thoughts and tracing their precursors and consequences; and recognizing and challenging cognitive distortions. While these approaches involve self-observation, it is not to look at one's appearance or performance but to notice, nonjudgmentally, one's subjective experience.

SEEKING AND CREATING SUPPORTIVE ENVIRONMENTS

The women's greatest strides in recovering followed their having sought out or created an environment—physical or relational—which supported their efforts to be in touch with their experience.

Isabella found such an environment in the natural world: "It just gives me a sense of beauty and makes me feel really peaceful, and I like to just go out there and think that there is this beauty and wonder on the earth, and it seems like a really positive energy for me. I went on a spiritual retreat in June, in the mountains, and just focused on nature and beauty, and it was wonderful . . . I think that helps you to get centered. To reach into yourself."

Similarly for Gita, moving out of the city and taking walks in the woods promoted tuning in to her senses:

I needed time alone, and I really decided I wanted time in a place that was within the natural environment. I moved out to a suburb and lived in this guy's garage. It had a pretty view of a pond, and it was in this open conservation land, and I walked and I walked and I walked. It was just beautiful. I've always found that when I was really sad and really troubled and really lonely, that nature and being in the woods or being with animals really helped. Because it put perspective on all this craziness of humans. So I think that that was part of it, that I purposely went to seek that.

The respite from city life permitted respite from social and parental pressures as well. In this context of retreat, Gita was able to ask herself what she really wanted in life and to sense her answers to that question: "I lived by myself and I had to really face myself . . . I was really alone and really looking at myself but also really looking, thinking about what I wanted in life. And I actually—and this is how I met Paul—used personal ads. And I think that really empowered me because here I get to say, 'Well, what do I like, and what do I wanna meet in somebody who would be my friend?' And so I really examined what was important to me and where I was going and what I was doing."

Claire received no formal treatment for her eating disorder, but, through a commercial weight-loss program, she learned to keep a food-mood diary. Keeping the diary helped her realize that she had to create conditions in her daily life that helped her to tune in to her needs:

I did the diary thing every now and then of writing down what I was eating. And I knew when my worst times of day were, it was always in the evening. Or, if I was ever coming home at four, five o'clock in the afternoon, that was always a particularly dead time as well, but generally it was getting home in the evening.

And how did you manage those times?

Just by slowing down. I would come indoors, and I would have a cup of tea, and I wouldn't eat. I would sit down, and I would drink a cup of tea first—I would drink it probably pretty quick—before I would do my food. And then I would do a meal, and I used to try and make it balanced . . . And I was being careful about how much protein I had. I had become aware that if I had a proper amount of protein, I didn't stuff myself with cakes. And I thought, "I actually feel better when I have a nice meal. And I feel sick when I eat cakes."

For all the women, finding and creating conditions in which they could tune in to their senses required continuing attention and effort. In the dailiness of life, they needed to slow down enough to sense what they needed and to imagine ways of responding to their needs other than by bingeing and purging.

None of the women recovered while in a residential college. Several noted that the environment of a residential college exacerbated their tendency to live life from the outside in, with a focus on appearance and comparison. Leslie says: "College was a very unhealthy experience. I learned a lot, but I think about how unhealthy it is to put 1,700 people in one place who are all trying to be perfect, and it wasn't a good experience for me." In college, and particularly on athletic teams and in dance troupes, the women felt pressure to overcommit and overachieve and found little support for honoring their limits. For instance, Gita got validation for her excessive exercising: "They were looked on as good things. 'Oh, you're gonna run five miles? Wow!' Or, 'Now then, you have to run seven miles.' 'Wow! You're an amazing runner.' It was something that was virtuous."

Although some women took important steps toward recovery during their college years, they did not make the full commitment that recovering required until they took a leave of absence or graduated. Those who returned to college after having considerable treatment did not fully recover until after they graduated. These findings could be consistent with any of the following explanations: that the context of a competitive residential college, and of college athletics in particular, promotes reliance on external appraisals of self-worth; that a residential college presents conditions which exacerbate a tendency to experience oneself as not good enough and which trigger overwhelming shame in people with a core sense of shame; that the academic and extracurricular commitments of a full-time student leave her unable to fully invest her time and energy in recovering; that recovering is enabled by a level of development that is likely to be attained only after the college years. It is beyond the scope of this book to assess the adequacy of these explanations.

Meg found that her active college life was not conducive to tuning in to her senses. She decided to enter a residential treatment program, where, away from other demands, she could focus on recovering from her eating disorder. She prized the tools she was taught and the time to practice using those tools in a supportive environment: "I had seven weeks to see it work. And to feel a little bit of pressure to make it work. And other people were doing it too. So it was an environment. I think given that information in a vacuum, or with no other supporting factors, you might dismiss it."

After her stay at the treatment center, Meg returned to campus to finish her last year of college. But she quickly fell back into old patterns:

> I was not able to use the tools that they had given me and everything I had learned to take care of myself when I was back at college because it was just old environment and old habits, and I was still wanting to get the good grades, and I was still rowing and had the same sort of pressures on myself. And I just wasn't able to relax any of it. So I was slipping, like I started sleeping all the time again, staying inside, not going to classes. Started bingeing and purging again. I just started losing the light at the end of the tunnel and decided that I couldn't go back in the spring.

Meg arranged to complete her requirements off-campus, at a college near her hometown. Back in her hometown, she set up her life to refocus her attention on recovering: "So I went home, and I didn't live at home 'cause I wasn't ready for that yet, with my mom, or with my dad for that matter. But I had an apartment, and I had a part-time job, and I took the two classes, and I saw a psychiatrist twice a week, and worked on my recovery. On getting better. That was my sole purpose for being there. And that's really what enabled me to function in the world with what [the treatment center] had given me during that time."

When I ask her what about this arrangement turned out to be helpful, she replies:

> There was no pressure. Just all the things that I have a hard time with were gone, like living with people. I was able to live by myself, cook my own food,

see the psychiatrist and make that a priority and not something I had to fit into my schedule with classes and this and that . . . I was able to continue some stuff with my mom and my dad that I had left off, that we really needed to work on . . . Just to talk about things. And I would go to work, and I'd come home at five o'clock, and the way to my house was by my parents' house, so I would stop by, my mom and I would have tea or something, and we would talk for like an hour. Sometimes I'd stay for dinner, sometimes I wouldn't . . . It was just getting to know each other again, and sort through things, and just get reacquainted.

While Meg's avoidance of the things that were difficult for her could have been counter to her learning to manage under the stresses of real life, the fact that she continued to recover indicates that her "avoidance" was in the service of simplifying her life so that she could continue to focus on listening to and being in touch with herself and thereby consolidate the gains she had made during residential treatment.

After Isabella's hospitalization, she decided to have no contact with her abusive husband. At that time she also lost her job. Away from husband and work, she was able to focus on herself:

> I totally cut myself off at that point from Ron. I told him I couldn't see him at all. He was constantly calling and writing and stopping by and sending presents, and I just didn't respond at all. So I just kind of got away from that pressure. And I was able to just think on my own a little bit. At that point, too, I lost my job so I didn't have a job . . . I was so stressed out and so tense, so anxious, that I just needed some time to work on me. And it felt selfish at first . . . that I should just focus on myself, like I was really self-centered.

Isabella is not alone in saying that attending to herself initially felt selfish. As discussed later in this chapter, the women learned to differentiate between being self-absorbed and being self-attuned.

UNMUFFLING THE SENSES

To be in touch with their self-experience required that the women both create supportive external and relational environments and foster a supportive internal environment. Fostering a supportive internal environment required that they unmuffle their senses by discontinuing their use and abuse of substances, by getting enough nourishment, by letting themselves attain a naturally maintainable weight, and by getting enough rest.

During her college years, Gita relied on alcohol and caffeine to regulate her physical states and her moods, but those substances in fact left her increasingly dysregulated, unable to modulate her physical and emotional states:

> I would drink caffeine in the morning, and in order to calm down, I'd have to drink wine to go to sleep at night. And there was a period of time I could definitely have had three glasses of wine before I went to bed . . . And I think the caffeine and the liquor were definitely part of the problem. I'd have a glass of wine when I came home in the evening from graduate school to relax, and it would loosen my willpower and then I'd start eating. And then I'd eat too much, and then throw up, and then I'd do some work and then I'd go to sleep. So I think it affected my sense of my body, too. I didn't know if I was hungry or thirsty. And you would wake up starving if you had been drinking the night before or had had caffeine, so I never could tell, Was I really hungry, or was I not hungry?

Although those who discontinued or reduced their use of substances such as alcohol did not necessarily do so in order to be in touch with their experience, one result of such changes was keener self-attunement. Gita cut down on alcohol when she realized that drinking contributed to her outbursts of anger and to her dysregulated eating and sleeping. She also cut out caffeine. When she ate and slept in response to her body's signals and did not try to override them with caffeine and alcohol, she could sense when enough was enough.

When I ask what recovery is, Gita replies:

> The physical part of recovery was the underpinnings, I think. Getting my body healthy again. I had really not taken care of it, though I thought I was taking care of it by exercising. And to really get it to a point where I was eating a balanced diet overall and not taking a lot of stimulants or depressants or any kind of thing in alcohol or caffeine and just really cleaning myself up. Seeing what it's like just to be healthy. And feeling how that made me feel so good that it was hard to sacrifice that . . . I think I really started the health

kick before I finally got rid of caffeine, but I didn't really feel wonderful, in terms of my sleep patterns and energy levels, until I got rid of the caffeine.

Around the time that she stopped using caffeine and cut down on alcohol, she became pregnant. She experienced her pregnancy as a reason to maintain her healthier habits.

When I ask Meg what was helpful in her residential treatment, she says:

> Well, I guess, the whole idea of listening to my body . . . Everything goes back to that in some sense. We weren't allowed to have caffeine, and we got plenty of sleep. And it was just really respecting your body and learning to take care of it. And it's something that I still do now. I sleep more than anyone probably 'cause I know I need a lot of sleep. And people at work are always saying "God, you sleep so much," but I know I need it. And I drink much less caffeine than I used to, and I've really learned a lot more about my body. And I can hear what it's saying. I can listen to it.

When Rebecca committed herself to recovering, she stopped using cocaine and significantly reduced her alcohol consumption. She also had to let herself be adequately nourished. She says, "I was never underweight by the height and weight charts . . . even though I was starved." Because of her disordered eating, her mental processes had been impaired:

> I was so malnourished. When people say "How do you recover?" I mean, I hate that you have to put weight on, but you really have to be at a weight at which you can comprehend what somebody's saying to you. Even at the weight that I was, I still couldn't fully fathom because it had such a power over me, and I wasn't thinking straight . . . Because I was an excellent student when I was in high school, but as the years went by, my body was so depleted that in college, I just couldn't comprehend a lot of things. And I don't understand how I actually made it through college.

It was not until she was well nourished that Rebecca appreciated how compromised her body and mind had been: "I didn't have the glucose from my brain to function properly . . . I wasn't able to study like I could study when I was in high school. And I wasn't able to focus. And I wasn't able to do the things I could do before I lost all that weight. Very moody. It affected my mood tremendously." She believes that a malnourished person cannot make much use of therapy: "When people go into therapy, I mean, you can't think straight . . . You're not, mentally, brain cell–wise, capable of doing that, you're only gonna take out 5 percent of the total potential." Rebecca, who is training to become a dietitian, speaks with the conviction of personal experience when she tells clients that they must feed their bodies:

> Whenever people say, "Well, can you tell me how to lose five pounds?" my first comment will be, "Cut down on your fat. Increase your activity. And listen to your body." And people will be like, "What?" I counsel people, I have girls that weigh healthy weights but eat nothing, have diet hot chocolate five times a day. And I say, "You have to feed yourself. You have to eat this, this, this, and this." And the expressions on their faces when you're telling them that they have to eat. 'Cause they expect, "God, I wanna lose more weight, she's gonna tell me I'm gonna have to cut down on this. Oh, my God, how can I do that? But if I have to, I will." And when you say, "No, I want you to eat," they'll be like, "Wow." And again, always listening to your body. You need to feed your body. And I'm a living example of it.

Once Rebecca began eating properly, her body required a lot of food and time to be restored to health. She gained a sense of how deeply deprived her body had been: "I could never eat enough. When you get so out of control and you're just eating, eating, eating, it's kinda like your body is saying, 'Oh, my God, great, she's feeding me.' And you just can't feed yourself enough. It took me a lot of recovering to finally get to a point where I felt like I was actually nutritionally sound. 'Cause I think so many things were off balance."

Beth, too, felt deeply hungry while she was normalizing her eating:

> One thing that I think was really, really hard during that time was that my body was starving. And I was physically really, really hungry. I remember crying to my husband saying, "I am so hungry," like it would hurt. Even when I would eat, I would feel like I couldn't get full. I think it was 'cause I didn't eat any fat for years, no fat at all. And even though my weight wasn't like anorexic low . . . I feel like my body was physically just starving. So when I started eating three meals, instead of it filling me up, it made me more hungry. My body was like, "More!" And that was really hard because I felt like "Even when I eat more, it's hopeless." I think it took me like six months

of eating three meals before that hunger went away, and my body knew it would get food.

Several changes that fostered a healthier internal environment were supported by changes in Beth's external environment: "I saw a nutritionist . . . And that was nothing new, but this time I decided just to try to follow three meals a day . . . And running once a day instead of twice a day. That was strictly the result of me graduating and not being on the track team anymore. It was like my lifestyle changed. I was working. And trying to eat three meals regularly and go to bed on time. And go to OA. It really was something that took time."

It seems tautological to say that recovering from bulimia nervosa required that a woman normalize her eating. While normalized eating did not in and of itself constitute recovery, it was an essential aspect of it. Adequate nutrition was essential to unmuffling a woman's senses, and her senses had to be unmuffled before she could experience and bear painful feelings. Tolerating feelings was a prerequisite for working through the psychological issues that had led her to develop and maintain the bulimia.

LEARNING ABOUT PAIN AND RELIEF

To tolerate distress and discomfort, the women had to learn that pain is an inevitable part of life, not a confirmation of weakness. And they had to learn that painful feelings inevitably subside. Pain, whether physical or psychic, has natural limits and natural cycles. As predictably as a wave, pain crests and falls, ebbs and flows.

Rebecca learned to trust that uncomfortable feelings would ease: "It took me years to practice and fail and overeat and try to sit with feeling full. And if you can't sit with feeling full—. Even when I overeat now, I realize that that feeling's gonna go away eventually. It's not that I've gorged myself, it's that I've eaten a little bit too much, maybe I let myself get overly hungry 'cause I didn't have the opportunity to eat earlier, and I just have to sit with that feeling."

The women also had to learn that they could ease their pain by means other than bingeing and purging. In the excerpt just above, Rebecca seems to be replaying the self-talk with which she keeps herself company when she feels uncomfortably full. She reminds herself that she knows something about this feeling: it has not lasted forever in the past and will not last forever now ("that feeling's gonna go away eventually"). Without judging herself, she reminds herself of what led up to her present discomfort, as if trying to learn how to avoid it in the future ("maybe I let myself get overly hungry 'cause I didn't have the opportunity to eat earlier"). Now that she trusts her capacity to supply company and comfort, painful feelings are not so frightening:

> I think for a lot of the time I was using the purging to deal with those feelings. Like when I was in therapy and feeling those feelings, I remember leaving therapy thinking, "Oh, my God, I have to go eat. I just have to." I thought, "Oh, my God, this is making it worse." But I see feelings aren't as scary, I guess. I think for a lot of time I didn't have any feelings so I didn't know what feelings were. So then feelings kinda came about, and they gave me more of a reason to binge and purge. And then, now I don't mind feelings so much. I don't like feeling pain, I don't like feeling hurt, but—. . . I've gone through some crises that would've automatically made me revert to those behaviors, and I have no desire . . . I don't even, those feelings, those tapes don't play in me anymore.

Rebecca found a way to *have* her feelings rather than to *be* her feelings (Kegan, 1982), to have perspective on them rather than to be consumed by them. What enables her to tolerate psychic distress is her ability to keep herself company when in distress.

For Jessie, enduring discomfort involves slowing down enough to notice her state of being and then talking to herself with a nonjudgmental voice:

> As a bulimic and a binger, you tend to eat very fast. You don't taste your food. Because it's not really about food. It's about emotions and things goin' on in your life and suppressed feelings, and this food and this bingeing is a release for that, for all this pent-up stuff. So now that most of the pent-up stuff is gone, you kinda have to learn how to eat food just for eating food. And it's

not easy. It's still to this day, if you find yourself not thinkin' about it, and shovin' the food down your face, and then you're done and you think, "Oh, now I'm full." And when you're full, your first instinct is to throw up. And you sit there and say, "If I don't throw up, what is gonna happen to me? I just ate a meal. That most normal people would eat. But because I'm me, it fills me. I'm stuffed. So if I let this meal sit here, what's gonna happen to me? All right, I might gain a half pound. So I pay more attention to my body tomorrow, I pay more attention to how hungry I am, to how I feel when I'm satisfied, to what the food tastes like. Okay. So I'm just gonna sit here till this feeling of anxiety passes and tell myself that it's gonna be okay if I don't throw up." And it was. It's very hard. Sometimes you have to leave the house. Sometimes you have to clutch a pillow for an hour.

Jessie's clutching the pillow suggests that she holds herself in an effort to comfort herself and stay in touch with herself.

At times Jill sat on her hands until the urge to purge subsided: "I was so sick from making myself throw up that I wanted to stop. Sometimes I just sat on my hands to stop. Because I was really sick from doin' it, and I just didn't wanna do that."

The women sometimes sought out others' company to help them ride out uncomfortable feelings. Feelings are more bearable in the company of someone who will bear them with us. Jill says: "My friends were great. They were available, they would listen, they would let me just come sit at their house all day long if that's what it took. Which is what I needed. Most of my friends were like that . . . 'Cause sometimes that's all you need is just to be somewhere else, with someone else that you don't feel isolated . . . I was never really good at being by myself or being comfortable with myself . . . Good's not really the word, but I just, I couldn't stand being by myself."

CONNECTING BEHAVIOR AND FELT EXPERIENCE

All the women found it helpful to sense direct connections between their behavior and their states of being. They sensed both how physical, emotional, and relational states influenced their eating behavior and how their behavior influenced their physical, emotional, and relational states.

Discerning these connections in specific instances in everyday life gave them a sense of being effective agents in their own lives, able to affect their own states and behaviors.

For instance, when Amy kept a food-mood journal, she discovered that she ate to deal with uncomfortable feelings:

> It helped me see what my feelings were. So I would eat a lot when I was very aggravated, very stressed out. Kind of overwhelmed with things that I had to do.

> *And how was it helpful to make those connections between what you were thinking and feeling and what your eating behavior was?*

> Because I was eating as a result of how I was feeling. I was trying to basically calm that feeling down by putting food in my mouth, is what I was noticing. But I was also noticing that by stuffing my face, I was punishing myself for not being able to handle the feeling that I was having.

Rebecca recalls a particular moment of sensing how her felt experience affected her behavior:

> Even when I left the hospital that time—'cause I got booted out because of insurance—here my mother was, she came to pick me up . . . And I was supposed to get my prescription at the nurses' station, and there was something wrong with it or something. And I just started getting really defensive. And one of the nurses who knew me came around the corner—"Rebecca, you must be really scared 'cause you're leaving so early." And of course I broke down 'cause—but that's what it was, my way of dealing with it is being defensive, and putting up this barrier immediately. And here my mother just saw me being a bitch. She just saw me as being a snotty kid. "Here Rebecca goes again." She had no clue that what I needed was a hug.

> *Or someone to help name what you were feeling?*

> That's even what I take with me today. It's kind of hard to say that—"This is what's going on. This is how I feel."

Rebecca learned that when her feelings are acknowledged and validated, she settles down.

Like Amy, Rebecca benefited from writing about her feelings when she felt the urge to binge: "I guess through therapy, really being forced to connect feelings and behaviors and reasons. I remember Susan saying,

'If you feel the urge to binge, sit down and write about your feelings.' And in the hospital, they would do that a lot, too. And you'd think it's so stupid. 'What the hell do my feelings have to do with any of this? It's just, I want to do this, and I want to throw up.' And I think it was just through the whole therapeutic process."

Meg's learning what led her to binge and purge was fostered by the freedom that she had at the treatment center, which had a policy of no locked bathrooms and no restrictions on bingeing and purging. Such a policy is rare to nonexistent in inpatient and residential treatment programs today, but Meg found the freedom helpful. She also found it useful to have both structured and unstructured time:

> I have a lot of anxiety about having free time. And that's when I would binge and purge most. So, and I really think that being allowed to binge and purge was so important to my recovery because I learned what it is that makes me do it. If I wasn't allowed to do it, I don't think I would've ever made the connection between the two as well as I was able to there. Not just the emotional connection, but just the day-to-day functioning connection, that there are certain hours of the day and certain events, certain things that people do and say that would make me want to binge.

The freedom to experiment with tools she was given allowed her to learn, rather than just be taught, how her behavior and her experience were linked:

> I was allowed to use the information however I wanted to. And it was personalized. It wasn't like I had to do something a certain way that was very specific. It was very much, "Take this information that we're giving you, and use it the best way that you can." And so that's what I did. And now I have it for myself, and I still carry it with me 'cause it's very much my own . . . I really had so much to do with my recovery that I don't see how recovery can be looked at as some sort of, like you can't piece together something and say, "Okay, this is what you're gonna do, and this is how it's gonna work." That there has to be freedom and flexibility and opportunity to create your recovery.

Abigail learned that when she eats in response to hunger rather than in response to stress, she feels satisfied and consequently does not feel vulnerable to bingeing:

I think my body gets what it needs, maybe on a chemical level. I'm eating properly, I'm eating healthfully, so it doesn't call for any nutrients that I might misinterpret and go for sugar. And then two hours later it still wants the fat or something that I need to live. I have this belief that when you eat in a way where your body's ready to eat, where it's not stressed out but it's ready to eat, that your body gets the message that it's fed. And that if you eat when you're stressed out, there may not be a recording of "This is a meal."

Having sensed the link between her behavior and her felt experience, she now regards "getting bingey" as a cue that she needs to eat well: "I've learned that, if I start getting bingey, what I do now often is I take myself out to meals, just so I'm eating well-rounded, good food, and I'm enjoying it. Rather than trying to diet, and skip meals and eat for my emotions, like eat for my anxiety rather than for my body."

Isabella recalls being frustrated that no one would tell her how to acquire self-esteem: "I'd ask all the doctors, 'How do I get it? Just tell me how . . . Whatever, just tell me, and I'll do it so I can get this thing called self-esteem.'" When I ask how she would now answer people who ask the very question she once posed, she says it was helpful to make the connections between small accomplishments and feeling better about herself: "Self-esteem is not something that you can measure objectively. It comes in such small amounts . . . I guess it's just the support of one little step at a time, and everything, every little accomplishment counts, however small it is. To just reinforce that every little step feels good, and it's working toward the goal."

Sensing effectiveness in small steps meant sensing it in tiny instances in the moment-to-moment activities and relationships of her everyday life. Summing these experiences over time helped her feel better about herself. When I ask how she even began taking those small steps, she replies: "Basically, using my positive affirmations. That was one thing that was helpful. And not having to be perfect, it wasn't all or nothing. So if I [binged and purged] once a day instead of five times a day, that's okay, that's an improvement . . . And basically writing it down and journaling, trying to look at it positively, whatever I was doing, try to look at it as a step forward." Taking pride in the small steps she took, as opposed to focusing on her failures, helped counter her tendency toward all-or-nothing thinking: "I always used to think it was all or nothing, black or white. Everything in life was like that. And just getting to the point where things could be in the gray area and be okay. I didn't have to be perfect or crumble apart. So it was just allowing myself to let go and take small steps and appreciate each of the small steps . . . And then once they start linking all together, you feel better and better."

SHARPENING THE SENSES

The women learned to discern and discriminate among particular sorts of self-experiences. Sarah learned to differentiate among feelings, physical sensations, and behaviors with her therapist's help: "She's not gonna take 'I threw up' as a reason, or as a feeling, or as an answer to a question. She's not gonna. She's gonna push me. 'That's just not good enough.' 'How are you feeling?' 'Well, I have a stomachache.' 'That's not a feeling.' She wasn't gonna take that as an answer and then let it go. Which is exactly what I felt like I needed. 'Cause I couldn't do that to myself."

Many women learned to discriminate between being selfish and being self-respecting, between being self-absorbed and being self-attuned. As Claire became more self-attuned and self-respecting, she was able to tell the difference between loving her boyfriend and tolerating his hurtful behavior:

> I had left the relationship because I was finding it abusive. I didn't like the fact that he gave attention to other women. He used to say, "Well, you know what I'm like. If you want to be with me, you want to be with me." And I used to think it was my problem. And I started realizing it was his problem. I was all right . . . And I thought, "Why do I have to take this?" It's difficult to separate that, but I know I still love him. We went through so much. So I'll never stop loving him. But I'm not in love with him. I'm emotionally dependent on him, as he is on me, as we both know we are. But that doesn't necessarily mean that we're going to be together. And there are people whom I can feel good with that aren't going to be treating me in that way.

While her parents were away on a sabbatical, Gita came to distinguish between a desire to visit them and a desire to spend time in the rural setting where they lived: "My parents live in a house in the forest, and I think I often went there to be in the forest but ended up being with them, too. And though I like being with them, I think what I was really seeking may have overlapped with the social part of it that maybe I didn't need at that instant. When they were away, I sought it on my own, and I got that peace."

Several women found that cognitive-behavioral monitoring helped them identify their internal states. Kate says: "My therapist had these sheets where she wanted me to keep track of when I ate, what I ate, why I was eating. Was I really hungry? Was I upset? Was I whatever? . . . So that was the beginning part. It was just a matter of learning to eat just when you're hungry. Or at least—if you're eating when you're not hungry, at least to know why you're doing it."

When Jessie stopped depriving herself of food, she learned what she really likes to eat:

> You discover an awful lot about yourself when you let yourself eat anything you want. 'Cause when you're deprived, you fantasize about Twinkies and ice cream and pizza. Yet when you have the freedom to eat that, you discover that you don't even like half of that stuff. I have discovered that I really like good, healthy food. I still like junk every now and then, but when I forget and I think, "Oh, wow, I want a Twinkie," but I can have it because I'm hungry and that's what I want, and I go get it, I go, "This Twinkie's gross. I don't like Twinkies." And I thought that was a pretty amazing thing. After years of fantasizing about all this stuff, when you let yourself have it, you don't even like it.

ACTING AND SPEAKING

The women experienced freedom of choice and freedom of voice as they learned to act and speak on behalf of their needs, preferences, and limits. In small ways and large, they learned to make self-respecting choices rather than to be bound by the compulsion and fear that had ruled their lives in the form of the eating disorder.

Rebecca began to let her eating be guided less by external gauges of rules, restrictions, and numbers and more by her internal gauges of appetite, hunger, and fullness. She attributes her ability to make this shift to years of trial and error in noticing her personal limits and preferences:

> They would say, "At breakfast, have a meat, have a starch, have a fruit." Do most people have that for breakfast every morning? No. And I would do that, I would have cottage cheese, I would have a bran muffin, and I would have fruit in my cottage cheese. Now to me that was a normal breakfast. But I look at that now and that's a lot of food to me. Like this morning for breakfast, I had cottage cheese with a banana and some wheat germ, and that's all I had. But it's taken me years to give myself the liberty even though I had the nutritional knowledge to do so.

Rebecca's progression suggests that if someone is profoundly disconnected from her internal gauges, or if she routinely overrides them, those gauges cannot serve her well, and she needs external guidelines to help her normalize her eating. But external guidelines are best used in the service of learning to rely upon internal gauges. Like training wheels on a bicycle, guidelines enable someone to remain safe while she is developing skills and a sense of balance. If she does not outgrow them, however, she never learns to trust herself and never knows the pleasure of true competence.

One self-respecting choice women made was to avoid or exit from difficult situations. Several women, including Gita, chose not to keep in the house foods on which they were likely to binge, not to attend food-focused functions, and to avoid leaving too many unstructured hours in their day:

> I think in the beginning it was just a matter of avoiding some situations altogether. Because I've gradually presented myself with a lot of these situations again, and now I can handle them. But I think I had to just not get into them for a long period of time before I could face them again and deal with them appropriately. Because it was habits, it was weird habits and weird sequences of the day. It became a routine almost at some point. It was just

terrible. "Oh, now I got a chance. I gotta use it." "I have two hours. What am I gonna do?" It was a way of using two hours.

Avoidance, like any coping strategy, becomes a problem when it is relied upon to the exclusion of other strategies. But, as one strategy among others, avoidance can be used in the service of wellness.

Meg now voices her needs and preferences when she orders food in a restaurant:

And this is something I learned at the [treatment center]. That you're out to eat, people are serving you, it's okay to ask questions and ask them to do things differently. So people don't like to go out to eat with me 'cause I'm always like, "Can you tell me exactly what's in this?" And "Can you use a little bit less cheese?" And "Can I have milk instead of cream for my coffee?" When I'm getting ready to order, people are like, "Okay, let's get out the book because it's gonna take a while." But I get what I want. And I feel comfortable. So it works for me.

Some of the women's self-respecting choices were not specifically related to food, such as when they acted and spoke on behalf of establishing their psychic separateness, as discussed in Chapter 3. They had to learn to assert their needs, preferences, and limits, even in seemingly small instances. For example, Abigail's bulimic symptoms had been a way to express her wants and needs. In recovering, she learned to voice her preferences and take responsibility for them:

I noticed lately that it's a protection . . . Like I couldn't go do social things because I ate too much so I would stay home.

Which protected you from what?

Not feeling good about me, maybe . . . Or maybe if I didn't really want to go, it was a way of making the decision without my really saying what I wanted. But because I had eaten, it was more passive. Because I had eaten, I couldn't go. When I really just didn't want to go.

With her sister, Isabella voiced her need for help in keeping in touch with her feelings:

If she saw me starting the bingeing, to just talk to me about it, not to tell me to stop, but just to say, "What's going on? How are you feeling?" To focus back on the feelings and not on the food. That was basically it, just talk about how you're feeling. 'Cause when you start getting into the bingeing, you cut off your feelings. It's just a mechanical thing. You're not feeling, tasting, you're not doing anything. So that's really helpful, if someone can just stop and say, "How are you doing?" Just for her to ask me that every once in a while, even periodically throughout the day.

Meg asked her boyfriend to help keep her connected to her own experience. Like Isabella, she taught him the questions to ask. She also voiced her need to have her sense of timing respected:

> I remember having very specific things for him to say when I told him that I had binged and purged . . . I think I just wanted him to say, "Why did you do that?" . . . And I told him that if I said, "Oh, it was just 'cause I was hungry," or "I ate too much," that he shouldn't press it because I wasn't ready to talk about it but that I probably would be able to talk about my feelings eventually. And that sometimes if he said "Why?" I would say, "Well, this and this happened, and I was feeling this way," and that that was what we wanted to get to eventually.

GRIEVING THE LOSSES

Recovering, although a triumph, involved real losses for the women: of a once achieved and still desired body-type; of the comfort of familiar roles; of relationships that did not withstand the changes that recovering brought; of the conviction that others could know their needs without their having to voice them; of the ambition to be superhuman; of the seeming simplicity and safety of living a passive or disconnected life.

For Rebecca, recovering required that she gain some weight. It was helpful to her that her therapist predicted her feelings of loss and grief:

> It's hard, 'cause it still hurts me inside that I can't be what I would ideally like to be. It's like a loss. Susan, my therapist, talks a lot about that. You lose something. You lose, and you have to come to grips with that. It's kind of like a grieving process. You lost that body that you'll never have again, but what you've gained from it all is so immeasurable in comparison to what you lost. I would cry, "I can't fit into these clothes." My mother would always say, "Get rid of the clothes." So I'd get rid of a lot of the clothes, but there's some

few dresses, size threes, size fives, that I just keep for posterity's sake. Just 'cause I liked them. But ninety percent of the clothes that I had I've gotten rid of. Because I can't, it's just, it's painful to think that I can't be like that . . .

I was looking at pictures this morning, too, and I'm like, "God, did I look great." I mean, sometimes I looked really sick [*laughs*]. My face is really, really drawn, but I'm like, "God, what I would give"—or not give— but I would like to still have that. The clothes I could wear, I could wear whatever I wanted, whenever I wanted. It's a tremendous loss.

I ask, "What would you say to someone who's still actively bulimic about that loss and about bearing it, about being willing to make the changes anyway?" She replies:

That you basically have to if you really wanna live. Being bulimic is kinda like Russian roulette—it's gonna catch up to you sooner or later. If it hasn't. I think of all the terrible things that I'm gonna have to face down the road. I look at wrinkles on my face, and I think, "Oh, my God, I wouldn't have those wrinkles if I wasn't purging and dehydrating myself." But I think the worst part is that the whole process is so hellish. It's hell. I can't explain it any better than it's pure hell . . . Not only do you ruin yourself, but you've hurt a lot of people, and it's just a terrible, terrible, terrible thing to have to live. And—I think most bulimics would say this—the body I had was a lie. It wasn't my body. It was something that I created, but it wasn't who I was supposed to be. It wasn't, I could not have been that weight if I wasn't bulimic. And I lived a lie. I just lived the biggest lie you could ever imagine because I deceived so many people because they thought I was something that I really wasn't. In many ways. Physically, and emotionally, and psychologically, it's a huge, a big lie.

Rebecca's experience suggests that when we keep our body below its naturally maintainable weight, we feel trapped—trapped in a body that is deceptively and dangerously small and trapped in a big lie that, like all lies, requires never-ending thought and energy to maintain. In letting herself be the size her body was meant to be, Rebecca experienced both loss and liberation: "I've gained a lot. See, the bulimia is negative in every way possible except for the physical, really, 'cause I had nothing going for me besides that with respect to being bulimic. Nothing. I didn't have the relationships that I have now. I didn't have my own honesty that I have now. I just didn't have my own sense of self or self-esteem or self-worth."

Rebecca's relationship with her boyfriend was challenged when they could no longer remain in the roles of sick one and well one:

> The bulimia I know really destroyed Robert in a lot of ways and made it a really difficult relationship. But it—and I've come to realize this—gave both of us a focus. So after recovering, the focus was gone. And Robert had to begin to focus on himself, and that's created a lot of stress and a lot of things that need to be addressed but that he's not able to address at this particular time in his life . . . So I get really angry because he needs therapy, he needs to look at some things, the way he feels about himself. And if I don't know that, who knows better than I?

Meg lost her relationship with her boyfriend because although he was just what she needed when she was bulimic, as she became healthier the relationship no longer felt healthy: "I had changed so much, and he was perfect when I had an eating disorder because he was there, and he was very supportive and did what I wanted and asked for. But after that, I needed more, and that wasn't there, and we didn't work anymore."

Meg also had to grieve the loss of her belief that if others would only try hard enough they could sense her needs without her asking for things directly:

> I remember reading . . . that people with eating disorders have this infantile idea that others will understand their needs and act on that. I remember believing this, that if I had to tell someone what I needed, then it wasn't worth getting because they didn't know. I also feel that sometimes now because I feel like I'm perceptive, and I know what other people need without them telling me. And that's not always the case, but I think—I thought this more at the time—but if people just tried hard and were perceptive of other people and thought about other people more than themselves, then they would know. But that was exactly the problem, was that I was thinking about everyone else and not myself.

Beth grieves her dream that she could be superhuman. Although she knows that the cost of superachievement was too high, she still misses her drive to be Superwoman:

I used to work two jobs, and I kinda prided myself on my self-sufficiency, and I looked down on people who couldn't do as much as I could do. I just was Superwoman, like "I can run twice a day and work a job and be in school full-time." And that's been hard for me to let go of. That for me to stay in recovery, they say HALT in the [OA] program: You can't get too hungry, angry, lonely, or tired. I prided myself on being able to starve myself and work two jobs, and it's been a process of letting go of that, that I can't have that, I can't. I can't be in a job that I work sixty hours. That's not an option for me as a recovering food addict, that's not an option for me to work sixty, eighty hours a week. And that was something I could see myself really wanting to do, be some great person. And I always had wanted to go to the Olympics and be great. And I really had to let go of ideas of myself as being better than everybody else. I always believed that in order to be okay, I had to be great. Like write some great thesis that was published all over, or win the Olympics. And I've had to let go of some of those things. And I'm glad that I have, but sometimes I'm still feeling, "Oh, man, I'm never gonna be the workaholic of the office." Or sometimes I think, "Will I even ever go back to school?" I don't know. That I've just had to accept who I am. That's been hard.

When I ask what has helped her accept that, she says: "That my life is so amazing today, lookin' at what I have, and not what I don't have. Seeing all the good things in my life and accepting who I am . . . I think I've gained self-acceptance. I don't have to do those things in order to be okay. In letting go of those things, I've realized 'Why am I always looking toward when I have that great degree?' That today I have the most amazing life. To me, my life is amazing."

I ask, "What amazes you?" She talks about that very day and how much of it included relationships with people: "And just that I feel like the most important thing in my life today is that I can help someone else, and I can go through life without hating myself. And really enjoying it . . . I have a life that's just so full of people and of helping other people, and just living, going through things, and being a part of other people's life . . . I always wanted that. I always wanted to care about other people and be in their lives. And I just feel so good." While Beth's caring for others may be a reaction to her own need to receive care, or an effort to garner approval, it seems to give her genuine pleasure and pride as well as a sense of competence in her relational ability and a confidence that she matters to people.

In recovering from her eating disorder, Beth has lost her protection from having to make active choices in life:

> It exonerated me from responsibility because if I binged and threw up, I would let myself say, "Well, I can't go out tonight with people 'cause I hate myself," or I'd say, "Oh, I can't go to this party tonight 'cause I'll eat at the party, so I'm gonna stay home and close my door and just be at home." And so it gave me a lot of excuses to not live my life, to not show up . . . "Oh, I'm too sick, I can't get a better job than I have. When I have a year of recovery, then I'll look for a new job, then I'll go back to school, then I'll take responsibility for things I don't want to take responsibility for." Even now, when I think, the times when I want to go back to that behavior is when I'm scared of life.

In recovering, Sarah felt that she was "entering the world of people." But once in that world, she discovered that the capacity to feel, while it allowed her to create more meaningful relationships, left her vulnerable to rejection, loneliness, and longing: "Being in the world of people is really what felt so good, but also felt like, 'Well, now that I'm connected and with these people, now I can really feel what it's like to be alone,' where before I just never bothered to make the connection."

Amy misses the sense of legitimacy and distinction that being bulimic gave her:

> What do I miss? In a sick kind of way I'd have to say the fact that the bulimia was abnormal, in that you are like a special kind of person for being bulimic, that you are looked at by society as "an unfortunate thing happened to you, and now you have to get treated for it." Maybe I miss that, that something was wrong with me. You know what I mean? That I needed special attention. Being bulimic. Maybe that's what I miss is the special attention . . . When I read about the bulimia, about it being among movie stars, and it being a problem, and you need to get help, I was like, "Oh. I have a problem." I was always a normal child, I never really had a problem. I was fat, but I never had this like serious problem that needed attention.

CLAIMING THE GIFTS

Recovering brings not only grief but gifts, including pride and self-respect, as well as a sense of freedom. As the women recovered, they claimed those gifts more fully.

Given that a core sense of shame is a primary impediment to sensing self-experience, and given that pride is the counter to shame, it makes sense that recovering would entail feeling pride. At the end of my second interview with Rebecca, I say, "I'm impressed by how much you worked at this . . . It's just clear that when you entered therapy, and you finally were ready, you really put your heart and soul in it." She beams and replies: "I totally did. A hell of a lot of work. And I don't deny myself all that work that I did at all. A hell of a lot of work."

Jessie, too, looks back with pride at all that she did to recover: "I like to talk about this. I do. Every now and then when you sit down and have a good conversation about it, and you talk about the painful things, it reinforces that 'Yeah, I'm strong. I'm still over it. I can still talk about it to a stranger, and I'm not embarrassed. And it doesn't hurt me anymore.' And I'm proud of myself. It was a big accomplishment in my life . . . 'Cause it was very, very difficult."

Leslie expresses pride in having identified her disorder and taken herself seriously enough to seek help:

> All those physical symptoms that people saw in me but didn't make a connection, I've started spelling out to other people, and they just say, "Wow, I see that in people in my own dorms." People saw it in me, too, but they just never put the pieces together . . .
>
> I think I'm pretty proud of the way I grabbed the bull by the horns. 'Cause during that whole period that was so awful the only thing I had to feel good about was the fact I was doing something about it. I often say to people, "The first step is the hardest step, and you can take it, and you have something to be proud of." But that was the hardest period of my life, the hardest thing I've ever done. So I guess I do feel pretty good about the fact that I drove myself to do it, I didn't have to have someone pushing me from behind. If anything, I had my parents pushing me from the front saying, "It's not that big a deal."

As noted in Chapter 2, many of the women are grateful that they got sick enough that they had to face the psychological difficulties their symptoms had signaled. Leslie is one example:

> I've been through it, I've survived it, and I really feel like I'm so much better a person now for what I had to go through. I have a sensitivity to other people I don't think I had before. I was a beanbag, and I would do whatever people told me to do, but I wasn't sensitive to their feelings. I feel like I look at everything from both sides now, left and right and right and wrong, whatever. And I think that that's something that happened through the process that I don't judge anybody until I know the whole story. And it's because I've been there. I've been judged and I've also been with people who didn't judge me . . .
>
> I really learned something. And my whole life has changed because I went through this. Realistically, maybe I would have never developed an eating disorder, but I always would have been unhappy. And I would have always had this crappy relationship with my family. And I would have always pushed men away. That could've happened. It just all culminated and turned into this eating disorder and forced me to do something about it.

She goes so far as to say she does not want to recover completely:

> I don't think I'd ever want to fully recover because if I fully recovered, I might forget what it was like and what it felt like. I would never want to lose how much I have to attribute to what I've been through. I need that whole experience to remind myself that I'm human, and I'm gonna screw up every once in a while, and that it's okay, and that people care about me for who I am. Took me a really long time to figure out who I am. And I don't want to get caught up in that game again, wanting to be what other people think you are. So no, I don't think you ever do [fully recover] 'cause I think it's always, it's such a significant part of who you become.

Like Leslie, Abigail attributes her deeper appreciation of human difficulty and of her own complexity to having had and recovered from bulimia nervosa:

> This makes me a lot more sensitive to treating not just eating-disordered people, but I wonder, well, if this is true about the eating disorder, it must be true about other things, people with disorders . . . I really think that what's more important is the underlying self, or lack thereof . . . This has been such

an important part of my life, it's not just a disorder, it's an important part of who I am and how I've expressed myself. Or how I've limited myself and managed affects and feelings . . . What I've gotten out of it has just been so much more. Everything that I think I will enjoy in the future I think I've found through this process of recovering from bulimia.

Abigail, too, is grateful that the disorder brought her pain to such a pitch that she had to deal with fundamental issues in her life: "I think of it lately as a good thing because it brought me—I don't know that I would've gotten into treatment if I hadn't been symptomatic and it hadn't been such a pain in the ass. That maybe I would've kept putting it off, getting into therapy. And that the core issues—maybe I'll be able to have good relationships, where I'm authentic in my relationships and I can feel safe being close with someone."

The women feel a sense of liberation. Gita says: "Basically, to have that obsession gone . . . I don't think about lunch now. I don't plan it at five o'clock in the morning 'cause it's not that important. If I need something to eat, I'll go have something. So it's the freedom from an obsession and the not feeling worried about weight the same way . . . I'm not obsessed. I still do all those things. I still eat, I still run, but with a whole different perspective. It's not compulsive."

Isabella feels she has her mind back: "Food wasn't on my thoughts in every moment during the day. I could think about other things, I could concentrate. Before I couldn't concentrate on anything. I couldn't accomplish anything 'cause all I was thinking about was what I was gonna eat next, how I was gonna get rid of it. So not having food as the center of your thoughts, you feel free."

And Leslie, too, enjoys her new freedom: "I just love being able to think about something else other than how much pain—. When I went through this whole process, all I could think about for a while was my eating and obsessing about my eating and my weight, and then it moved into only being able to think about how much pain I was in. And then it moved into putting the pieces together and getting my life together and convincing my family that there was a problem. But now I just so appreciate being able to care about other things."

The Nature of the Process

REMISSION OF SYMPTOMS

As the women learned to sense self-experience, they were able to know their internal states more precisely and to tolerate and regulate painful self-experience. They therefore did not need to binge to disconnect from uncomfortable feelings or purge to undo a binge or to reintegrate.

The women's accounts indicate that there were various patterns of ending bingeing and purging behaviors. Two women stopped abusing laxatives cold turkey. One, after years of treatment and trying to diminish her bingeing and vomiting gradually, stopped both behaviors the day she committed to following an Overeaters Anonymous program. The other ten stopped gradually, over months or years. Of those ten, three made stopping purging their primary effort; in their experience, the bingeing gradually stopped once they were no longer undoing the binge. For three others, the primary effort was to stop bingeing and overeating; in their experience, if they did not binge or overeat, they did not need to purge. The remaining four decreased their bingeing and purging more or less in tandem.

Of the thirteen women, eleven sought treatment at a point when they met full DSM-III-R criteria for bulimia nervosa (APA, 1987). One sought treatment when her symptoms were within a subclinical range. One did not enter treatment.

Some women found that moderate exercise helped them stop bingeing and purging. But for others exercise became a substitute for vomiting or laxative abuse. That is, it served as a effort to achieve a weight or shape that was not naturally maintainable, to abuse or punish themselves, or to numb themselves by exhaustion or intensity of experience.

AMBIVALENCE

Given the women's impediments to and impairments in sensing self-experience (see Chapter 1), it is no wonder that they were resistant to sensing self-experience and ambivalent about recovering. The women make clear that they did not resolve their ambivalence before beginning the process of recovering but rather recovered despite their ambivalence.

As described in the Introduction, Isabella experienced profound ambivalence about giving up bingeing and purging. Many of the women report having been unable to imagine other ways to cope. Isabella longed for a clear procedure to follow: "You don't know what it is. It's not knowing those steps, the exact procedure. At least for me it was. 'Cause I was the type that wanted to know 'Okay, what do I do? Let's do it. Let's get it done.' I was always the list person." She eventually learned to sense self-worth in the smallest of steps: "I don't know if it was conscious, it wasn't like 'I'm working toward self-esteem.' It was little step by little step. It's 'This made me feel better. Today. So let's try some more again tomorrow.' It's working at what felt good, what made you feel better and better, and trying different things that helped you to do that. To feel more positive . . . If you did some of these things, eventually it would happen."

Jill's ambivalence about changing was in part due to her fear of empty time and psychic emptiness:

> I didn't wanna give up the behavior 'cause it's like "What will I do with my time?" It was like this big fear I had—it was the same fear I had when I quit drinking—like "What am I gonna do with my day? What am I gonna do with my time?" Well, I don't have enough hours in a day anymore to do everything I wanna do, or enough days in the week. But I couldn't see what I would do with all this time I would have. That was my big fear. "What am I gonna do with all this time?" How would I deal with anger, with all this rage? I don't think I consciously thought about how would I deal with it, but it was just the fear of giving it up, totally giving up the behavior.

Despite her ambivalence, Jill took steps toward recovering: joining an eating-disorders group, paying for that group, and investing effort in her therapy. She was surprised one day to discover that those steps had taken her some distance toward health:

> I think the ambivalence was always kinda there. Until the one day I woke up and said, "Gee, I am getting better . . . Wow, I'm doing some of these things,

I'm really getting better" . . . I think I was trying to think of the last time I had binged or purged. Those were the real quantitative things, and I hadn't done it in a while. I could see it, I could see measured improvement. At first it was really measured by the amount of food I ate, or didn't eat, or the fact that there was a package of Oreos sitting in my cabinet in my kitchen at home, and I had been at work, and I had totally forgotten about those Oreos till I came home. Because that was something I would just think about all day at work. So little things like that, that I didn't really see, but then I just one day realized, "My God, I didn't think about those the whole day. I can't believe it." I didn't eat all that food. Or I didn't make myself throw up. That was the stuff that came first. As I was able to tackle some of that stuff, and become a little bit more confident or trusting of the process, then I think the ambivalence lessened.

While in college, Rebecca participated in eating-disorder groups but did not invest fully in recovering. Looking back, she analyzes her ambivalence about engaging in therapy:

My mother had asked me after I had gotten out of college, . . . "Rebecca, why didn't you just tell me that you couldn't do it anymore and that you needed some time off?" And I said, "Mom, I couldn't." I had this plan of my life that I was graduating from college in that particular year. One semester later just wouldn't fit into my life. And I look back, and I should've taken a semester off, I should've gone in the hospital then, but I wasn't ready to do that. And I didn't even want to face how bad the situation really was . . . I was too hard on myself, I was too much of a perfectionist. Everything was always planned for me. I always knew what I was gonna do. From high school you go to college, everything was mapped out in my own head. Nobody else told me I had to be that way, but that was just what I had structured for myself. So to change that would be kind of like failure, and failure would be the utmost in feeling terrible. At that point, it was worse than having the eating disorder.

When Meg was in college and her eating disorder was out of control, she "knew what I was doing was wrong" and yet was intent on keeping up her high-achieving life and staying thin: "I would steal my roommate's food, so people knew, but I was still, I just didn't want any help. I knew what I was doing was wrong, but I didn't want any help. Went to the counseling service a few times 'cause my friends forced me to go, but I never stuck with it. I was managing still to compete in sports. I was a varsity athlete in college, and I'm not really sure how I managed to do that. So my body was still something that was really important to me, staying in shape, and staying below a certain weight."

Meg, like Rebecca, took halting steps toward recovering while in college: joining a group, going reluctantly to the counseling service, participating ambivalently in an outpatient treatment program. As discussed in Chapter 8, those steps may have prepared them to invest more fully in treatment later on.

PRACTICE, PRACTICE, PRACTICE

Sensing self-experience required practice in three senses of the word. First, the women needed *trial-and-error practice* and experimentation to learn how to sense self-experience. Rebecca says:

> The rest of it has just been practice of the techniques that I've learned. You just constantly apply things, and if something doesn't work, then you try something else. And it's just very personalized . . . But it's so hard because you being the sick person and the unstable person, who are you to decide what's gonna work for you? So that's why the process of recovery can take years and years and years because it's just giving yourself the opportunity to try different things and allowing yourself to fail and allowing yourself to just keep on plugging. That's all that you can do.

Second, the women needed to *put into practice* specific, practical suggestions of how to connect to their self-experience. For example, writing down their thoughts, feelings, physical sensations, and behaviors before and after eating helped them slow down enough to discern immediate connections between their felt experience and their behavior. Writing also helped them notice patterns of connections. Writing exercises were especially helpful when they occurred in the context of coaching and company. For instance, Jill says: "I can remember the revelations that would come with some of the particular exercises that I tried. So that would be kind of exciting. That's why it was good to be in the group, because that was the kind of stuff I could share with the group. That wasn't really something I'd share with my friends."

Third, sensing self-experience is an ongoing, *abiding practice.* It is not an accomplishment like learning to ride a bicycle that a person masters once and for all. Like meditation or cardiovascular exercise, sensing self-experience is a way of life that requires routine practice to sustain its benefits. Rebecca recognizes the need to keep noticing connections between emotions and behavior in everyday life:

> Even to this day, I try to make connections as to why I'm doing things . . . I'm still defensive, and I know my defensiveness is a lot of expression of my own fear . . . And after I get sarcastic or explode, I can look back and say, "You know, I was feeling such and such." It wasn't that I was angry about the dishes not getting cleaned, it was, maybe I felt that [Robert] was acting like my father. Or doing something that brought up another feeling that was a fear or something that I just didn't feel comfortable with . . . It's like going to school twenty-four hours a day, eight days a week . . . They're just little things that you can look at in retrospect and say, "Oh, my God, look what I was doing." It's a lot of looking back at what you've done or the way you've behaved or what you said. Just little, tiny increments, tiny, tiny, minuscule increments of trying to do it a little bit differently.

REALISTIC EXPECTATIONS

The women emphasize that recovering is not easy and is not over and done with once and for all:

> It's taken such a long time to get there. It's not like overnight, "Whoops, I stopped doing this. I'm okay, I'm fine, everything's peachy, and the sun's shining" [*laughs*]. Not at all.   (Rebecca)

> It wasn't easy. It sounds really simple—it sounds very television movie type of thing—but it wasn't an easy thing to do.   (Kate)

> I've been in this therapy for three and a half years, and I have come a long way, but I see this as being a life's work. It's great work, and it's getting to know myself and nurturing myself and expressing myself . . . that seems like

something that for this period of my life is what I need to work on. Valuing myself . . . It sounds very easy, but it's very difficult.   (Abigail)

As discussed in Chapter 7, the women have continuing vulnerabilities to psychological aspects of the disorder, and they need to continually commit themselves to sensing self-experience.

The women also stress that recovering takes time. While it could seem disheartening to realize that recovering is a long and difficult process, knowing this helped the women develop realistic expectations for themselves and counter feelings of disappointment, failure, and shame. Jill says: "You fall into that trap of wanting an instant cure, and, perhaps because I'd already been in AA a couple years, I realized there was no instant cure, that even though I quit drinking right away, I realized what a long process it was to get better . . . It's not something that's gonna happen overnight."

Gita, like Jill, advises patience, emphasizing that it takes time to establish a baseline of true health and vitality: "At every level there was something that was askew, and it took a while to even those out. It wasn't like the day I stopped, or the week after I stopped drinking caffeine that I felt better. It was a long time before I really, but you have to have the patience to let that have a chance . . . To get to that point of health again and say, 'Oh, it is good.'"

Sensing Self through Relationship

Relationships were essential to the women's process of recovering. The shift from observing and objectifying themselves through their own or others' eyes to listening to and being in touch with themselves (discussed in Chapter 5) was made possible through their relationships with others.

VOICE

The women relied upon the internalized voices of themselves and others to sense their self-experience, in particular to evoke a sense of self-with-self and of self-with-other. Many, including Rebecca, internalized another's voice and eventually experienced it as their own:

> Again, I can only go back to Susan, that what's inside of you is the most important thing, and it doesn't matter what the exterior is. You're only beautiful if what's inside of you is beautiful . . . What your body is is just a capsule for your soul. The whole concept of spirituality and your soul, and that that's what we're meant to be, we're not meant to be these physical beings of beauty. And it's just a shell, it's just an outer coating. To really identify with that, and really, truly believe in that, I think really was one of the many steps in recovery.

Rebecca describes the process by which she took in her therapist's voice:

> I'm a person who kinda tape records certain things in my head and I replay them through time . . . What I've retained and what

I've considered valuable and put into my own little treasury of things to take with me and kinda try to live by have a lot to do with what came out of Susan's mouth. And it amazes me how much I did retain, and that I did. 'Cause they're things that I try to practice. Things that to this day—and we're talking, five years ago that I heard these things. So it's really, it's mine, it's mine. I've done some reading, and she really clicks with a lot of other things that are out there, but I think it's always easier to hear it from somebody's mouth. Especially someone that you believe in. Because you can read a thousand books, but it's not the same thing as getting it verbatim from somebody who is trustworthy and has gotten you this far basically.

Rebecca internalized not just her therapist's words but her therapist's voice. As if learning a new song, she kept replaying what her therapist said until she knew it by heart and took it to heart: "So it's really, it's mine, it's mine." She recounts an instance of making her therapist's voice her own:

I remember Susan always saying, "Having two cookies or whatever is fine. Now, if you eat, say, a box of cookies, that's okay to do it once in a while, that's no big—if that's what you really, really, really want, and your dinner is gonna be a box of cookies, then have the box of cookies." But I would think, "She's crazy. This lady's crazy." But all those things, even though at the time when I heard them, I probably wasn't able to put them into practice, I still retained them, and they're absolutely true. Absolutely true.

When Amy talked with a friend who had an eating disorder, she incorporated her nutritionist's voice as her own:

I have a friend that still does it. And I know she does, but she denies it. And I told her, "I went and I saw a nutritionist, I saw a psychologist, it's made my life completely different. It's really not good for you, you've just gotta stop doing it and start taking care of yourself and stop punishing your body" . . . 'Cause that's how Monica had phrased it to me was that I am punishing my body, I insist on beating up my body and punishing my body for whatever reason. That I was treating myself very badly and why would you wanna do that, basically beat yourself up?

Jessie felt worthless partly because she feared that, like her father, she would be an abuser. To this day she can replay a conversation with her therapist that helped her believe she was not destined to abuse her own children. She uses her therapist's voice to evoke the sense of being okay she felt in her therapist's presence:

I think people with eating disorders generally have a very negative opinion of themselves. They could always do what they're doin' well better. I could always look better. I could always have a better body. I could always do a better job at work. I could always be a better daughter. I never felt really like I was worth anything . . .

And a big thing, too, was my fear that I would in turn molest children . . . Not because I ever had any urges, but because you think people who are victims of child abuse usually abuse children—you know, physical beating abuse . . . And I think I carried that with me for many, many years, and that made me feel like a horrible person. It's almost like I turned that on myself even before I did anything. I was feeling horrible for something that had never happened . . . But you're terrified that you're gonna. And she showed me that that was not true, that I didn't have to suffer for that.

How did you come to believe that that wasn't true?

We worked on that for a couple of sessions with, "Do you have friends with children?" "Yes, I do." "Have you been alone with those children?" "Yes, I have." "Have you had any urges toward those children?" "No." "Have you ever touched those children where you shouldn't have touched them?" "No." "Did you have any desire to touch them where you shouldn't touch them?" "No." "Have you changed any diapers?" "Yes." Things like that.

She basically had to give me a real-life situation that I had been in and keep drilling that and keep bringing up situations that I had been in or that I could possibly be in and say "How do you feel? What do you feel? What would you do?" And it was always, "No, no, no, no, no. I have no desire." And gradually, it came into my mind that "Gee, no, I'm not like him. He didn't bring me up. All I have are his biological genes. And psychologically I don't feel like he was. I don't wanna harm anybody. I'm aware of it, so if I ever did feel it, I would get help." And just gradually I became aware that this was not going to happen. That I don't have this in me.

And that was an enormous weight lifted off my shoulders. 'Cause that was a concern for me for my own children, "Oh, my God, what am I gonna do to my own children?" And she said, "Don't you realize that the first step is that you're aware that this might have ever happened in your life and that you're protecting your children before you even have them?" And I thought, "Well, yeah, gee, that's true." And that alone really was a boost for me and how I felt about me as a person.

Daniel Stern (1985) talks about language as a means by which functions that were performed by others become part of the self: "The word is given to the infant from the outside, by mother, but there exists a thought for it to be given to. In this sense the word, as a transitional phenomenon, does not truly belong to the self, nor does it truly belong to the other. It occupies a midway position between the infant's subjectivity and the mother's objectivity . . . It is in this deeper sense that language is a union experience, permitting a new level of mental relatedness through shared meaning" (172).

Stern describes the "crib talk" of a 2-year-old girl as her father put her to bed and then after he left the room:

> As part of the putting-to-bed ritual, they held a dialogue in which the father went over some of the things that had happened that day and discussed what was planned for the next day. The girl participated actively in this dialogue and at the same time went through many obvious and subtle maneuvers to keep daddy present and talking, to prolong the rituals. She would plead, fuss-cry, insist, cajole, and devise new questions for him, intoned ingenuously. But when he finally said "good night" and left, her voice changed dramatically into a more matter of fact, narrative tone, and her monologue began, a soliloquy . . .
>
> It was like watching "internalization" happen right before our eyes and ears. After father left, she appeared to be constantly under the threat of feeling alone and distressed . . . To keep herself controlled emotionally, she repeated in her soliloquy topics that had been part of the dialogue with father. Sometimes she seemed to intone his voice or to recreate something like the previous dialogue with him in order to reactivate his presence and carry it with her toward the abyss of sleep . . . This, of course, was not the only purpose that her monologue served (she was also practicing language!), but it certainly felt as though she were also engaged in a "transitional phenomenon," in Winnicott's sense.
>
> Language, then, provides a new way of being related to others (who may be present or absent) by sharing personal world knowledge with them, coming together in the domain of verbal relatedness. (172–173)

199

This child seems to use not only language but voice to internalize soothing. She uses her voice to evoke a sense of her father's voice and a sense of how she felt with him, of me-with-Daddy. As Anna Romer (2000) observes, we internalize experience through our senses, and our memory of experience is evoked through our senses "as when a particular bar of music releases a flood of feelings" (141). *Evoke* derives from "voice." Voice is, by nature and definition, highly sensory, highly evocative.

Stern considers language development an interpersonal process by which "the infant and mother create a being-with experience using verbal symbols" (172). Self-talk is self-soothing because it is evocative not only of other but of self-with-other. Self-talk is the means by which the sense of comfort and security one experiences in another's presence is transmuted to the capacity to soothe oneself. Self-talk keeps one company. The etymology of the word *company* leads to its sensory roots: "with bread." Breaking bread is synonymous with keeping company. Women with bulimia nervosa overuse food as comfort not only because of the sensory, comforting experience of eating and the associations of food with comfort and company, but also because they have not internalized a self-accompanying capacity, an ability to evoke a sense of comfort in the absence of bread or company.

Craig Johnson and Mary Connors (1987) suggest that the therapist of a bulimic provide a mantra of sorts to help the patient reintegrate following a dissociative experience:

> Bulimic patients often appear to lapse cognitively under the pressure of strong affects. It is often helpful to suggest a single word that might help patients organize during these times. We use the word perspective to attempt to teach patients to focus away from the immediacy of their affective state. Some striking changes in symptomatic behaviors have been observed as patients begin to rehearse using the word. Apparently, if a therapist uses the word frequently, the patients' later use of the word may evoke a memory of the therapist or the therapeutic holding environment. For character-disordered patients who have difficulty with evocative object recall, the association between the word and the therapeutic environment is sometimes sufficient to help soothe them when they feel in danger of losing control. (244)

Again, while words may help someone reintegrate, the women suggest that it is not only words but the sound of voice that evokes the soothing sense of self-with-therapist.

Ana-Maria Rizzuto, in considering the connections between voice and words, or what she calls "sound and sense," says, "I believe that the central factor in the therapeutic action of psychoanalysis is the communicative power of the analyst's voice" (1995, 6). She notes that where words, in the form of an interpretation, allow a patient to feel seen, voice allows her to feel touched. Psychotherapy relies upon what Rizzuto calls "exquisite attentiveness to affect and words" (1988, 385) to enable a person to integrate sound and sense:

> The analyst's emotionally meaningful interpretations offer the analysand a triple experience. First, the analysand recognizes that, as a self, he has been "seen," heard, and known in his private reality (the content of the interpretation); second, the analysand experiences that, as an object in a relationship, he has been reached and "touched" emotionally (there where before he stood alone, conflicted or shamed); finally, the analysand registers, as a bodily self, the sound qualities of the analyst's voice, which reach emotions and developmental impressions beyond what can be made fully conscious by the semantic meaning of words. (1995, 6–7)

Uniting affect and words helps someone communicate with herself and with others "by restoring to the patient's words the fullness of their meaning" (12).

As discussed in Chapter 1, the integration of words with their affective resonance is especially healing for a bulimic woman who tends to dissociate language and affect. Rizzuto observes that bulimic patients are especially attuned to voice:

> The patients' conscious and unconscious passive and active disregard for words contrasts sharply with their exquisite attentiveness to the non-verbal signals emitted by the analyst. Their ears capture every modulation of tone of voice, pitch, intonation, and matter of speech in the analyst's words. They are equally alert to the analyst's timing and type of movements, gestures, or facial expressions. They hope to "catch" in those manifestations the analyst's "real intentions" and meanings—so absent for them in his/her words. (1988, 370)

Rebecca illustrates this keen awareness of a therapist's words and voice. She vividly recalls her first phone call to Susan:

I had called her from work, and I had called her from a pay phone after getting the referral from the hospital. And I remember the conversation. And she was so empathetic. I was on the phone for I would say less than an hour, but it was a long time. And here I was at work, and I just remember—it probably wasn't even that long, but it seemed like forever—'cause it was just, this person was listening to me, and here I was saying all these things to this person who I had no idea who she was. But it was just her demeanor, and her tone of voice—that's all it can be over the telephone—it just, she was very caring. And "Oh, my God, I think maybe I can get some help here."

A young woman I had been seeing in therapy for over two years said to me one day, "It must be hard for you that I'm not getting better. What must your colleagues think? We've been meeting for so long, and I'm still bulimic." At this point, uncharacteristically, I snapped at her: "*Don't recover on my account!*" I knew something powerful had just happened. Although I felt the urge to apologize, I did not. I knew that I had to allow her to have her own experience of the moment. To apologize would have been intrusive. And so I waited. In our next session she told me, "What you said last time was the best thing you've ever said to me because I knew you really meant it." And I could tell from her voice that *she* really meant it. She heard the congruence of my words and voice, and I heard the congruence of hers. The question "Whom is this actually for?" was central to this woman's life. What others did ostensibly on her behalf was all too often on behalf of their own needs, and what she did for them was all too often on behalf of her need to be loved. So when the question of whom her recovering would be for arose between us, it was essential that my voice carry my conviction that her life, her body, her eating disorder, her choice of whether to recover, and her recovery itself were her own.

Like the note that shatters the glass because it resonates with the frequency of the structural bonds holding the glass intact, voice has the power to release energy when it resonates with a person's experience. That energy, which manifests in tears of relief or a sigh of understanding or a grin of recognition, creates a bond between speaker and listener and between sound and sense.

Replaying others' voices in their minds and doing role-plays in which they spoke about their experience were among the forms of self-talk the women used to take in others' voices and to sense their own. Kate says:

> For myself, and I think it's probably true for a lot of people who go through this, you're not gonna be able to face the issue and deal with it until you can say it out loud. To somebody, even if it's to your own face in the mirror. But until you can hear the words actually come out of your mouth that "this was a painful thing for me." Or if you have really negative feelings about some member of your family that you think God's gonna strike you dead if you say it out loud. I think that before you can stop stuffing down inside you symbolically with the food, you actually have to physically—you're doing something physical to keep it inside you so you have to do something physical to get it out. So saying exactly what it was, I think you have to do that . . . I actually a couple of times went to the cemetery and said it out loud up at my father's gravesite . . . I would actually go and have conversations with him about things that were going on in my life at that time that, if he were alive, I would wish I could say to him. So I would go up and do that.

Kate also participated in psychodramatic exercises with her therapist: "She would be my father, and I would have to say things to her about how angry I was about whatever." In the following excerpt, her use of metaphor suggests that Kate now knows that her subjective experience is a real force with which to reckon: "You have to be able to hear yourself say the words before you can close the loop. The loop is still open, so until you can come full circle, you have to say it out loud . . . I definitely think it has to be some sort of physical exorcism, if you want to call it that. 'Cause you can have the thoughts, but thinking them, you're still keeping them inside. You're using food as a way to push the thoughts back. And push the feeling back. So there has to be a contradicting force to get them out."

Lyn Mikel Brown and Carol Gilligan (1992) emphasize the capacity of voice to connect self with other and self with self: "Voice, because it is embodied, connects rather than separates psyche and body; because voice is in language, it also joins psyche and culture. Voice is inherently relational—one does not require a mirror to hear oneself—yet the sounds of one's voice change in resonance depending on the relational acoustics: whether one is heard or not heard, how one is responded to (by oneself and other people)" (20).

Voice identifies both *how* we are and *who* we are. Voice conveys anxiety, joy, sorrow, upset, ease. Each person's voice has a distinctive, identifiable signature determined by, among other elements, its pitch, timbre, and cadence. And so it is natural that the women would use voice not only to communicate their subjective experience to others but also to sense it themselves. Gilligan says: "By voice I mean something like what people mean when they speak of the core of the self . . . It is composed of breath and sound, words, rhythm, and language. And voice is a powerful psychological instrument and channel, connecting inner and outer worlds. Speaking and listening are a form of psychic breathing" (1982/1993, xvi).

Journal writing was also a form of self-talk the women used. Kate found that hearing her own voice—whether by speaking with her therapist or in her group, talking to herself, or writing in her journal—helped her stay connected with herself and with others:

> But I kept a journal the whole time . . . So within that six months when I saw the weight kept creeping up, I would write about it in my journal and say, "Oh, shit, I gained two pounds today" and just try to work the whole thing out down on paper. And then I found that it was helpful to actually be able to look at it again and read it through. It was a lot of talking to myself, talking to myself in my own head. And then to Linda and the group 'cause they were the only other people that I really had to talk to about it.

Another form of self-talk was affirmations—positive statements the women repeated like mantras to calm, comfort, and refocus themselves. Many initially voiced their affirmations out loud, some in front of a mirror. At the treatment center Meg attended, each resident had to create her own affirmation. Meg believes her affirmation served as a "foundation" for her recovering:

> As silly as it seems, it was really good to start to believe the things that I said. For me the affirmation was realistic. It wasn't "I'm a beautiful, thin, attrac-

tive, lovely whatever, woman." It was something about how my body is very functional, and it's muscular and whatever, attractive and functional, and that I am caring and giving. And it's not so much the affirmation itself but that it helped me formulate ideas about myself. And that was a definite beginning. I think that was the start. I had to have some foundation to go from . . . I took a long time 'cause I wanted it to be concise and exactly what I wanted.

Meg is not alone in reporting that she felt "silly" saying affirmations. But like Meg, many women were surprised that something so seemingly hokey could actually be helpful: "It really does seem like such a basic thing. I never thought about how powerful it really was, but it was. Just because there was a point where I went through that big thing where I thought I was no one and had no personality . . . I thought I had no self. And when I could sit down and think of things that I really was, of who I was, it was just very, very helpful." Although she uses the words "thought" and "think," Meg implies that it was not just her thinking but her voicing and hearing "things that I really was" that enabled her to sense these aspects of herself.

Just being able to talk also helped Meg sense her experience. Being listened to by her therapists let her hear and know her internal experience: "They were definitely both great listeners. They made me feel comfortable enough somehow, they weren't judgmental at all, and I just felt comfortable to talk to them . . . I mean all along, I knew that there was this internal struggle, just all of this stuff going on inside of me that I couldn't label and I couldn't find words for . . . And just to be able to talk. I really like to talk and I am good at making connections myself and so I would just sit and talk and make connections."

AUTHENTIC AND ATTUNED ACTS OF CARE

The women sensed their worth when they realized through a specific, attuned act of care that their welfare mattered to someone. Both the noun and the verb *matter* derive from the Latin word *materia*, meaning "building material, timber, hence the stuff of which a thing is made"

(*Oxford English Dictionary,* 1971). Matter is substance—from the Latin word *substantia,* meaning "essence (literally that which stands under, i.e., underlies)" (*Random House College Dictionary,* 1975). To know that one matters is to trust that one is a person of substance. The women had not regarded themselves as people who mattered, as people of substance. For instance, Amy described herself with the metaphor of air:

Eighth grade though is when I started *ballooning* with weight.

I hadn't exercised in two weeks because of my work . . . I just felt like I was losing control. I envisioned myself as being a big *balloon,* and I cried last week to my husband, "I'm getting so fat, I'm afraid I'm gonna *explode*" . . . 'Cause I was starting to lose control, I was very unhappy. Putting on my skirts, I was like, "Oh, my God, I am gonna *blow up* again."

Equating her self with her body ("myself as being a big balloon") and her body with air ("I started ballooning"), Amy felt she had no enduring shape or size, no substance or solidity, and could therefore make no impact on others.

The women sensed their substantiality when they experienced their effect on others, in particular when they sensed that someone was moved by them—moved to action or evident emotion. For example, Abigail's first therapist saw her for a very low fee. That personal sacrifice evoked in Abigail a sense that her concerns were "really important to address": "They referred me to this social worker who was just really wonderful to me. She charged me like 40 doll—, she charged me some ridiculous sum of money, half of which the insurance paid, so I paid her maybe $15 or $20 a week, which was what I could afford. It may have even been less. And she just made me feel like it was really important, that this was really important to address. That she was ready to make no money to see me."

Similarly, her therapist's willingness to invest time on her behalf beyond the therapy hour helped Kate believe she really mattered:

The way that she has about doing it makes you truly believe that she genuinely cares about what happens to you. I guess that's it. That it isn't just for those fifty minutes that you're in there with her. She actually thinks about what you say during those fifty minutes and will expand on it afterwards. Or, if it was a really, particularly intense session, she will take the time to call you at some point during the week, even if it's for only two minutes, to say, "Hey, are you sure you were all right with everything that happened?"

Meg's eyes fill with tears as she recalls receiving acts of care from the people at the residential treatment center. Like Abigail and Kate, she felt she mattered when she sensed others' investment in her recovering:

The most helpful thing I think was just the environment. It was so supportive and nurturing . . . It was everything. It was the building, it was the whole complex. From the chef, the guy who made the meals who would take you in and show you how he was cooking anything . . . And from the administrators, who would show up every now and then and talk and ask us what was going on and if we have questions and explain to us how the whole institution came into being. To everyone in the middle, the more important people in our daily lives—the group people and the nutritionist and everyone was just there for you. It was amazing, it really was. And that's not something that you—I really get teary whenever I talk about it 'cause it's just, there was nowhere else in the world where I could go where I would feel like, where I had ever felt like everyone was doing something for me. And everyone was there for me. And even eventually, the people that you got to be friends with, they were invested in their own recoveries, but they were invested in my recovery as well, and I was invested in theirs. And so everyone had some connection to you, and you felt like you were important and that it mattered that you got better. And that if you slipped, there would be people there.

For Amy, whose nutritionist, Monica, used pieces of fruit to demonstrate the limited mutability of body-types, both the lesson and the act of care were powerful:

It was something about this woman . . . she was just so good-hearted, and just very sincere, and I knew that she really cared about me . . . I would really have to say that I think if I hadn't met her, maybe I wouldn't have gotten over it. I definitely don't think so. There was just something about this woman that helped me to see the light . . . and why I have to stop it. And she made me recognize that I am important. And that I really need to take care of myself.

How did she do that?

Just the way that she gave me that, the way that she explained things, the way that she talked to me, the way that she treated me, with great respect. Made me feel important.

Other acts of care contributed to Amy's feeling that she mattered, namely her physical therapist's arranging the referral to Monica and Monica's agreeing to see her for a reduced fee. Amy also sensed that her welfare mattered when Monica referred her to a psychotherapist: "She went on and on and on about why was I abusing myself, and she really felt that I should get in with a psychologist right away. So she gave me Sally's number, that's how I started to see her."

In high school, Sarah often stopped by her faculty adviser's office to talk: "She was interested in me as a person. She wanted to know me as a person. She wanted to hear what I was thinking about. She enjoyed me. I mattered to her . . . Knowing I mattered was important."

Claire says her relationship with her boyfriend was "a turning point." In time, Claire adopted his acts of care for herself:

That was something I started doing after the surgery when I wanted to start liking myself more. My partner would soak my feet and wash my legs. And I would feel sick when he did it at first. I really would feel sick. I'd never let him touch my legs in bed . . . And now I make it a ritual. Part of my routine before I go to bed at night—'cause the evenings, sometimes they're stressful, and I don't want to eat when I just feel very tense. And to have a bath, and to put bubble bath in, to soap your legs, and soap my arms, and soap my tummy, all the areas that I used to find really repulsive and used to cover up, and I used to have thoughts of slicing bits off of, I was making myself like them and touch them. And starting to do that, in getting over bulimia, was a good thing.

What made that possible to even start?

Somebody else doing it first. Was one thing . . . And I thought, "There must be a way that I can like myself." So I just tried to start being nice to myself.

CONCRETIZATION

The bulimic self speaks a concrete, sensory, bodily language. Given that bulimic women tend to convert psychic pain to physical pain, they need someone to understand their bodily communication and help them translate it into the language of emotional experience. And they need someone to help them make their emotional experience concrete enough that it feels sensory and real to them.

Amy's account illustrates how concrete, sensory, and bodily the language of the bulimic self is. Amy bought a book on nutrition and, reading a chapter on eating disorders, learned about the dangers of laxative abuse and excessive exercising. She recognized her own experience in the descriptions of physical symptoms of dehydration and electrolyte imbalance. She noticed that the co-author of the chapter was a nutritionist who worked at the clinic where she was getting physical therapy for a shoulder injury. During a treatment session, Amy asked the physical therapist how much the nutritionist charged. Thus it was when Amy recognized her physical symptoms, written concretely in black and white, and while her body was being attended to in a physical therapy session, that she felt able to inquire about another concrete, body-based therapy.

And I read this chapter about how it's not good for you. It explained to me about the electrolytes, and how come when you work out, your skin gets— you feel very drained, it's not good for you to work out after you've binged and purged. So I'm laying on the table, and I said, "How much does it cost to go see Monica, the nutritionist? 'Cause I don't think health insurance would cover that." She said, "$90 for 45 minutes is what she charges." I thought, "Oh, geez, I could never afford that." And this woman, the physical therapist, said, "Why? Do you need to see her? Why do you want to see her?" I said, "Well, I have an eating disorder." And she was like, "What?!" And she was massaging me. I said, "I binge, and then I take laxatives." And she's like, "Oh, my God, maybe you should go see her." And I said, "And I took them last night, and I'm just really sick of it because," and basically I tell this woman my life story. I said, "I'm just really sick of it, I've been doin' it for six years, and I'm tired of it. And I'm struggling." And she's like, "I don't understand why you feel that way about yourself. You're an average-looking girl, you're very fit. Let me talk to this woman, Monica, and see if she can get you a discount rate or something," she said. "'Cause I know that she works with people if they can't afford it." And sure enough, this woman Monica says, "I'll see you for $30."

By contrast with physical therapy and nutrition therapy, psychotherapy was not satisfying for Amy because it was not attuned to her present, bodily experience. She was frustrated by the pace of psychological change, which was not as concrete, quick, and complete as was restoring the use of her shoulder or stopping laxative abuse. Amy stopped going to therapy after a few months:

> Because I think what's the problem with me is that I look for concrete things to happen. Like I overcame this. That was a definite, it happened within a short amount of time, it's concrete, it did change . . . Like [Sally's] saying I'm never gonna be fully recovered or through this low self-esteem problem until I identify why I have that low self-esteem . . . With Monica, there was a definite end result that we were getting toward. And with Sally, it's like, "We're gonna just keep talking until something clicks with you," but that's it. And I don't really have much patience.

Beth, when I ask how she came to take her own pain seriously, recalls a concrete, body-focused exercise in which she witnessed other people with eating disorders speaking about themselves with cruelty and hatred:

> An experience that was incredibly powerful was in a group where people had to draw their body images on a piece of paper. You had to lie down, and people had to trace your body. And then you had to hang it up on the wall and write how you felt about all the different parts of your body. And then the whole group had to sit on the floor and you had to explain it to the group. And, oh, my God, it gives me chills here right now—my arms are just— because I remember seeing people who I had grown to love and care about as people, not as bodies, as people with kids, with hearts and souls and just, who cared about people pointing to their bodies and hating themselves so much, and saying, "I hate this part of me," and "This is my stomach, which had an abortion," "This is my butt, and this my vagina, which my stepfather sexually abused." And just so much self-hate, and I couldn't believe it seeing these people that I loved hating themselves the way I hated myself. And it

was okay for me to hate myself that much, but I just wanted to shake people and say, "You're not your body" . . . That was so powerful to me, to see how much pain, that they were doing the same things to themselves that I was doing to myself. But I saw them as whole people, as wonderful, caring human beings that weren't their bodies. And that was a really powerful experience where I saw my own pain by seeing other people doing to themselves what I did to me.

And saw your own hatred—?

In other people. And it was really sad. And you can only go on so long saying, "Well, I can do it to myself but I don't want you to do it," until that doesn't really make sense, that isn't logical. So that was a really helpful experience. And that's what I remember even more than what I said about my own body.

Beth appreciated that her therapist, Dr. Locke, asked her to give words to her tears, the concrete expression of her pain. She contrasts her therapy with Dr. Locke with "my worst experience definitely in therapy," with a therapist who seemed to want her to justify her tears:

Like instead of empathizing with me, she'd say, "Well, why do you think that?" Or just stuff like that . . . I felt like I was a subject, not a patient, not somebody who needed help . . . And I just didn't feel cared about or understood or like she had any understanding of what I was going through. I felt like I had to explain everything about myself. And then with Dr. Locke, it was so different. With Dr. Locke, I just felt like, when I would cry, she would say, "What are the tears about?" And I remember that, her saying that to me when she interviewed me for the group. I remember her just saying, "What are the tears about?" And it was like I needed someone to say that to me. Not to say, "Why are you crying?"

Sarah, who used to sit in therapy sessions feeling numb, once wrote her therapist a letter describing what it had been like for her growing up, terrified of her brother, who beat her nearly every day. When her therapist's eyes filled with tears as she read the letter, Sarah knew "it was worth crying over." The concrete fact of her therapist's tears helped her know that her experience mattered.

The women say that when the symptoms and consequences of bulimia nervosa were spelled out in concrete terms, the seriousness of the disorder felt more real to them. Beth, who is now a case manager at a counseling center, recommends that therapists ask specific, concrete questions to help a bulimic client sense the extent of her dysregulation:

> If you see a person who's bulimic, you need to clue into other addictive behaviors. Are they drinking? Are they using drugs? Are they promiscuous? If a person's bulimic, I would say that's a clue right away to other impulse kind of things, self-destructive things. Are they cutting themselves? Do they think about suicide? Are they on antidepressants, and if they are, are they the kind that they could overdose on? Do they think about wanting to die? A lot of physical stuff to be aware of . . . I've met people who have ruptured their esophagus, stuff like that, electrolyte stuff, their cheeks are swollen— pointing that out to people. And definitely looking for addictive kind of stuff. How many packs of gum are you chewing in between meals if you're not eating? How many Diet Cokes are you drinking? How much caffeine do you drink? How much do you sleep?

As noted in Chapter 1, Beth believes a bulimic woman needs to hear in concrete terms what is and is not normal because she is apt to know little about her body's needs and limits: "Like that it's not normal to sleep four hours a night . . . Or that it can be abusive to drink that much caffeine. You can feel really awful. And you can not sleep well, too. And that contributes, for me it contributed, to the bingeing and the being out of control." Beth also urges therapists to teach bulimic women concrete life-management skills:

> It was the first counseling experience I had ever had, and I liked it. She taught me really concrete things about time management and stuff, stuff I'd never even heard. It seems so concrete, but she made suggestions, like "Why don't you not try to lose weight while you take exams?" stuff like that. "Why don't you write down your schedule for the day?" And that's basically what we did . . . We were talking about this at work, I was talking with a social worker about how, to us, basic stress management is such like the ABC's so that we don't even think that we should teach it to people. We feel kind of stupid. But when that counselor at college gave me like "Write down your day, structure your day," that was great, that was something I never thought of doing.

Several women report that when therapists and others used concrete, direct terms such as "vomiting" and "fingers down your throat" in talking about bulimic symptoms, the plain talk reduced their sense of shame. When someone spoke directly about throwing up or stealing, the women trusted that the person could tolerate the truth of what they were doing. For Gita, it was a relief that her husband was so matter-of-fact about her symptoms:

> It took a long time before I ever just said the word "throw up" to anyone. I'd say things that alluded to it, and I would talk about "I just did it," but to be able to openly talk about it and describe the details of it, to have it not be a secret anymore was important.

> *Do you think that the other person can do things to make that basic talk easier?*

> By using the words. Paul does that, Paul's always done that. Very graphically, bluntly, and it kind of becomes funny. That it could be funny to talk about it was great. Then it wasn't this huge, horrible thing I'd been doing that I should be so ashamed of. So definitely it's okay—not okay, but it's not evil. So definitely that they use the words and be very open and direct . . . And that's always made it much easier for me to talk to him about it, too. He can talk about anything, and it's not gross. He sort of teases about it, which even makes it easier, and has a humor to it, which makes it less difficult for me to talk about.

Meg describes how she came to experience her self in concrete, bodily ways—through achievements, physical talent, and bodily impairments:

> My way of getting attention within the family was to succeed at things. It wasn't anything my parents necessarily set up except that I didn't feel recognized personally. Since I started being good at things at such a young age, I felt recognized only through my achievements. Whereas my brother, he was always sick, and so he got the attention that way . . . When he was little, he had a hernia . . . And then he had braces on his legs for a little while. And then he has a learning disability, and this learning disability and trouble at school caused insomnia in the fourth grade, depression, and so he was seeing a therapist then. And he got glasses, and he got braces, and he fell out of a tree and shattered his arm and was in the hospital for a month. Then he has the same back thing that I do, but he had it worse, so he was in a full body brace thing for a while. Just everything, he had a lot of things. And I never had anything. I didn't even have glasses, I just, nothing ever went wrong with me.

213

You were without—?

Yeah, attention.

In eighth grade, Meg experienced a devastating break in her friendships. As she remembers it, friends who were envious of her achievements tried to make her feel bad about her talents and triumphs. In the wake of this abandonment, Meg relied upon physical aspects of herself—her appearance, sexuality, and athletic achievements—to feel good about herself. When she was 15 she began having sex with a 16-year-old boy: "My body was accepted. Somebody wanted to have sex with me, and I still was a good athlete. My body was accepted in both those ways. So I guess that just became the vehicle for my expression of wanting to be right and be accepted through my body because those were the two things that during the time of crises were still, the body was still okay, it was still being accepted as attractive, and it was still functional, even if the inside was not."

She came to rely upon sex to feel affirmed by men:

> I began to feel that in order to know that somebody liked me . . . I needed to have sex with them. And so sex became this really important thing in a relationship. Like if my boyfriend didn't wanna have sex with me, I felt completely rejected, like so rejected that I couldn't sleep. Or, like with my boyfriend who helped me with the eating disorder, if he didn't wanna have sex with me, I couldn't even stay in the bed. I had to go into another room. 'Cause I felt this intense rejection . . . Just that the whole idea that, with the eating disorder, your body becomes your self. I had no self, and what I had was my eating disorder and my body, which I could focus on. And that's what outside people saw, and if they appreciated it, then I was accepted fully as a whole person 'cause that's what I believed I was, was really just this body.

IDENTIFICATION

Identification involves sensing oneself—seeing and hearing oneself—in another's experience. Identifying with people who had recovered helped the women believe that they, too, would recover.

When Isabella met women who had been severely bulimic and yet were recovering, she believed that she herself could recover: "I saw other girls, in the hospital and in my support group, who were further along in their recovery, and I saw that it was possible. Carol, my therapist, also had me speak to someone who was basically fully recovered. And I knew it was something that I could achieve . . . I saw that the women that I talked to were intelligent, successful people, and they just felt good about themselves. And they had been where I was at that point."

Besides helping women believe they could recover, identification helped reduce their sense of shame and isolation, as Rebecca describes: "It was just really nice to be in the company of other people that had the same problem or a very similar one. Just the idea of identifying with other people that, the things like stealing and bingeing all day, just knowing that other people were doing this . . . You have these bars around you, and you're weird, and you're strange, and you've got this problem that nobody else has. Part of the cathartic experience is that you're not alone and that other people can really identify with you."

When Sarah read Geneen Roth's books on compulsive eating, she identified with the workshop participants' narratives: "In the beginning I would read them on the sly, or read them thinking, 'This isn't necessarily about me. I'm just gonna read it because it might be.' And just crying through them because there was like, 'Oh, my God, this is it. I can't believe it.'" Identifying with Roth and the people she wrote about enabled Sarah to try Roth's approach of giving herself permission to eat what she wanted and as much as she wanted whenever she wanted it as a means of learning to read and trust her own gauges of enoughness: "I felt like this was so much me that of course this would work for me because of everything I read about her and about these people she's talking about. 'This is me, and so now I just need to do what they did.'"

Sarah worked on an eating-disorders unit of a hospital while she was in therapy and found it helpful to watch the patients feel. She felt as if she "didn't know how to feel" and was struck by the courage and strength that feeling required. Her identification with the inpatients' experience was accompanied by envy, however:

215

Working in the hospital then, I think one thing it did to me was reinforce for me that other people deserved more help than I did. And I would find myself getting jealous that they were getting all this attention all day long and that whenever they needed it they could start to cry and someone would be there. Or they could go get someone. Or in the middle of the night, or the times that were hardest for me which were going to bed at night. And they had all these people there . . . I wanted to be sick enough so that I would get whatever it was I wanted, but not so sick that I was out of control like these people were.

Leslie benefited from her nutritionist's disclosure that she too had been bulimic: "It helped with the shame a little bit. Here was this really successful, happy person, who had a family and had a real life, and she had made it through this. So it was something for me to look at. I didn't know anybody who'd ever recovered. All I knew were all the people at college who still had it. And I had never seen anybody successfully come out of it."

It was through identification that several women experienced horror or outrage at how they were treating themselves and sorrow and compassion on their own behalf. Claire, who was a nursing student when she was most severely bulimic, remembers an identification that scared her: "I kind of saw the elderly people having bowel problems, and I thought, 'My God, that's going to be me before I'm 30.'"

As discussed in Chapter 4, Claire's identification with Frankenstein's monster and with Frankenstein's fear of the monster helped her accept herself. After her gynecological surgery, Claire also identified with the painter Frida Kahlo as she tried to sustain compassion for herself as someone who had been hurt:

I might not be a mom, was what I was told by the doctors. And I didn't have a role model, I knew nobody else who was like this. I was a freak. I was dirty, I was soiled, I was unnatural. And I discovered the artist Frida Kahlo . . . She was married to a guy called Diego Rivera . . . one of the famous Mexican muralists. He was older than her and not monogamous. And she was very beautiful when she was young. And she was an artist. And when she was a young girl, she had been in a tram accident. And a rod had pierced her vagina and come out the side and broken the spine. And a lot of her art is about sexuality and pain—it's quite gory, it's quite bloody. It's very, very powerful . . . While I was convalescing, I went to the exhibition, and found her art . . . I was really completely taken with it. Here was somebody who knew what I was feeling. Here was somebody who was drawing what I was feeling.

I ask her about her favorite paintings:

My favorite, favorite, favorite is of her in a bridal gown. They were all self-portraits that she did. And it's pink and white—she was very into traditional Mexican dress. So very feminine, very attractive, but quite violent. And she has this wedding dress on. She's looking very beautiful. But she has tears coming down here. And there's a portrait of Diego Rivera in the middle of her head here. And I've always liked it, I've always liked it.

Can you say what moves you?

It was summing up when I was growing up in the relationship with Tom. That this man was the center of her life, and yet he gave her a lot of pain. That children and being a woman is the center of her life, but at the same time it's giving her a lot of pain. The two are intertwined. Visually, it's violent pain, and you can tell from the expressions it's very emotionally intense. So it's this balance between the want and the pain.

That Claire, who did not have any psychotherapy, used identification to sense self-experience speaks to the power of identification in the process of recovering.

Identification with children also helped the women. Leslie recalls seeing herself in her niece:

My brother had gotten divorced, and he had custody of his daughter. And his life was less than pleasant. And I was looking at his little girl, who was at the time 6 years old. And she was so perfect. She had to be an adult, basically, at 6 years old, taking care of him. And it was painful for her to make mistakes in school. And I was seeing myself. And I said something to the effect of "I look at her, and I see me." And no one caught that except for the social worker [in a family therapy session]. And she stopped everybody and said, "Wait a minute. Explain that. What are you seeing in her, what are you afraid is going to happen to her, and how do you think she's like you?" 'Cause I know my parents would have just gone, "Phh, that's not such a bad thing to be. You're a straight-A student, you got through college" . . . but I saw myself, it was like a reflection, and it really scared me.

Identifying with her niece helped Leslie understand how emotional neglect had left her at risk for an eating disorder:

I never remember being unhappy. I'd look back and I'd think, "How did this happen to me?" . . . I was just looking at my life and my childhood and thinking, "I had it good. I have two parents who love me and love each other" . . . And then I looked back and I thought, "That was me." I was so painfully afraid of making mistakes, and my parents thought this was great, but I would spend an entire evening opting to do homework instead of watching television or playing with my friends because I didn't want to make mistakes. I wanted straight A's. They never pushed me to get straight A's. This was something they could never understand. "Why do you drive yourself so hard? We're not making you do this." It took me a long time to recognize that I just wanted them to say, "Hey, that's great. You got all A's. That's terrific." They never did that . . . My brother would come home flunking out of school, and they'd say, "We know you tried your best." And I'd come home with straight A's, and they'd acknowledge that they got my report card. And that was another thing that the family worker did was made them realize that what they perceived they gave me in terms of a lot of credit and admiration, I didn't pick up on it. I never saw it. You know where it went was they told everybody else how proud they were of me, but they never told me! And my mom said that in one of our sessions one day, "I tell everybody how proud I am of you," and I'm, "How come you never tell me?"

DISIDENTIFICATION

The women appreciated others' genuine curiosity about their eating disorder. This regard helped them to disidentify from their eating disorder, to *have* it (and have perspective on it) rather than to *be* it (Kegan, 1982). Curiosity is opposed to what Edward Shapiro (1982) has called "pathological certainty," the conviction that I already know what I am about to hear or see. When someone conveyed an openness to learning about the women's experience, their sense of shame was diminished, and they felt encouraged to be curious about the eating disorder and about their self-experience more generally.

Leslie was pleased that her roommate read up on eating disorders:

> She was great in that she really educated herself the way I had, and she read everything that I had.

And that didn't feel intrusive or—?

> It really didn't. It didn't because we talked about it as if it were somebody else. Like, "Did you know this?" Like it wasn't me. And she was really interested. And I was very interested in the subject whether it had to do with me or not. It just was fascinating that this was happening, that it was something that was real.

Their talking about eating disorders without acknowledging that Leslie had one may seem odd, but doing so may have allowed Leslie to disidentify from her bulimic self, to know that it was part of, not all of, herself.

Similarly, Leslie, when asked what advice she would give parents, says she wishes her own parents had expressed more curiosity about her experience:

> I guess for my parents it would have been one, to not be judgmental because they were incredibly judgmental. And two, to ask a lot of questions if the person's willing to talk. I was at the point where once I'd told them, I thought, "Well now they know, so I can talk about it." And they didn't ask questions . . . They didn't ask, "What do you need?" or "What can we do for you?" "How are we involved in this?" So I guess my recommendation would be just to ask questions once the person comes to you or if you find out. 'Cause I felt like they were uninterested.

Leslie's family therapist did express curiosity and tried to cultivate that attitude in family members: "One thing she did that I will never forget is my family had, like I said, they had a tendency to push pain away. Things that aren't pleasant they don't want to look at it. They also have a tendency to not hear you if you're speaking about your own pain. They minimize it, or they just don't hear it. And she wouldn't let that happen. She'd say, 'Whoa, stop. Did you hear what she just said?' And then she'd make them react. 'What do you think?'"

Gita, who teaches problem-solving strategies to her elementary school students, learned to approach problems in her own life with disidentification and curiosity. She recognized that by stepping back she could discern ways to respond to distress other than by bingeing and purging:

> I think that's what I really have learned is not the specific details of whatever's going wrong for me today or whatever food problem I'm having, it's how I handle it, and stepping back to look at how I'm handling it, not the feeling good or bad or guilty about the details. So, it's removal, again . . . I guess it's a basic thing about learning that I believe in, that I've discovered . . . I ought to give examples. Well, mainly the self-talk kind of things that if there's a mistake, let's say I did overeat and I felt bad about it, and I wanted to throw up. Well, "What are some other solutions? Write, do the brainstorming." I do this with kids all the time. "Let's brainstorm some ideas. Okay, let's look at all the ideas, and what's the best compromise with all the different perspectives involved?" . . . And looking at it as a problem that's away from you, it doesn't make you good or bad.

Her practice of "removal" allowed her to disidentify from her bulimic urges and behaviors and freed her to be creative about how to respond to her needs and feelings.

Filling out a health questionnaire as part of a medical exam may have helped Gita disidentify from her bulimic symptoms and may thereby have countered the shame she felt about needing help:

> I think that that was always so hard for me, to be able to talk about those things, about myself. Or to seek help . . . It's taken a long time, and I sort of fell into asking for help. I think she was ready to give, and then the questionnaire put me in a position to ask it 'cause I didn't know how to ask in a way that I didn't feel like I was imperfect or that this was a huge flaw. I always thought that asking for help meant that you were inadequate, weak, and low. That was my big problem. I didn't wanna be that, so why ask for help 'cause that means you are that way.

RESPECT FOR ONE'S SENSE OF TIMING

Respect for someone's sense of timing, as my colleague Suzanne Repetto Renna has pointed out, implies an ultimate trust in her being and a belief in her basic right to live her own life, make her own choices, and learn from her own experience. But it is difficult to trust the sense of timing of someone who lacks or disregards an internal gauge of enoughness. Nevertheless, the women indicate that within the bounds of safety it is important to respect which changes a bulimic woman is and is not ready to make at a given time.

When I ask Beth if there are things people could do to help bulimic women take their pain seriously, she associates to meeting with a counselor at her college:

> I look at the therapist I had in college, Dr. Locke, and I don't think I would've lived through college if it wasn't for her. And I don't think she could've done anything to make me get well or anything, aside from what she did, which is say, "You need more help." She took it seriously enough that it forced me to do the same thing. I thank God for her because I knew that every week there was some place I could go and just cry and be heard and be understood. And there was one person, she was the one person who I could trust. I didn't trust anybody else.
>
> If it hadn't been for her, I wouldn't have made it through college. Just that she sat with me. And I don't think I was really, I didn't understand things. I didn't understand why I did it. I just didn't understand much about it, or about the level of self-hate I had, or the background that I had come from, and how it contributed. As a therapist, I think about it sometimes, and there wasn't any great interpretation that I even remember. In fact, I don't even remember specifically any session, I can't really even remember. I think I was in so much pain, I can't really even remember words, but I do remember feeling there was somebody who understood and who supported me.
>
> It might've been helpful if she had suggested that there are places like OA to go. I don't know if it would've helped or not. Who knows if I would've been ready? But I really think just the fact that she was there and cared about me. And listened to me. I had trust that I didn't have with anyone else, that I didn't have with my parents . . . Just having someone that I trusted, who listened to me, and who didn't judge me. And who didn't condemn me, or even force me to change. 'Cause I really, I don't know if I could have.

Dr. Locke eventually told Beth she needed more care than the college counseling center could provide, and she recommended to the dean that Beth take a medical leave of absence. She respected Beth's timing, but only within the limits of Beth's safety.

Asked what advice she would give women who are bulimic, Gita talks about the importance of attunement and timing:

> It depends on the stage where they're at . . . It depends on the person. If they're really struggling with the throwing up part or struggling with the eating part or something else. You have to give them strategies at the stage that they're ready for. If someone had told me to eat healthy food in college, I would not have been able to listen at that point. But maybe giving me strategies of talking to myself at that point. That "It's okay to make mistakes," "It's okay to fail," "It's okay—." More self-esteem things at that stage. And then start dealing with the symptoms. But I think kindly presented. I guess at the beginning I was very competitive and afraid and thought that people wanted me fat, so that there's sort of a paranoiac stage that you have to be careful of because I think that bulimics can be scared away from health at that point. But after they've asked for help, I think caring and loving and looking at self-esteem and concrete strategies.

She stresses the importance of remaining responsive to timing: "And then backing off a bit. The kind of therapy like the group therapy that I had to go every week was not necessarily the best. Maybe being there, but more flexibility."

Like Gita, Abigail says it is important to offer someone with an eating disorder options so she can choose the forms of care that are attuned to her needs:

> Certainly you find books at the time of life where you can use them . . . I would love to be able to give someone something and say "Read this and this'll be the light." But I think that when people are ready to—and I don't mean that they should suffer until they're ready—but that things should be dangled. To dangle the different things in front of people and see what they pick up then. They may pick up a yoga class, where they can go and just feel okay about their body for what it is for an hour a week . . . Or maybe it might be for someone else a different thing.

Leslie, too, talks about the importance of trusting someone's own timing:

> Give 'em space . . . Friends need to look out for the warning signs and try to push them into getting help but at the same time not crowd 'em, not

smother. Because my friend did smother me. I think one of the greatest things that my therapist said to me is, "I'm not going to make you stop doing this. You need to be doing this. So you're going to keep doing this until you don't need to do it anymore." If she had tried to make me stop, I would've just dropped out. Well, 'cause I knew I couldn't. And my friend was trying to make me stop.

Meg, too, stresses the importance of communicating availability and caring without trying to take control:

What people focus on mostly is "How can friends help? How can I help someone?" And my general response is that it's really difficult if they don't wanna be helped . . . I really don't think there is any way that you can help someone, I mean really help someone, like change them, 'cause it's not possible . . .

But I just tell them to continue to do what they're doing, which is get more knowledge for themselves about it and don't confront the person with any anger, just gently tell them that you think they have a problem, and that you're there for them, to talk to them whenever they need someone. Maybe give them a list of therapists or a bibliography, a list of books or something that they could read if they wanted more information. And then that way you could feel like you've done something and you've given something that maybe they'll look to at a certain time.

And then back off for a little while and see what happens. Don't dwell on it, and don't drill them about it, because that's gonna make them probably go further underground with it and begin to hide it from you. If they confided in you and they start feeling like you're pressuring about it, they're probably gonna hide from you, and that's the last thing you want. You want to be a confidante.

Once the women sought help, they needed to focus on present experience before they could explore the psychological origins and dynamics of their bulimia. Caregivers who did not understand this priority were experienced as frustrating and were typically fired. For instance, when Leslie first sought help, she wanted to focus on getting control of her eating, not on making connections between her eating disorder and her family: "I went to the health center at school—and, it's funny, now that I have some clinical training, I see what happened. Immediately the therapist started asking questions about my mom and my dad and my family,

223

and I said, 'I don't wanna talk about them, I'm the problem, I've got a problem here.' Went to her once and said, 'I'm not going back to her.'"

She asked the health center for another referral: "And they referred me to a nutritionist. Off campus. Who was wonderful. She had been bulimic. And really worked with me around trying to just at least get the eating under control. To structure—I had lost all concept of what normal eating was, even in that few-month period. I didn't stop the bingeing and purging but at least I felt I connected with somebody. And she gave me the name of a therapist."

Once she felt met on her own terms, she felt prepared to begin psychotherapy:

> I thought the woman in the health center didn't know very much about counseling. "Is she nuts? It's not my parents' problem. It's my problem." So I decided that I would go find somebody who did know something about eating disorders. See, I also thought that I knew how to treat it, I guess. So I think it was a nice transition for me to go to the nutritionist. She did not try to do psychotherapy on me. She just tried to help me get my life in perspective. And when things stabilized just a little bit, she gave me another person's name.

Gita stopped attending a therapy group that was frustrating, even harmful, for her: "We talked mainly about our pasts, and I felt so bad blaming my parents 'cause I felt that that's what the doctor sort of encouraged me to do: 'Oh, look, you've been treated this way, that's why you're that way.' And all the girls in the group were the same way: 'My mother did this to me,' so I really, blech. In fact, I'd go home afterward and throw up." The therapeutic approach that was a better match for her at the time was present-focused, cognitive-behavioral therapy in which she learned to trace her thoughts, feelings, sensations, and behaviors, identify patterns among them, and generate alternative, constructive responses to her experience.

When Isabella remained symptomatic after seeing a therapist for three years, she decided she needed concrete strategies to counter her negative thoughts and beliefs: "We didn't work on my thinking now, we just dwelled in the past. And I had gone over that so many times. I was ready to move on to today 'cause there's only so much you can do about the past, and now you have to move on, dealing with today."

Sarah recalls being "horrified" by her therapist's questions about her family: "And she's the first person who suggested to me that there were reasons why I wanted to be fat. And I just looked at her, I was horrified. Just absolutely horrified. She's the first person who would ask me questions about my parents, and I would say, 'What does this have to do with them?'" But unlike Leslie, Gita, and Isabella, Sarah did not fire her therapist. The therapist was willing to shift gears to talk about Sarah's present concerns, which included her uncertainty about which college major to choose. The therapist's questions about her family, while not attuned to Sarah's immediate experience, did pique Sarah's curiosity, and the two later returned to the work of linking Sarah's past and present experience.

Over time, and in most cases through therapy, most of the women attained a deeper and more integrated understanding of their eating disorders. The two who seem to have little psychological understanding, Amy and Claire, are the two who have had little or no psychotherapy and have the most fragile or incomplete recoveries. Amy was in a psychotherapeutic bind. She liked the quick, concrete change of stopping her laxative use but was too impatient to stick with the slower work of psychotherapy. She can recall her therapist's formulations, but they are received, repeated knowledge, not experienced, integrated knowledge: "Sally basically just focused on my whole background growing up, what my childhood was like. And she basically came to the conclusion that my father had a lot to do with the image that I had. She thinks that this taking the laxatives and bingeing was kind of my way of rebelling against my upbringing or something like that. We never really came to a good conclusion on that."

Amy's concerns about herself are still body-focused: her weight, the shape of her breasts, and a newly diagnosed crossbite. Her body and psyche are linked, however, when she talks about needing to set limits in order to take care of her body and mind:

Even the past three weeks, when I called you and said I really can't come up, it's because I had been putting on weight, I had been feeling miserable, I hadn't exercised in two weeks 'cause of my work and the commute. I just felt like I was losing control. I envisioned myself as being a big balloon, and I cried last week to my husband, "I'm getting so fat, I'm afraid I'm gonna explode." And I hadn't felt that way in a long time . . . I'm like, "I'm just gonna lose my mind, I have to go to the gym, I really have to start getting my peace of mind back together" . . .

Is being able to call me and say, "This isn't going to work. We have to do this differently," is that something that's new for you?

That *is* new because before I would just go ahead and just do what I already, I wouldn't back out on something. But now I'm very open, and I'm very assertive . . . And recognizing that I have to take care of myself and that my body is important and that I need to take care of it, I can't keep abusing it.

Amy is engaged by my acknowledgment that she had respected her limits by asking if we could delay our interview and meet in her home instead of my office. She seems proud of her self-respecting act. She might well benefit from exploration of her present self-experience, and in particular from curiosity about how she experiences her sense of a psychic limit in physical terms: "I'm afraid I'm gonna explode."

The importance of attending to present experience before attempting to make psychodynamic sense of the disorder is understandable given that bulimic women avoid sensing self-experience to avoid overwhelming affect. Only when a bulimic woman trusts that someone will keep her company in the face of present pain can she dare to experience the painful feelings that psychodynamic psychotherapy inevitably entails.

Belief in One's Potential

As discussed earlier, the women needed to believe they could recover. They needed to experience a sense of potential—a sense of what the process of recovering would be, what would make it possible, and who they would be once they had recovered.

The women found it helpful when others believed in them. For Jessie, being believed in by a supervisor contributed to her sense that she could make contributions in her job and was a worthwhile person:

> In the beginning, in most businesses, training is virtually nil, they just kinda throw you in and you kinda swim. I wasn't doin' too hot there in the beginning 'cause I was drowning . . . And she saw that when I did learn something, I ran with it, did a great job and was organized and precise and accurate, and she took a real interest in me. And she built me up. And she showed me that I could do a damn good job . . . To have an outsider take an interest in you like that and build you up—and when you have a bad self-image, you kinda take pride in whatever you do because you're trying to find some way to justify that you're not all as bad as you think you are. And here I was doing this good job, and people were writing memos about me, saying that I was doing a good job. It was like, "Wow! This is kinda good."

Like identification with others, the creation of images—which is a form of concretization—helped give physical form to the women's belief that they would recover. Images typically arose in the context of relationships and gave a woman a sense of her own potential. Meg recalls an image that came to her during a meeting at the treatment center in which, by identifying with another group member, she realized that she feared she had no self:

> I was listening to someone who was going through a real crisis about her personality and herself and who she was . . . And this brought up in me the idea that I didn't know who I was. I was able to just be a chameleon and be whatever anyone wanted me to be, or what I was supposed to be. And the way I thought of it then, the image I used then was that I was living inside a car with tinted windows. And on the outside everything looked sleek and fine, but on the inside—no one really knew what was on the inside. That sounds now like a very basic discovery, but it was just the hugest revelation to me that I had no self. Or I didn't know what that self was. And at the time I felt like I had no self. I really did. I felt like, I was just horrified at the thought that I had no idea who I was. I wasn't really anyone. Did I really have any friends? Did I have any relationships? Because I didn't have any basis to have those things. And so that was just the starting point of the recovery really.

She shared that image with the group and received a response that inspired another helpful image:

> All I did really was sort of break down and tell people about this. And there really wasn't much of a response except that you have to understand that what you've been doing, that's where your self is, in all those things, in all those relationships. And it's not that you have no personality and no self. You just have to start to put it together. And find it. In pieces . . .
>
> I have a lot of images from the time, and the image that I had then was that here were all these people who, I picture them as having like little glowing spots. It's not the greatest image, but little, just little suns. And people had these, and they were me. But there wasn't anything in the center. But when you would put them together they would make one big whole sun. And so I had to go around and start collecting them, and putting them together.

The image of gathering her Meg-ness to form a whole self helped quell her fear of having no self and allowed her to sense self in all that she was already doing and enjoying.

Meg says that images helped her know her own experience and communicate it to others: "I'm not that big on images, like I don't think in images now. But then, I think in order to convey my ideas to a whole group, it was easier to use images than to try and use words. And so I started doing that there. And I don't do it now. And I don't really know where they came from. But they seem to have fit so perfectly at the time. Now the whole car thing seems a bit cliché, but at the time it seemed like exactly what I was thinking, what I was feeling."

Meg is surprised to realize during the interview that the image of the sun is an enduring one for her: "It's really funny because I remember that image now, and I've thought about it, but in the past. But last summer, I got a tattoo, and I got a sun—and I had never made the connection before." She seems amused to discover this continuity in her experience.

Abigail, comparing herself with her psychiatric patients, used both an imagined image and photographic images to help her reconnect with her authentic self:

> All of a sudden they come in because their feelings are overwhelming to them. And they want medicine. And all of a sudden you become acquainted

with this whole part of yourself that you've been treating with these toxic substances. Like lots of food, drugs, and alcohol. So it's becoming reacquainted with yourself . . .

I have a sense of myself as a very young child as having a lot of spirit. I had this little private life. And that is voice. I did this bodywork a couple of weeks ago at the yoga center where I had this image of a tulip bulb . . . that was wrapped up, kind of gnarled up in its roots or something so it couldn't grow. So the roots couldn't plant, and the plant couldn't grow. The part of it was there, I just needed to release it and let things come . . . I went to my parents' house a few weeks ago, and I was looking at some pictures of when I was younger, and there was joy, and there was something there. There was a spirit that I could feel that was there as a kid . . . So I think that as a child I still had this life and this spirit that I could recultivate and draw on.

When I ask Leslie what advice she would give women still struggling with bulimia, she talks about finding a mental image of one's potential:

Try and find that hope, try and have some sort of—no matter how cloudy—some mental image of what you want your life to be like. For me, all I wanted was to not loathe myself all the time, that's all I wanted. And I never really thought that I'd get there. I thought that it would get easier, that it wouldn't be so bad. But I got there. I really did get, I don't hate myself anymore. I give myself a break. I laugh at myself now . . .

I put this picture out here of what I—I didn't set my standards quite so high as my social worker did. She was saying, "This is what you can have. But we've got to go through the swamp to get there." My image wasn't quite so bright as hers. I just wanted it to be better. But I think even having any kind of image helps.

EDUCATION ABOUT CHANGE

The women appreciated being informed about what to expect during treatment and recovery. I can identify three ways in which education about the process of change helped the women sense their experience.

First, hearing her therapist describe the nature of recovering and what she could expect from the therapist and from herself fostered a woman's belief in therapy, in the therapist, and in her own capacity to recover. Belief in turn fostered her engagement in therapy by enabling her to understand the rationale for her therapist's interventions. For instance, Sarah found it helpful when her therapist explained how Sarah's purging interfered with their work:

> What she would start to say to me is, "When you come in and you tell me that you purged, we have to stop focusing on what you need to focus on. Because I need to deal with that behavior. Because you're hurting yourself, and I need to stop. And you're totally taking us away from what we need to be doing. And so you're just delaying what you say you wanna get to, which is talking about your family and having some feelings and working through some stuff." And that made a lot of sense. She had to say it a lot of times in a lot of different ways.

Her therapist taught her that symptoms can function as defensive structures: bingeing and purging divert attention from painful feelings and painful realities. Sarah describes how she internalized the connection her therapist impressed upon her:

> I think I knew after Annie confronted me that I wasn't gonna throw up anymore even though it had kept occurring to me. And sometimes I'd think about it even more than just a passing thought. I thought, "I can't do that because if I throw up, then," and then I would think about all the consequences. "It would be a step backwards because all I do is complain about not being able to feel. And I hate sitting in therapy not being able to feel. And what am I doing? I'm just numbing myself out. It's not a tool that's ever worked before to help me feel, it's just making me step backwards. And maybe the longer I hold off and don't throw up, the closer I'll get to being able to cry in therapy."

Knowing the rationale for the constraining policies in the inpatient eating-disorders program enabled Isabella to trust that they had a purpose: "We had very limited free time. And they explained it all to us, and what they were doing. I didn't like it. None of us liked it. 'Cause they were in a sense very controlling, and you felt like a child. They controlled what you ate, when you ate it, they watched you eat it. You couldn't exercise, you couldn't walk quickly down the hall. You couldn't go to your room by yourself. You couldn't go to the bathroom by yourself . . . But they would always explain to us, 'This is why we're doing it.'"

Second, being told what to expect in recovering helped the women recognize and sense their experience as it unfolded, much as anticipating particular landmarks helps one sense where one is on a road trip. For instance, Meg found it helpful to realize that there were progressive steps she could take, a path she could follow, to develop alternatives to bingeing and purging:

> They just gave me the tools. The bathrooms are open, there's food available all the time, and they don't ask you not to binge or purge. But what they teach you to do is to—. . . at first you binge and purge, and then, it's almost like an honor code, you have to come to the group and tell the group that you did that, and then talk about it. And then the next step in that progression is that maybe you binge, and then you go find someone, or you tell the group. You talk about it and try to prevent the purge by replacing it with talking to someone. And then eventually when you get the urge to binge, you go to someone before you do any of it.

Amy found it helpful that her nutritionist made predictions about her weight and her feelings:

> She's like, "Every day I want you to log in this book every single thing that you eat. Eat how you normally eat. And we're going to monitor, you're going to do this for two weeks, eat like you normally eat, and you will see that your weight is gonna stay the same" . . . And she says, "You're going to go through ups and downs, and you're going to be tempted to take the laxatives, but open up the book and start writing to get yourself away from it. Just remember how bad they are for you, what they do to you" . . . "You might hit a big crash, and you might even overdose on a whole box of laxatives again . . . but it's gonna take time to get over that, and it's supposed to happen that way, you are supposed to go through real lows where you think that you're getting nowhere."

> *So then when you hit those, you could remember what she was saying?*

> Right, I remembered what she was saying, that "Okay, now I'm hitting a real low." But I never took them again.

Third, as Amy indicates, having a sense of what would be difficult helped the women tolerate the discomfort inherent in change. When they knew what to expect, they could anticipate the discomfort, recognize it, and remind themselves that it would ease. For example, when Amy binged and felt the urge to purge, she listened to the internalized voice of her therapist:

> She said I'm going to go through a lot of lows and a lot of highs. And she was right. Because the day after, I stuffed my face till I was blue in the face. I got in the car, and I was driving toward the drug store to get myself some laxatives. I'm driving there. And then I get to a red light, and I'm sitting there, I'm like, "I've just gotta get these laxatives. I don't want to gain weight." And then I start thinking about this woman—'cause she was a very nice woman—and I start thinking about this woman, and I'm starting to listen to what she's saying, I'm hearing it in my ears, and I'm like, "No, forget it, I'm not gonna do it." So I didn't do it. So from that day I never took laxatives again.

Gita, who identifies cutting out caffeine as an essential step in her recovering, found it helpful that her husband and father-in-law warned her about withdrawal symptoms: "It took both Paul and his dad saying 'Stick with it, you're gonna have withdrawals where you're gonna have headaches and you're gonna feel tired, but you'll be tired for a week, and, and then, if you can survive that week, then you're okay.'"

COACHED PRACTICE

The women appreciated active coaching and guidance in specific activities and strategies, including creating and saying affirmations, writing in journals, keeping food-mood journals and using them to identify what led to particular behaviors, and anticipating difficult situations and rehearsing how to handle them.

When I ask Kate what advice she would give therapists, she replies:

> Patience [*laughs*]. Patience is a big one. You can't be tentative with somebody with this problem. You can't be afraid of confronting whatever issue

you think is pertinent at the moment. Linda would always couch it by saying, "I know this is gonna be difficult for you to hear," or "I know this isn't easy for you to talk about, but we're not gonna be able to move forward until we do this, until we resolve this." "You can't get from point A to point B without doing this. You have to travel this road to get where you're going."

Kate alludes to several coaching functions her therapist served: believing in her potential, evoking a belief that she could reach her potential, anticipating discomfort, providing a rationale for doing difficult exercises, being persistent, and offering encouragement.

Jessie, too, valued her therapist's persistence:

Be tough . . . Don't let us off easy. If you ask us a question and we try to avoid it, persist. Because we wouldn't be there if we didn't want to be. In most cases. There are some cases with teenagers where you're forced, but we wouldn't be there if we didn't wanna be. And I think it's just difficult for us to answer some things. And if you let it go, it lets us off the hook. Be persistent. 'Cause you'll get it out of us eventually. 'Cause that's why we're there. And I think if you're persistent, we'll build up a comfort level and then be more ready to let it flow.

Can you say what the "it" is?

The "it" is all the emotions, and the bad, and the hurt and whatever. I'm convinced that most eating disorders are caused by some early life incident. And that you normally suppressed until you're ready to cope with it. And the "it" being that negative thing. Be it somebody pickin' on you when you were a kid that made you feel an inch big. And gave you a bad body image. Or be it sexual abuse by a family member, or physical abuse, or mental abuse, or you don't feel like your parents loved you because they loved your brother better. But somethin' there is bad. And that's the "it."

Gita advises therapists to help bulimics anticipate and rehearse situations in which they would be apt to binge and purge: "I think caring and loving and looking at self-esteem and concrete strategies of, 'You're confronted with a situation, what do you do?' 'You're at a party, your favorite food is being served, and you know where the bathroom is. Are you going to eat it and then go puke, or how are you going to handle that situation?' You know, play-acting or facing real situations that that person deals with."

The women also found it helpful to be coached to observe their self-talk and to talk to themselves in constructive ways. Gita's therapist recommended exercises adapted from *Feeling Good,* by David Burns (1980/1999), which helped her trace her negative thought patterns and steer herself toward self-respectful thoughts:

> She gave me sheets, and you're supposed to write down a sentence, something that someone had said to you that bothered you, or something that you were saying to yourself, and follow it out . . . Just sort of a process of thinking things through in a rational way when you're hit with that and your gut's going "Arahhh!"

> *And how is it helpful to do that?*

> It made me realize that I had sort of set up cycles in my mind that were not helpful to myself. And part of them related to the bulimia, like, "Oh, I ate too much, da da da." Just spirals that would end up with me hurting myself.

> *And once you identified them as this kind of spiral, how did that help?*

> How'd that help? I guess you could stop, you could hear yourself saying them at other times, and you'd say, "Wait a minute. This is what got me down there before. I'm not gonna say that. I'm gonna say something else to myself." Like, let's say I said I was fat. "Well, last time you said you were fat, you ended up throwing up. Why don't you say, 'Okay, maybe I'm fat, but does it really matter?'" Or just going a different track. Not always ending up in the same spot. Hearing that record and moving in a different direction.

Gita found the written exercises and the recommended book helpful in themselves: "She gave me so much to take away that I could work with, too. And that was nice. That would be something I recommend is a strategy to take away—a book to read and papers to fill out. Even if I didn't use them, it was something I could do if it got desperate. And maybe it'd be easier to throw up first and then go do it, but still, at least it would be something to do in addition."

Listening to other people's responses to experiences that were difficult for her to handle enabled Gita to internalize more constructive voices:

> *How did it become possible to answer that question—"But does it really matter that I'm fat?"—in some way other than "Yeah, it does matter"?*

I guess hearing other people say it. The therapist at that point would say to me, "You could say to yourself this." Or Paul would say, "Gita, it doesn't matter if you're five pounds overweight. I gained ten." Just hearing that other people have different ways of answering that question. I think a lot of the times in my life I've been surrounded by people that are very much like me in that attitude. I used to live with women. And in dance classes, we'd all spiral together. And in the group therapy, we would all spiral together.

Taking stock of their progress was another coaching function the women found useful. When a therapist tracked and reviewed the changes they had made, they were able to discern shifts in themselves that they might otherwise have overlooked or discounted. At a point in Leslie's therapy when she was feeling discouraged because she was in so much psychic pain, her therapist reframed her pain as progress and helped her credit herself with that progress: "She made me trace all the stuff that I had sort of put out on the table and talked about. And I started to see that things were getting better. I was being more honest, I was being more assertive. I was doing things that I had never done before. And I really started to believe I was getting better. I couldn't track the progress myself. I was not seeing it."

Sustaining Recovery

Which aspects of bulimia nervosa are most persistent? The women's accounts help us answer that question and understand how women sustain their recovery in the face of the more tenacious features of the disorder.

CONTINUING VULNERABILITY

Although the women's behavioral symptoms had remitted for on average about two years, they remained vulnerable to psychological aspects of the disorder—a sense of inadequacy and shame (not being enough), a sense of deprivation (not getting enough), and dysregulation (not knowing when enough is enough)—as well as to interpersonal difficulties, difficulty in sexual relationships, and dissatisfaction with their bodies. The difficulties, defenses, and deficits that contribute to a person's developing an eating disorder are profound, and so it is no surprise that the women continue to reckon with them even after they no longer have a clinical disorder. Rebecca says: "When I thought of recovery, I thought everything would be over. But I am Rebecca, and Rebecca is— even though the bulimia is gone, I'm still the same person dealing with these other issues that are similar to or have some parallels from before."

A SENSE OF INADEQUACY AND SHAME

Many women continue to have feelings of inadequacy, of not being good enough. Leslie says: "You know how an alcoholic's always an alcoholic? I guess I'll always be bulimic. I never say to someone, 'I was bulimic.' I say, 'I'm a recovering bulimic.' Because it's always there even if you deal with whatever drives you to do it. So I think it pops into people's head every once in a while, this feeling that I'm not good enough." Leslie does not keep a journal because she fears someone might read it and think her concerns were not important: "I tried last summer to start it again. I thought, 'I have no record of my life and where I've come from. It's all up here [*points to her head*], and I oughta put it down and just have it.' I'm not dedicated enough to it to do it. I bought one of those little books that have blank pages, and I just feel stupid that someone's gonna pick it up and go, 'I can't believe she actually thought this was worth writing about.'"

She says: "The hard part was letting myself be human. It's still hard. Not thinking that I have to live up to these incredibly unrealistic expectations that I created for myself." She gives an example of how she is still trying to be superhuman:

> This stupid Ph.D. program. I catch myself in the old trap sometimes. The other day I was thinking, "I can't do this. I can't work 45 hours a week and go to school full time. Nobody's capable of doing this. I'm not learning what I should be learning." And I heard myself saying that, and at first I was a little bit ashamed that I couldn't do it all and immediately went to talk to my adviser and said, "I don't think I can do all this, something's got to give. I don't know exactly what it's gonna be, but something's got to give." And as soon as I said it and I realized that she wasn't looking at me like, "Khh. You can't handle it?" it was okay. It's just for so many years I have assumed that people were gonna look at me and think, "Khh, you're weak, or you're not good enough." And she didn't. She said, "I can't believe, you're the only person I know who's doing this right now."

Nearly every woman expressed concern that she was not qualified to participate in my study: that she was not recovered enough, or had not been sick enough, or both. Abigail says:

I guess I want to make it clear that from the position of recovery, when I was thinking about whether I should do this interview or not, on the one hand, I was wondering if it'd been too long since I'd recovered. And the next second, I'd wonder if I'm really in recovery 'cause it's still very present with me . . . 'Cause I don't know how to get totally in the clear or if that's possible. But I don't want to misrepresent myself, and I think all the things that I've described have been like really little baby steps. And sometimes I step backwards.

Just a few minutes later she wonders whether she qualifies for the study because she was never hospitalized for her eating disorder: "On the questionnaire that you sent there were questions about hospitalization and stuff. And I guess I just had concerns about whether I'm not really sick enough."

Abigail, like Leslie, still has trouble allowing herself to be human: "There are some times where I see myself, there's this grandiose [self] and then there's this really inadequate self, and then to develop this sense of just being human, and somewhere in between, somehow is very hard to do. When I was growing up, making mistakes was very difficult. It wasn't handled well in my family when somebody made a mistake. And now I've learned just to, it's hard, but just to allow myself not to do everything perfectly."

Even though Rebecca now has roles and activities that are meaningful to her, she still relies on productivity and approval to compensate for her sense that she is not enough:

I used to wonder, "What am I gonna do if I'm not bulimic? I'll have all this free time. What will I do?" Because I fit it into my schedule every single day no matter what. And I always said, "There's no way possible I could not be bulimic because what would I do?"

What's the answer? What do you do?

I still keep myself overly busy . . . My sense of identity kind of revolves around my sense of accomplishment . . . I need to feel like I'm doing something and being productive and getting some type of acknowledgment and just feeling fulfilled. And I know I need to still work on that and feeling fulfilled myself, inside.

A SENSE OF DEPRIVATION

Many of the women remain vulnerable to feelings of deprivation, of not getting enough. When I ask Sarah what aspect of bulimia nervosa has been hardest to change, she replies:

> I think being able to live with that feeling that I'm never quite gonna be filled up. Whether it's by food or by another person. Because there's a lot that I can get from my relationship with Annie, my therapist, and in my new relationships with people. But I can never get what I didn't get from my parents when I was little. I can't go back and get that. So I'm able to tolerate that more than I ever could before, which is new. But . . . I think I'm always gonna feel that way, with people, or something's always gonna feel like I didn't get enough.

Sarah, just graduated from a master's program, is in tighter financial straits than she was during graduate school. She now experiences deprivation more around money than around food:

> The thing that has happened with food, at least in the past year, is that it has become very connected to money. And the less money that I've had as the year has gone on, the more food has this whole different meaning to it. Now it's connected to "I can't eat this all now because I can't afford to go grocery shopping for the next week." So it's been really hard because, in order for me to get better, I had to not deprive myself. And so if I wanted ice cream every night of the week, I went and got ice cream every night of the week. And I can't do that now 'cause I don't have the money. And so, to me, it's been a real positive sign that I can just say, "No, I'm not gonna get ice cream tonight" and not feel so deprived that the next day I have to go buy six gallons of it. That I can kinda let it go. I think it's just 'cause I have no choice. I don't have the money, and there are so many other things that are more important to me than food . . . There's my car payments, my school loans, health insurance that I didn't have to pay for before.

Do you experience it as deprivation now?

> I experience it as deprivation in terms of money . . . I guess I experience it in terms of deprivation, but in terms of the food, it's not as bad. I'm able to take it or leave it more than I ever could before. So if I'm down to the wire and I don't have time to go grocery shopping, and all I have is peanut butter, but I

didn't want peanut butter for lunch, tough, I'm just gonna have a peanut butter sandwich for lunch. And that I've been doing okay with that. 'Cause once I eat it and I'm full, I'm perfectly happy, it doesn't matter what I ate. And I never used to be able to have that attitude. I wanted what I wanted. And even if I ate something and was full but I still didn't have what I wanted, I'd have to go get it, even though I was now full. So that's been different.

Jessie feels deprived of a loving father and her childhood innocence:

I grieved for my lost childhood. I feel like it was robbed from me. To this day, I will always be a little melancholy about the fact that I don't have a daddy. I have Howard, my biological father, but he's not a daddy. I have friends who are very, very close to their fathers, and in a way I'm a little jealous. I have the world's most wonderful mother . . . And we have this bond that is so incredible. People say to me, "I wish I got along with my mother like you get along with your mother." But what I always wanna say to them is "But I wish I had a dad."

Jessie regards her sense of deprivation as, in part, a product of a scarcity mentality which can lead her to eat compulsively, without tasting her food:

I have a very close girlfriend who has a 3-year-old daughter, Alison, who's a riot. I'll go over there sometimes at dinnertime and eat over, and she'll say, "Alison, do you want supper?" "No, I'm not hungry." A child doesn't know that it's suppertime and you're supposed to eat, hungry or not. Most adults have it in their mind, "It's lunchtime. Well, I'm not that hungry, but it's lunchtime, better go eat lunch" . . . You don't even think, "Am I hungry or not?" . . . A little kid doesn't think that way. A little kid thinks, "I don't care what time it is, I'm not hungry, I'm not eatin' that now." But an older person would say, "That could be gone tomorrow. I'd better eat that right now." A little kid doesn't think like that. A little kid thinks there's an endless supply of ice cream in the freezer. They don't think it's gonna be gone.

Amy still feels deprived of a body she never had and of the life she imagines she would have had with that longed-for body:

I always wonder what it woulda been like if I'd never gotten fat, what would I look like, what would my life have been like if I hadn't gotten fat? . . . I think I would've been much more athletic, I think I would've definitely gone forward with dancing. And I would've done very well at it, and not become professional with it by any means, but I would've really gotten into it because I really enjoyed it a lot . . . And I think I probably would've had a lot more boyfriends. And I don't think my self-esteem would be so low. I probably would've been, I definitely would've been more confident, maybe accomplished more.

Meg feels deprived of her hope that she could once again be a star athlete as she had been in high school: "That's something that's still with me, is the idea that someday I'm gonna be a professional athlete. I have never given up the hope that, and sometimes I grieve a little bit about it, and then I say 'No, I still have time.' But as I get older, it's something I realize is not realistic . . . I am sort of in the process of giving that up now, too. I have one more try left. I'm gonna try triathlons. I've done them before, and I feel like I just have to try one more thing, one more time."

While for young men, normal growth and development make them bigger and stronger and better equipped for competitive sports, for many young women, the normal growth and development of puberty change their bodies in ways that leave them less well suited for certain types of competitive athletic performance, including gymnastics, ballet, and running. As Meg's body changed and her running times slowed, her sense of identity was challenged:

Unfortunately, that's at the root, I think about it on the surface, about wanting to be an athlete really badly and that being important to my sense of who I am. But I've never thought about the idea that I will really have to grieve when I decide to give that up because it will be a big loss to me to decide that I'm not gonna be an athlete, an athlete is not who I am. And in some sense I hold on to that just through my job, I'm a physical education teacher . . . Because when I was in high school, when I was in ninth grade, I was really good. I was good enough that I was in the paper all the time, and people interviewed me, and I was the best thing they'd seen in a long time, and I was gonna be so great. And it just didn't happen, and so I guess I still hold on to the idea that somewhere I am really great at this and I just have to find it.

DYSREGULATION

The continuing difficulty in sensing when enough is enough takes various forms. Several women avoid stocking certain foods for fear of overeating or bingeing. Meg says: "I would really like to be able to keep food in the house, like cookies or things that I could serve guests, but that I would feel comfortable having them around. That I wouldn't eat all of them, or that I wouldn't eat too many of them. I basically only keep raw materials in my house—rice and pasta and things that I can't eat without doing something to them."

Meg's theory about this vulnerability to dysregulation is that she is easily overwhelmed by external stimuli:

> Somebody mentioned to me that bulimics are overstimulated by sensory stimulation. Like seeing food is actually just so powerful. Or smelling food, or touching it. But I think it's true with me with everything. My senses I feel are very sharp. I can pick up conversations—in a restaurant, I can hear a conversation on the other side of the room. And I notice things, I'm very attentive . . . There's really something to the whole sensory aspect of food and just the world in general that it can be really overwhelming to feel like you're being bombarded with images and sensory perceptions all the time.

Meg's theory fits with the model of recovering as a process of coming to sense one's subjective experience: if outside stimuli are too compelling, it is difficult to consult one's own experience. Conversely, if one has difficulty orienting to internal experience, external stimuli are especially disorienting.

Meg is particularly vulnerable during unstructured time, when she is prone to feelings of nothingness and to being overwhelmed with or preoccupied by painful feelings. She explains why she has anxiety attacks in anticipation of vacations: "That there's no forward motion . . . I'm just so future-oriented, and I think vacation, there's nothing to look forward to except the end of vacation. There's no goals, and so I set goals for myself, that I'm gonna exercise twice a day, or that I'm gonna eat well, things that I can control and focus on. And it's a sense of lack of control, not having any regimen or schedule."

Sarah's vulnerability to a sense of deprivation contributes to her vulnerability to dysregulation. On a vacation, her scarcity mentality contributed to her staying in the sun too long:

> I felt like it was the only vacation I was gonna get. And I love to go to the beach, and I love the sun. And so I overdid it like I always do. I was lying there on the beach just soaking it up thinking, "There will never be a time where I feel like I wanna leave. I will never feel like I've gotten enough." And I hated myself for thinking that . . . I hate that it never seems like there'll be enough. Well, I proved to myself that there was enough, because I was in the sun so long that I got totally sick . . . All of a sudden I opened my eyes and realized I was nauseous, and my leg was huge, it had blown up like a balloon from this bug bite, and so I didn't know what had happened. I think it was a combination, I was dehydrated, I had been in the sun way too long, I was having a minor reaction to the bug bite. I overdid it, and it was like, "You know what's enough now." But it takes that for me to be able to start to think moderation.

When Jessie recently felt herself in danger of losing control, she returned to her therapist:

> My life seemed to be out of control. There were things going on at work that I couldn't control . . . I felt like I couldn't control this house, I felt like everything was out of control. And what I noticed was I was trying to control my eating again. To stop it. I was restricting myself. And I said, "Uh oh. Better call Helen." And what I said to her was "It's like my life is out of control, so I'm controlling the one thing that's familiar that I know for a fact I can control. Which is my eating." And she said, "It's very good to be that aware. And catch this before it manifests itself back into something again."

DIFFICULTY GAUGING ENOUGHNESS IN RELATIONSHIPS

Many of the women continue to have trouble negotiating "enough" questions in their closest relationships: What is too much to expect of someone? What is too much to expect of myself? What do I do when I feel I am not getting enough in a relationship or feel too much is being asked of me? These questions are associated with feelings of deprivation and inadequacy: if one needs or wants more than others can provide, one can feel deprived and exposed as having inadequate internal resources. If one cannot provide all that another is asking, one can also feel inadequate.

Sarah's difficulties in relationship derive in part from her fear of deprivation. As discussed in Chapter 4, a confrontation by a friend led Sarah to realize that she tends to take more than she gives for fear that she will not get enough:

> Now that I know what I do, now I can change it. Before I never really had a handle on what it is that I was doing that was putting me in bad situations with people and making other people get mad or making me feel too needy or too whatever it was.

> *When you say "Now I know what it is," what do you mean, what is the "it"?*

> The "it"? I think what I said about sometimes I really don't feel like there's room for two people in a relationship, that I just feel like I need all the space and that the other person just needs to be the strong one and be the one who's there for me.

Abigail speaks to the other side of Sarah's problem—how to include her own needs in a relationship rather than being exclusively focused on the other: "I think it's a struggle with declaring yourself . . . I guess there's something about feeling comfortable with my hunger, my power, taking what I need and not worrying about the other person. I still do that to a large extent. So I don't know if that's okay to do. Aren't I supposed to be nice? And certainly you can't just go around being selfish . . . That happens in many, many places in my life. That sense of 'What are the other people gonna think of what I do, say, look like?' rather than 'What feels good to me?'"

Meg links her interpersonal difficulties with her perfectionist thinking:

> Like if I don't return a movie when it's due, I'll have a hard time returning it for three months . . . 'Cause I didn't do it correctly the first time so then I can't face up to the fact that I've done it this way. I guess that's a little bit of perfectionism, too . . . But it's also in interpersonal relationships. I want things a certain way, and if they're not that way, then they're not the right way. If I set expectations, and if they're not met, then there can't be any sort of gray area, there's no like, "Well, that's okay. It's not exactly what I wanted,

but—." It's more like "That's not what I wanted. It's wrong." So compromise is difficult.

Deciding that if she does not get exactly what she wants then what she gets is "wrong" protects Meg from the sense of deprivation she would feel if she accepted something that did not perfectly match her preferences. It also protects her from the shame attendant to wondering whether she is worthy of what she wants. In aiming for perfection in her relationships to avoid deprivation and shame, Meg paradoxically sets herself up to feel that she does not get enough and is not good enough. She is bound to be disappointed with others and with herself because perfection is humanly impossible.

Meg's difficulty tolerating feelings of nothingness contributes to her interpersonal troubles. She sometimes provokes an argument with her boyfriend just to counter those feelings: "I guess just the whole idea of not necessarily enjoying the status quo or enjoying vacation. I am generally euphoric, but if things are just going along, it makes me uncomfortable. I can find something to argue about pretty much all the time, or be excited about it. I can't stand just nothing, what I feel is nothingness but is really just, that's reality."

As noted in Chapter 2, although Isabella still tends to seek her worth in others' eyes, she tries to be more self-respecting by focusing on relationships with those who truly care about her:

> I've still made the mistake of trying to get it from men, whether it's the sexual relationship or just trying to get that love from anybody I can. But I'm also working at that. And getting it more from myself and from people who I know really truly care about me for me. Before I wanted to have lots of friends and just have everybody love me . . . Oh, I used to get really upset, everybody had to like me, or I would just go crazy. If I knew there was somebody who really didn't care for me that much, I really tried to work so hard on making that person like me [*laughs*]. I was trying to find my self-worth in other people's acceptance.

Meg has difficulty sensing separateness in an intimate relationship. She also tends to overwhelm people with her neediness:

I guess I'd really like to work on my interpersonal relationships. Just mostly I guess with my boyfriend, or with men in general . . . I have a really hard time being individuals in the relationship. I will generally just go back to the old way of feeling like I have to do whatever this person wants or become whatever. And I completely give myself up when I'm in relationship. Which is really unhealthy. At least now I know I do it. And I can hold back sometimes, but I don't like to be alone. I don't like to have no one, and when I have someone, I generally overwhelm them with my needs for attention and affection. And that's why I'm working on it, but that's something that's really important.

DIFFICULTY IN SEXUAL RELATIONSHIPS

Several women report continuing problems in their sexual relationships. Meg craves constant affirmation from men: "I definitely really enjoy when people are attracted to me and flirt with me or whatever. That gives me a sense of worth that is in some sense unhealthy—I know that it's also real and normal and healthy, but a little bit too much at times— where I've cheated on my boyfriends more than is appropriate— although not that any of it was really appropriate. But just because I feel like so overwhelmed when someone's attracted to me, that my body is good-looking."

Sarah, who experienced chronic physical abuse by her brother and chronic devaluation of women by her father, is frightened by the prospect of a sexual relationship. She has wondered whether she was sexually abused as a child. But she believes that whether or not she was sexually abused, what she knows about her abuse history—that her brother beat her and her father devalued women—was "bad enough" to account for her difficulties:

> And I'm at the point now where I don't think that there was anything particular that I don't remember. That I remember everything that happened, and that's bad enough. And that it's okay that that's all that happened, I can still be as fucked about sex and have only that have happened.
>
> *And when you say "all that happened" what are you—?*

Little things that turn into a big picture when I finally start talking about them. My father and my brother walking around in their underwear. My father commenting about my body. My brother and I fighting and me remembering it in a sexual way even though I don't remember anything explicitly sexual happening. What else? Just the tone that sex had in our house. My father loved to watch movies that had violence in them and sex in them. And would stay up late at night and watch dirty movies on HBO. Things that by themselves, "Yeah, so what," but—

At the time of our third interview, Sarah has recently placed a personal ad and begun dating, with the encouragement of her therapist. She is enjoying meeting men but is wary. She expects that in dating she will learn more about her fear of sexuality:

I still wonder about is there something I'm not remembering, though I'm less hung up on it. And I'm also assuming, like Annie said, through this process of dating that if there's something there, this is when we'll find out . . . I don't think I'm hung up morally about sex, but a lot of my thoughts come from the way the church thinks which is the way my father thinks, which is if a guy flirts with me at work—and this just happened recently— my first reaction is, "Oh, that's nice, and I want to flirt back." But I can also have that extreme reaction of "All he wants to do is get in my pants." I go from him saying something nice to me to assuming he wants to rape me. In a second, there's nothing in between—zoom!

Leslie, who was raped by a boyfriend at age 16, is now in a loving relationship but is still at times uncomfortable having sex:

I'm in a really wonderful relationship now, but I realize, every once in a while I freeze up, and I don't want to be touched . . . I do recognize that I feel sometimes like I don't want to be wanted for my physical appearance, that I'm not comfortable with that. So I think I probably still have some more work to do there . . . From time to time, I still have problems with the fact that what I feel is like when I was 16, this guy, all he cared about was my physical person. That all the things I thought he cared about—like my personality and how much fun we had together and whatever—I had led myself to believe he cared about that, and all of a sudden, I was proven wrong. That wasn't what he cared about, what he really wanted to do was have sex. And so that comes back to haunt me every once in a while. Every once in a while I feel like Ted is pushing all that good stuff aside, and this is all he wants. And I know that's not true. But I can't shake the feeling sometimes.

DISSATISFACTION WITH BODY SHAPE AND WEIGHT

Many of the women remain dissatisfied with their body shape and weight. While that dissatisfaction may be intense at times, most report that it is not the ever-present, disabling preoccupation it once was. According to Peter Cooper and Christopher Fairburn (1993), two aspects of bulimia nervosa—"overvalued ideas about shape and weight" and "dissatisfaction with body shape"—are typically confused with each other. They found that "change in body shape dissatisfaction was closely associated with change in mood; and change in the overvalued ideas was closely associated with change in self-esteem" (385). In fact, as the women recovered, it appears that dissatisfaction with body shape did persist while ideas about shape and weight underwent more enduring change as the women's sense of worth came to reside in more fundamental aspects of themselves.

Amy and Claire, the two women who have had little or no therapy, are most preoccupied with body shape and most prone to excessive exercising. Amy, in particular, is painfully obsessed with the shape of her breasts:

> I say to my husband, Mark, sometimes—he thinks I'm really a nut—"I'd like to know what it'd feel like to have firm boobs." I'd like to know what it would feel like to not have to wear a bra everywhere I go. I'd like to know what it would feel like to go in and try on bikinis and not have to buy the underwire cup bikini with the little bit of padding so that my breasts don't look in bad shape . . . I do realize that it's very materialistic and it's not important whatsoever. I don't know why I continue with it. It's not like Mark is saying to me, "Oh, I wish you had firm breasts," by any means. He's not. It's me. It's all me.

Rebecca regrets that she had to gain weight to recover. But even though she liked the attention she got with a thinner body, she never truly liked her thinner body either. She now accepts her body because she knows that being thinner came at the price of her honesty, her relationships, and her health: "I don't think I'll ever like my body. I didn't like it when I weighed 105, I didn't like it when I weighed 120, I never liked my body. I appreciate it more now in some respects, but I don't know if I ever really will say I like it. Because I don't like it . . . I guess it's coming to an acceptance that that's who you are. It may not be what you consider ideal, but it's just kind of coming to accept that it's who I am."

CONTINUING COMMITMENT

MAINTAINING CHANGES

The women had been recovered for between one and four years, on average two years. Maintaining the changes they had made requires an enduring commitment to sensing self-experience. They continue to make conscious efforts to sense self-experience and to notice cues of disconnection from self. Many had not expected recovery to require such long-term attention. When I ask Abigail how she pictured recovery, she replies: "That today it was here, tomorrow I was completely comfortable with food. Just poof. I didn't realize how much continual effort it would always be . . . I think that I always have to watch that part of my life and that when things are stressful that it's likely that that's some of the ways in which I'm gonna deal with stress, is gonna be about food. And that I have to watch that I'm taking care of myself."

To maintain the changes she has made, Abigail pays close attention to signals that she is losing control and losing touch with herself:

> I care enough about myself now where when it starts to careen, when I feel more out of control when I'm around food or when I'm eating, that I need to do something to put the brakes on and regain whatever, even if it's taking myself to a place where I can recognize again that I'm devaluing myself . . . No matter what's going on, need to take a long weekend, or to read a book that will remind me . . .
>
> *What do you stay alert to, what are your signals that—?*

Eating in the car. If I'm doing it a lot. Or eating a lot of stuff like frozen yogurt to the exclusion of other things . . . Not eating nutritionally valuable meals. I can do that for a day, and that'll be fine. But, if I continue to do it, I think it's that thing about my body wants something else, but I can't interpret it or won't allow it to have what it wants so I keep going for other things.

When she starts to feel out of control, she literally brings herself back to her senses: with the sound of music, the glow of candlelight, the smell of food, and a sense of wonder about the food:

Sometimes I'll go out to eat, lots of times by myself. That's probably one way that I do it. Another way is to make dinners for myself where I sit down, and I have a candle, and I have music on. One thing that I've done recently that helps with this is, at the yoga center, I started doing this conscious eating thing, which I thought was hard to do all the time, but it's really helpful, like mindfulness in living . . . You look at food, and you think, "How does this smell? This is gonna become a part of me, this is gonna become my cells, my hair. Where does the food come from?" That appreciation for how it's grown and just that we have all these different foods. It's incredible to think about how amazing food is rather than to think of it as your enemy . . . That's something you need to practice all the time.

Jill, too, notices her danger signals:

I can feel when I'm slippin' back into the behavior, which is really amazing. Like I'll just go for ice cream, "I've gotta have it, I want it now, I want it," and I don't even think about it, I just start eating it. I usually don't even eat that much, but I know I'm fallin' back into it. I can feel it so usually I can stop myself . . . It's that "Don't get in my way, I want it, I've gotta have it now, my life's terrible, I hate it, blah, blah, blah, so I want this ice cream, and I'm gonna eat it, and I want it now, and I've gotta have it, and the phone can't ring, and no one can talk to me, and if you get in my way, I'm gonna—." It's that, drive isn't the right word, but almost like that. It's like a frenzy or something.

She now uses self-talk to coach herself toward knowing what she is experiencing that is behind the urge to binge:

Usually it's nowhere near the extreme it used to be, it's not even close . . . but I can feel it. If I start gettin' like that I'm like, "God, what am I doin'?" and

I'll say, "All right, well, go ahead. Go ahead, get a bag of Doritos, eat the Doritos." So I'll start eating. And then after a handful, I find it's really not satisfying, it's not solving my problem. Like, "What is the real problem here?" "What am I bummed out about?" or "What am I angry about?" or "What's goin' on?" And I just seem to stop. And I seldom follow through. I really just stop.

It sounds like part of it is that you know to ask yourself those questions?

Yeah. Maybe I've trained myself or something. I think it comes from the awareness though that this just isn't what I want to be doing anymore.

For Jessie, maintaining changes requires continually affirming her sense that she is worthy of care:

I think it's very easy to relapse. It's very easy. You have to really, really want to do this for yourself. You can't wanna do it because your mother wants you to stop. You can't wanna do it 'cause your husband wants you to stop. You have to do it because you want to stop. Because it's such a day-to-day challenge. Because the opportunity is everywhere . . . You can get food everywhere. And there are bathrooms everywhere. So it's constantly staring you in the face. And you have to tell yourself, "I'm a wonderful person. So I'm at a fried clam store? And it's far from home? And I want to eat all these fried clams. Well, because I'm such a wonderful person, I'm only gonna eat enough to satisfy me. And if I want them again tomorrow, I'm worth the ride back here to get it again tomorrow." You really have to, and it's hard. Because there'll be days when you don't feel that wonderful about yourself.

She expects that situations that are difficult now will become easier to handle: "This is the first time since I've recovered that my life is crazy. Now I think the next time my life is crazy, it will be different. Because I've been through it once. And you draw from experience. So I think as you gain more experience as a recovering person, you apply it more as situations arise over the course of your life. So I think every situation will continue to be different. And maybe even easier." But she suspects she will always need to be prepared to talk herself through difficult times. The nature of her self-talk indicates that she knows the value of disidentifying from her eating symptoms as a means of getting perspective on them:

I still think once a person with an eating disorder, you always have the potential, if you're not continuously aware of what's goin' on. You need to be in touch with yourself. You need to be honest with yourself. You need to be able to sit down and say, "All right, Jessie, what's goin' on?" "What's goin' on in life, and what are you feelin'? Obviously you're feelin' somethin' 'cause you're getting these bulimic urges again. Or you're gettin' those anorexic urges again. And you know that that's just a cover for somethin' that's goin' on." And you try to be honest with yourself and think, "Well, I really hate my job." But instead of comin' out and saying "I hate this damn job" and kickin' your desk, you take it out on yourself. So you need to say, "That's not the right thing to do 'cause you don't deserve this." And you deal with it.

She finds it helpful to know that she can return to her therapist for "booster shot" visits. Just knowing that her therapist is there helps her be responsive to her own felt sense of enough:

Like with my stress [at work]. I was flipped out. I was just stressed. I was comin' home. And I expected my house to stay clean. Because everything else was busy. I didn't wanna have to clean my house. I would come home and my house would need to be cleaned. I would go to work, the work has to get done, this one's out sick, you have to do this by this deadline, and get this done, and my mother was comin' for dinner, and I was just like this [*physically tenses up*]. And I said to Helen, "What do I do? I have to come and talk to you, I don't know what to do. Before it channels itself inward, I need to know how to deal with it." And she did. And sometimes it's just one visit. And it's enough. Like this time. But you have to feel that you are worth it. You have to say, "I'm worth this. I deserve to go find out how to handle this. I deserve not to relapse."

Isabella finds it helpful when people close to her prompt her to notice her self-experience:

What advice would you have for friends or lovers of people with bulimia?

To focus more on the feelings in talking about it. Even sometimes now I'll get quiet. The person I'm seeing, he'll just look at me, and he'll say, "Are you okay? What are you thinking about? How are you feeling right now?" And that's really helpful. I didn't ask him to do that, he just seems to do that. So it's just focusing on how you're feeling in the moment and keeping in touch with that and not losing that. 'Cause if you do, you get into that escape mode.

When I ask Leslie what advice she would give people who are strug-gling with bulimia, she cautions them to remain open to sensing their experience: "Once you open up, to stay open. To fight the instinct to close. I personally think that's the worst thing that ever happened to me are the times that I shut down and thought I was okay. I wasn't okay, I was just shut down. So to just be diligent and really work on it. 'Cause you'll know when it's better. You just know."

Beth finds it helpful to "take quiet time" in which to pray:

When I feel really inadequate, I lie down, I take quiet time, and I ask God to please help me to feel adequate and to be grateful for what I have instead of looking at what I don't have. And that fills that hole right away, when I feel like I don't fit in. Like I'll go to a party, and everyone has these beautiful clothes, and I'll feel, "Oh, my God. I don't fit in." I just have to ask God to help me to believe that I am okay just as I am and that I'm me, and I'm the only Beth there is, and it's okay that I'm not like everybody else . . . I know if I feel inadequate in any situation, I can go in the bathroom, and I get on my knees and ask God to help me to let go of that feeling and to trust that I am okay. I am right where I'm supposed to be.

She has learned to attend to feelings before they get out of perspective:

'Cause I feel like if I got into that feeling enough, then I'd go binge again. If I let that feeling grow and grow and grow, like "I'm inadequate, I don't have the right clothes, I'm a loser, I'm fat, I'm ugly, I—blah, blah," it would just grow and grow and grow and grow and grow until the point where I'd say, "Screw it. I'm just gonna binge on that cake." And then the next thing would be to throw up. So I feel like when I have those feelings, even a little bit, I have to immediately use kind of the tools that I've learned from OA to not let that feeling grow.

Although recovering requires a continuing commitment to sensing self-experience, the women do not regard that as a burden. Remaining connected to their experience also enables them to live richer lives. When I ask Isabella whether it's been hard to discover that to maintain her recovery she needs to keep on attending to herself through her med-itation, journal writing, affirmations, and self-talk, she says that, quite the contrary, she enjoys attending to herself and finds that doing so affirms her sense of self-worth: "Now it's something like 'I feel so much better, but I want to keep this up for myself because I'm worth it.'"

Similarly, Beth appreciates her commitment to her A Way of Life (AWOL) group, a small, closed group of OA members who meet regularly to work through the twelve steps: "It's really such a gift . . . And I've changed incredibly since the day I started AWOL. For me, that's where the recovery has been, that's where my faith has grown . . . People have even commented, 'You seem so much more relaxed.' I was just so tense all the time. And that's changed. Through AWOL, I take a half an hour of quiet time to pray every morning, and it's changed my life absolutely."

RESPONDING TO LAPSES AND RELAPSES

Bulimia is an episodic disorder: lapses and relapses are common in the course of recovering. The women's symptoms at times diminished to a subclinical level and then returned to clinical severity. None, however, suffered a major relapse following a symptom-free year. Two brief lapses, by Rebecca and Meg, illuminate the process of recovering from lapses.

A single-episode lapse helped Rebecca confirm her commitment not to binge or purge. It occurred just after she learned that her husband had been using cocaine. The news came as a shock to her, especially since the couple had made a pact to stop using cocaine:

> In August, I did overeat once and I did purge. It was kinda good that I did it 'cause I hadn't done it in so long, and it really made me realize that it wasn't doing anything for me. It doesn't provide anything. It's not a quick fix, it doesn't, the problem's still there. It just makes you feel miserable and gross and disgusting, physically and emotionally. And I hadn't done it in so long that I'd forgotten that. I wanted to see if it did for me what it did for me years ago. And it just didn't. But I was in a situation that I felt so out of control . . . If I could deal with this situation, then I can deal with anything. I never feel that that's something that I'll ever do again. I really, I can't live with that. I refuse to live with bulimia in my life. It's not a part of me, and I refuse to ever let it be a part of me. I have too much living to do, and it took up too many hours of my day.

In response to their difficulties at that time, she and Robert returned to Rebecca's therapist for several couples sessions.

Meg attributes her lapse to anxiety about the future and about an impending spring vacation. To recover from the lapse, she used a number of strategies to connect with her experience, including self-talk, talking with others, disidentifying from the disorder, and normalizing her eating:

> I told myself that this was probably normal. That it probably happens to people and that I shouldn't beat myself up about it. Because part of it was that I was getting so mad at myself for doing it that that was creating more anxiety about the whole thing. So I just had to say, "I'm not bulimic again. I'm just having problems dealing with some things, and this is the way that I'm trying to deal with it." And I thought about how it wasn't making me feel any better. And I just started thinking about what the real problem was, the anxiety over the future. And I made some phone calls to therapists. And just the idea of getting myself out of it, just starting to climb out of the hole made me keep going . . . What else did I do? I stopped restricting food. That was a big thing. Because I was—I use the word anxiety a lot, but I have a lot of anxiety about this vacation I'm going on just because of vacations. Also that I'm gonna have to wear a bathing suit. And so I was semi-dieting, which I know is—sometimes I can do it, but at this point in time, it was ridiculous for me to try because it was just setting myself up for failure. So I stopped doing that, and that helped. It was just going back to things that I knew. That I can't restrict myself, and I do have to talk to someone. I can't deal with it all myself.

Continuing Consolidation

The women's accounts of recovering extend far beyond the remission of eating-disorder symptoms. The post-symptom portion of each woman's account is an essential part of her recovery. Sensing self-experience requires continuing practice and consolidation.

Many of the women had assumed that recovering consisted of stopping the behavior. They did not imagine that recovering would mean feeling better about themselves. Isabella says: "In the beginning I didn't think so much that it was the self-esteem. I thought it was if I could just stop bingeing and purging. So I have stopped that, but it's an added bonus because I feel really great."

The women consolidate their gains over time. Sarah, at our first interview, felt disconnected from her feelings. By our second interview, seven months later, she was feeling much more present to her emotional experience and much more intimately connected with her friends and her therapist. By our third meeting, one year and five months after our first, she was starting to date and said she was at last dealing with issues that had been at the core of her eating disorder: "It has so much more to do with what I'm doing now in terms of taking these risks and dating than food stuff . . . It has so much more to do with being able to be a whole person. And being able to take this risk and open up this whole area of my life that I've kept closed for whatever reasons, some of which I might not even know yet. Just to allow myself to experience all of that. Just to allow myself to experience things and feel things and have real relationships with people."

Gita, who in our first interview said, "I could always be thinner," is less concerned about her weight a year later:

> It's amazing, I noticed the other day that I hadn't weighed myself for a month. It's great that I can forget it now. I would weigh myself three times a day before. I was very tied to it. Now I'm more free. Now I use it more as a monitor of just general health . . . I can go a month, and I'm still the same when I get on, that some days I might eat a lot, some days I don't eat a lot, it's just I eat when I feel like it, and I've trusted that, and I end up being exactly the same and no problem and nothing to worry about.

Gita is learning to say no (that is, "enough"):

> We also worked on saying no. That was another big problem I had, and at work, people ask me to do a million things, and I'll get overworked, and then I don't act. And I don't wanna hurt their feelings, so I couldn't say no. And now I'm really realizing that I can't help anyone if I'm fragile. And saying no is all right. And Paul's also helped me with that, though it's still something I'm working on. Saying no to people is difficult. I really wanna help people

and do as much for everyone else as I can. And if I've let people down, it makes me feel awful. But I can't look at it as letting them down. I have to just realize it's "No" and okay.

Some of the women look ahead to the next steps in the consolidation of their recovery. For example, Rebecca knows she needs to nurture herself:

> That's something that I know I really need to focus on a lot more. And I think that's a part of, a small part of, the bulimia, or that whole attitude that I'm not able to nurture myself as well as I should be able to . . . I think, "Well, why should I do something just for me when I can do something to make more than one person happy?" Or "How can I dare fathom spending a hundred dollars to do something that gives me pleasure? My God, I should save that money, or I should buy groceries with it, or do something much more practical."

When I ask what occurs to her as a way to nurture herself, she replies: "I would like to start horseback riding again. But I know that's very, very expensive. But that would be very, very nurturing." She sounds wistful, full of longing, as she imagines how it would feel to ride.

Implications

When we talk of discovery, we tend to use the metaphor of sight: we see; we observe; we inspect. Discoveries are unveiled, illuminated. New findings are revealed. But in phenomenological research, the metaphor of discovery is that of sound: we listen; we hear; we discern subtle changes in vibration. Discoveries reverberate, ring true. New understandings resonate.

Mary Belenky and her colleagues, the authors of *Women's Ways of Knowing*, found that when women describe how they know, the metaphor of listening prevails over visual metaphors. Many who study women's development rely on listening closely to women's voices (Brown and Gilligan, 1992). Attentive listening is an intimate act which yields intimate knowledge.

My interviews with these women yield knowledge which is not so much new as known and in need of reclamation. When we come into intimate relationship with an object of study, what looked new and intriguing from a distance can sound familiar and ordinary up close. To my mind, that is the case with much of what I describe in this book, including the elements of pivotal experiences, the component processes of change, and the helpful relational experiences. Belenky and her colleagues note their realization that what was novel in their work was not their seemingly newfound knowledge but their readiness to listen to a seemingly ordinary voice and learn what it had had to teach them all along: "The stories of the women drew us back into a kind of knowing that had too often been silenced by the institutions in which we grew up and of which we were a part. In the end, we found that, in our attempt to bring forward the ordinary voice, that voice had educated us" (20).

When we listen attentively enough to personal knowledge, the most ordinary voice becomes extraordinarily original, not in the sense of being new but in the sense of being an origin, a primary source. When we listen closely to primary sources and discover understandings that resonate deeply with our experience, we swiftly integrate our new comprehension with our old conceptions. The ostensibly new knowledge feels so basic, so essential, that we soon act as if we had known it all along. And in a sense we had. Bessel van der Kolk, Lars Weisaeth, and Onno van der Hart (1996) observe that rediscovering what is already known is part of an age-old cycle by which each generation reclaims essential truths. The women's primary accounts of recovering bring us back to our senses as clinicians, researchers, and human beings and back to the essentials of how people change and heal.

IMPLICATIONS FOR TREATMENT

THE COMPLEXITY OF RECOVERING

The women's accounts make clear that the process of recovering is multiply determined: it requires a convergence of six essential elements and a combination of helpful efforts and experiences. Recovering is also multiply situated: these elements, efforts, and experiences occur not only in formally therapeutic contexts but also in life outside clinical offices and treatment centers.

When we consider the paths into an eating disorder, we recognize that psychological, sociocultural, biogenetic, familial, developmental, and life experiential factors all contribute to a person's developing and maintaining an eating disorder (Levine, 1987; Strober, 1991, 1994). Yet when we consider the ways out of an eating disorder, we seldom acknowledge a comparable complexity. In most writings on treatment, recovering is described only in terms of formal treatment, with no consideration of the interactions between formal treatment and the rest of life. Descriptions of treatment also do not consider much complexity. Most written works on treatment focus on a single approach, and few consider how different treatment approaches interact in lived experience. (Three excellent exceptions are Tobin and Johnson, 1991; Johnson and Sansone, 1993; and Garner and Needleman, 1997.)

For instance, Meg did not make much progress in an intensive outpatient treatment program because she maintained her overcommitted schedule of activities as a student, athlete, and ROTC member. In that program, however, she did confront her ambivalence about changing: "When I was in the outpatient thing, they really emphasized that you can't just give it up because it's a big part of your life, it's a lot of who you are, and it's a coping mechanism, and if you just stop doing the behavior, there's gonna be this big void there. And you need something to replace it, and that's a gradual process, and all this sort of stuff. And I remember writing letters to my eating disorder. In the very beginning. Which made me think about why I liked it and why I wouldn't wanna get rid of it." She eventually realized she could not recover without fully investing in the process. She dropped out of the outpatient program, radically trimmed her list of commitments, and entered a residential treatment program.

Meg regards her stay in the residential treatment center as essential to helping her make good use of her subsequent therapy: "But I don't think if I was a newly recovering person and just going to therapy, if you would've put me in with a therapist, that with that alone that it would've done me any good. I think the whole [treatment center] experience and having just a whole base and a context and an understanding of all of the issues that were involved, then I was able to work from those with the individual [therapists]."

Rebecca's first individual and group therapy did not feel helpful, because "until you're ready to really deal with it, until you are able to face it, you're not going to." But looking back, she sees that they did prepare her to make good use of therapy when she was ready to change:

I think the first psychologist that I saw when I just started with the eating disorder gave me an introduction to what therapy is all about. Because it's like a foreign world, it's something that takes you a while to just get familiar with, the whole atmosphere, never mind the individual that you're having the therapy with . . . I think I had gotten into the swing of things a little bit more about what's going on and what's going to be expected of you . . . So I think all of it grows upon each other one.

The women's accounts challenge traditional approaches to treatment-outcome research. They indicate that we need to study not only which symptoms change over time and in relation to which treatment variables but also how people subjectively experience the process of change, including interactions among treatments and interactions between experiences in treatment and experiences in other domains of life.

The concepts of predisposing, precipitating, and perpetuating factors, which we use in etiologic models of eating disorders, may also help us understand the process of recovering. We need to ask the following sorts of questions: What predisposes someone to recover? What precipitates recovering, and what perpetuates it? Of the six essential elements of recovering, do the three elements of agency precipitate the process? Do the three elements of commitment create a climate that sustains and perpetuates it?

INGREDIENTS OF EFFECTIVE THERAPIES

The women's experiences do not indicate the need for a new treatment so much as they help us understand why and how people with bulimia nervosa respond to different treatment approaches. Today, cognitive-behavioral therapy and interpersonal therapy are considered the treatments of choice, in particular for short-run to medium-run reduction of symptoms (Fairburn, 1993, 1997; Fairburn et al., 1991; Herzog et al., 1992; Wilson, Fairburn, and Agras, 1997). But other therapeutic approaches have also demonstrated value, including psychodynamic psychotherapy (Boskind-White and White, 1987; Geist, 1985, 1989; Goodsitt, 1983, 1985, 1997; Sugarman, 1991; Sands, 1991; Rizzuto, 1985, 1988;

Tobin and Johnson, 1991), experiential therapy (Hornyak and Baker, 1989), narrative therapy (White and Epston, 1990), family therapy (Root, Fallon, and Friedrich, 1986), the twelve-step approach of Overeaters Anonymous (Johnson and Sansone, 1993), and medication (Garfinkel and Walsh, 1997). The women's accounts indicate that recovering is fundamentally a process of coming to sense self-experience and that elements of various approaches may foster that process.

For example, among the ingredients of interpersonal therapy (IPT), as described by Christopher Fairburn (1993, 1997), are education about the process of change—specifically about why IPT does not focus on eating behaviors and about how the effects of therapy continue to accrue for months after the therapy has ended—and coached guidance in attending to the feelings accompanying role transitions and interpersonal disputes. IPT enables a person to act and speak on behalf of her needs, preferences, and limits; to sharpen her ability to identify needs and feelings; to grieve ungrieved losses; and to take pride in developing interpersonal effectiveness and in decreasing her bulimic symptoms. Fairburn suggests that as a person begins to feel effective in her relationships she can look beyond appearance to gauge her self-worth.

IPT also appears to foster a belief that one will recover. A therapist conducting manual-based IPT therapy for bulimia nervosa is taught to convey a conviction, backed by data from treatment-outcome studies, that IPT is helpful to people with this disorder. This conviction no doubt promotes belief in the therapy, in the therapist, and in one's ability to recover. The therapist is expected to explain that the time-limited nature of the therapy enables the client and therapist to focus their minds, "thereby making both work harder" (Fairburn, 1993, 361). In being told that she needs to "make the most of the opportunity by giving the treatment priority in your life" and that "not doing so is likely to limit the progress that we can make" (Fairburn, 1997, 282), a client is encouraged to invest in the process of change.

The women's accounts also have implications for understanding how and why medication can be helpful. Relief from depression, anxiety, or obsessive thinking may help someone attune to her self-experience by giving her biochemical support for tolerating the negative affect that accompanies focusing inward. Medication is not invariably helpful, however. Four of the women took medication related to treatment of bulimia nervosa; two found it helpful; two found it unhelpful or harmful.

TIMING

In treatment-outcome studies of cognitive-behavioral therapy (CBT), only 50 percent of the subjects stop bingeing and purging, even under the very best of conditions: with therapists well trained in conducting formal, manual-based CBT; with enough time to complete the treatment; and with subjects who are motivated enough to participate in the treatment and the research. Issues of timing can help us understand why even the most successful treatments do not always succeed.

Stages of Change

According to a transtheoretical model of change derived from studying how people relinquish addictive behaviors such as smoking (Prochaska and DiClemente, 1982; Prochaska, DiClemente, and Norcross, 1992, 1994), there are five identifiable stages of change: precontemplation, contemplation, preparation, action, and maintenance. The model also indicates that there are ten processes of change and that a given process is most relevant during a specific stage of change. It appears that the effectiveness of any therapeutic approach depends not only on the particular diagnosis and the particular person but on the particular stage of change the person is in when she seeks help.

Some researchers have found this model useful in predicting the course of change for people with bulimia nervosa (Franko, 1994; Levy, 1997). The transtheoretical model of change may help us anticipate what sort of help a particular bulimic person would actually find helpful at a particular time. For instance, cognitive-behavioral therapy might be a good match for someone who is moving from the preparation stage to the action stage but a poor match for someone in the precontemplation or contemplation stage.

William Miller and Stephen Rollnick (1991) drew upon the transtheoretical model to develop what they call "motivational interviewing" for use with people with addictive behaviors. They emphasize that "motivation is a *state* of readiness or eagerness to change, which may fluctuate from one time or situation to another," and they note: "This state is one that can be influenced" (14). Their observations are consistent with my findings that the felt sense of enough, which defines a state of readiness, may endure only briefly and that the timing and nature of the response to that felt sense of enough can influence what happens next.

Windows, Doors, and Steps into Care

When we are concerned about a person with an eating disorder, we need to be alert and responsive to moments when she herself feels a need or desire to seek care. Such *windows of opportunity* are typically characterized by her felt sense of enough. It is important to listen for, name, affirm, and respond to her felt sense of enough. To confirm that her subjective sense of a limit is a trustworthy gauge, we need to validate her sense of enoughness: *Yes, this is enough misery. Yes, you have tried long enough to do this alone. Yes, you are sick enough. Yes, you matter enough.* To promote her curiosity about her experience, we need to express our own curiosity about how she came to experience a sense of enoughness and what moved her to take a step directed toward getting care. Because the window of opportunity may open only a crack and only for a moment, our response to a person's effort to get help must be timely.

Acknowledging someone's needs does not necessarily mean that we must drop everything to accommodate her. What matters most is that we recognize and appreciate her experience and respond in as timely and attuned a way as we can. For instance, when a person calls a therapist wanting an initial appointment within a day or two, the therapist may not be able to make an appointment within that time frame. The therapist can, however, speak with the person briefly by phone, affirm the importance of her having taken the step of calling, acknowledge the unfortunate but real limits of his or her availability, schedule the soonest appointment possible, arrange an interim appointment with another provider if necessary, and promise to call her if an earlier time opens up. Similarly, I know of nurse practitioners with crammed clinical schedules who fit in a new patient for a fifteen-minute appointment within a few days of her initial call, even though that is not enough time for a full medical history and physical exam. The brief but timely appointment allows the provider to meet the patient, rule out or attend to any urgent medical situations, and signal to the patient that she is being taken seriously.

Access to inpatient and partial hospital programs is limited by insurance coverage and, in some regions, by the scarcity of such programs. Under these conditions, someone like Rebecca, who, as discussed in Chapter 2, sought inpatient care when she felt she had tried hard enough to recover with outpatient resources alone, would probably not qualify for insurance coverage for inpatient care. But her experience suggests that it is important that people have access to the level of care they feel they need when they feel the need for it so that they can experience a sense of agency and effectiveness in their efforts to get help. Rebecca engaged productively in the inpatient program partly because she entered it in response to her own sense of enoughness.

A timely and attuned response is no guarantee that a person will enter into care. But a failure to respond, or an untimely and unattuned response, runs a serious risk of leaving the person feeling shamed, discouraged, and defeated.

Given the priority of medical safety, one of the first steps a person needs to take is to consult with a medical provider who can evaluate her medical status and provide the care necessary to keep her safe. But unless she is in acute medical danger, a medical consultation need not be the very first step. There are many possible *doors into care*, including that of a physician, nurse or nurse practitioner, physical therapist, psychotherapist, nutritionist, psychopharmacologist, or group therapist. Once a person has entered the network of care, the provider she encounters can help her connect with other members of a treatment team as needed and as she is ready to connect with them.

Referral services, hotlines, eating-disorder associations, and educational materials and presentations can be useful first points of contact, antechambers where someone can meet a guide who will point her toward doors into care. Twenty-four-hour answering services and hotlines have the advantage of being available in the middle of the night, a time when someone with an eating disorder is especially vulnerable to disordered eating and to overwhelming affect. Some of the women called a hotline or answering service at night or on a weekend to ask for a referral. They were able to take a first step toward help only when they experienced a felt sense of enough, which was typically when they were in acute distress. Had they waited until the acute distress passed, they would no longer have felt sick enough to seek help. For example, Sarah says:

> I had been thinking about [getting into therapy] but I always felt worse at night, and that's not when you could pick up a phone and call a therapist or call an agency or call someplace. And in the morning I'd feel better, and so I'd think, "Well, we'll see," and so I ended up during the day doing my exploring about where I could go for counseling in case I ever wanted to do it. And then ended up calling at night and leaving a message with the answering service because I felt like I had to do it that way or I'd never go . . . I called the answering service [of a therapist whose name I had] and asked for her, left a message that I wanted to make an appointment and didn't let myself go back on it even though the next day I felt better.

A woman's initial efforts to seek care may appear to be *small, first steps.* She may tell one person that she feels concerned about herself. But her seemingly tiny step needs to be acknowledged for the giant leap that it is for her. While a person with a serious eating disorder needs a team of caregivers, she might be overwhelmed by the prospect of having to assemble an entire team all at once. She needs help to take things one step at a time and to put first things first. Once she has made a first step, she needs support and guidance to prepare to take a next small step. For instance, if her initial step was to seek a referral, she needs to focus on specific next steps: making one appointment with one provider, keeping that appointment, and making and keeping one follow-up appointment. She may fear that if she seeks any help at all she will be expected to make a full and unambivalent commitment to recovering. She needs reassurance that caregivers will appreciate her ambivalence about receiving care and about recovering.

The Convergence of Six Essential Elements

If, as my clinical experience suggests, the convergence of all six essential elements of recovery is rare, the implications are serious. As in Claire's and Amy's cases, the absence or mistiming of even one or two elements may result in an incomplete or fragile recovery. Bulimic women and their caregivers need to be mindful of which elements are missing, introduce or foster missing elements, be alert to moments when missing elements spontaneously appear, and cultivate them once they are present. More specifically, caregivers need to affirm a woman's felt sense of enough by way of a timely and attuned response to her acts directed toward getting help. And bulimic women and their caregivers need to create an abiding context conducive to sensing self-experience, foster a belief in the possibility of recovery or a sense of being believed in, and promote investment in the process of change.

Timeliness in Psychotherapy

Timely and attuned responsiveness is of course essential throughout treatment, not just at the beginning. Sarah, who resumed purging after having stopped, appreciated the reaction of her therapist, Annie, to the communication, in the form of intensified symptoms, that Sarah needed more intensive therapy:

> I went home at Christmas break . . . and started purging when I was home. And then came back and told her, and she just laid into me like no one has ever laid into me before. "Why weren't you talking about this?" Just "Why?" and "What?" and no one had ever asked me why before. And she asks me why constantly. And at the beginning, I probably got defensive, but I don't get defensive anymore because, first of all, she confronted me, and I was getting exactly what I'd wanted for years. Because I totally wasn't feeling ashamed about it. I was finally being seen. I was finally feeling like she knew, the jig was up. That was it. And she knew. And her second response was, "How would you feel about coming to therapy twice a week?" And it was like, well, "Oh, my God, not only did she hear me, but she heard me loud and clear." She went beyond hearing me. She just, she absolutely knew.

Sarah contrasts Annie's timely, attuned, and active response with her previous therapist's supportive approach:

> Sonya never asked me about purging, and I hardly ever brought it up. And when I did, like if I had purged, I knew that there was something going on, but I didn't know what, as usual, and so I'd go in and I'd tell her that I purged, and she would miss it. She wouldn't take it seriously a lot of the time. She would just say, "Oh, you gotta expect that. It's not gonna go away completely." When what I wanted was for her to say, "What's so wrong that you needed to throw up about it?" So I didn't expect that Annie would do any different.

Annie's challenge was also timely and attuned with respect to Sarah's overall readiness to change: "See I don't know, if I had gone to her when I was 20 and first had started throwing up, whether she would have responded that way. I don't think so, I think probably she would've done what Sonya did which is just accept it and work with it and leave it alone."

ATTUNEMENT

Knowing about and appreciating the subjective experience of change may help caregivers attune to a person with bulimia nervosa. Knowing and appreciating their clients' experience requires that caregivers be attuned to their own subjective experience as well.

Doing and Being

The questions of what to do and how to be, considered in Chapter 4, are pressing ones not only for someone recovering from bulimia nervosa but for anyone who cares about her. Before recovering, the women were unable to *be* with their self-experience. They felt compelled to *do* something to vanquish physical and psychic distress. They did not know that all feelings, even the most intense, naturally and inevitably subside. They did not know that feelings are wellsprings of self-information, motivators of self-defining acts, and sources of energy. And so they tried to blot out their feelings by bingeing, purging, exercising, and other intense physical experience.

Therapists, too, feel the need to do something: to "do treatment" to bring a client's symptoms under control and to relieve her pain. Although I may rightly feel the imperative to do something when I sit with a woman with a serious eating disorder, particularly when her safety is in question, I need to consider not only my responsibility to her care but also my ability to respond to her states of being. It is my being with her in her pain that enables her to learn that she can tolerate—be with rather than avoid—painful states of being, which, after all, are part of life.

Even doing nothing can be a form of doing. In fact much of what we think of as nothing may in fact be *something*, something quite rare and powerful. Therapists-in-training learn that to help a client tolerate her experience so that she can work through it, they must heed this advice: "Don't just do something. Sit there." Jessie Taft (1933/1973) notes: "The word 'therapy' has no verb in English, for which I am grateful; it cannot do anything to anybody, hence can better represent a process going on, observed perhaps, understood perhaps, assisted perhaps, but not applied" (3). Attuning to someone's state of being is not doing something *to* her or *for* her but *with* her.

Doing is not always a defense against sensing self-experience; it can also be a means of becoming connected with one's subjective experience. Many clients do things that could be considered attempts to experience themselves through their primary senses: listen to music; paint their nails; create artwork; burn scented candles; take bubble baths; pet an animal; wear a warm, soft sweater; drink fragrant tea; take in the sights, sounds, and scents of nature. Some clients say that even a binge can begin as a sensory, pleasurable experience of the taste and texture of food, although it is apt to turn into a dissociative experience. Sometimes a client will call her therapist's answering machine just to hear the therapist's voice. If the client leaves a message (and she may not), it is in part to hear her own voice in a moment of distress. In a moment of intense emotion, sensing voice—hearing and/or speaking—helps her create a sense of being-with-other and a sense of being-with-self. Distress is more bearable when one feels a sense of company, of with-ness.

Therapists need to appreciate how sensory and concrete therapy with bulimic clients must be, especially early on. As discussed in Chapter

6, things that therapists actively do help clients be with their experience. The therapist of a bulimic woman needs to actively coach her to consult her subjective states of being. Such coaching can take the form of simply asking questions: "Let's pause for a moment. Can you focus inward and just notice what you are experiencing underneath it all?" If a client is stumped by such a question, she may find it helpful to be given a more discriminatory prompt: "Just notice whatever occurs to you, even if it makes no sense to you." "Just stop and notice what feeling seems hottest or feels most alive in you at this moment." Or, when she makes a physical gesture or facial expression that seems to spring from the core of her, the therapist can ask her to repeat it, this time noticing any feelings or words that accompany it.

The effectiveness of therapeutic acts depends on therapeutic presence: what I do and say is most effective in helping a client sense self-experience when I am emotionally present with her. One of my best gauges of her state of being is my own state of being in her presence. I must therefore attune to my own internal states and let them inform what I do and say. This link between being and doing can take the form of my pointing out the discrepancy between her presentation and my affective resonance: "I see you smiling, and I hear you saying that everything's fine. And yet, as I listen to you, I feel so sad."

In the current context of mental health care, there are many pressures to provide a standardized treatment for particular disorders, including bulimia nervosa. Many therapists work in managed care contexts where they are expected to provide short-term, problem-focused, behavior-oriented treatment that is based on doing rather than on being with. In severely restricting the duration of therapy, limiting its focus to symptoms and behaviors, imposing standardized treatments, and failing to support professionals' need to routinely reflect on and consult about their sessions with clients, managed mental health care threatens to inhibit therapists' ability to attune to their clients' subjective experience with the precision that they know to be so healing.

I recently observed to a fellow therapist that each time I meet a new client I feel as if I am dealing with an entirely new situation, starting at square one. My colleague said, in effect, "May it always be that way. The day you presume to treat someone as a typical case, you'll know you're in trouble." Overmanaged care leaves therapists at risk for treating a given client as a typical case rather than as an individual.

A therapist needs to remain open to each client's unique experience of her eating disorder and her life. For example, Meg resisted an outpatient treatment program that stressed behavioral charting and behavioral change but did not help her understand how those tasks related to her particular concerns at the time:

> They wanted to work more on the behavior first. And so they wanted me to do these food charts. And, you probably know, most bulimics hate food charts. Where anorexics will do them like every day, I will never do a food chart. I hate them. I don't want to face up to what I eat. "How do you feel when you're bingeing?" "Bullshit, I'm not gonna tell you! I don't really know, and I don't want it to be your business right now anyway!" And so they would get mad at me 'cause I wouldn't do the food charts . . . There was a nutritionist and the therapist, and they were both telling me that one couldn't work without the other and I needed to cooperate. And I said, "Well, I'm not then." I maybe talked to the therapist like once, but she was saying I needed to do this behavioral stuff first before we could really start working. And I didn't do it. So it didn't work . . . There was no flexibility. It just felt like "Oh, someone comes in, they have an eating disorder, they have to do this." It felt bureaucratic. That's exactly what I didn't need.

While Meg may simply not have been ready for treatment at the time, and while she admits that the outpatient program prepared her to invest more fully in her subsequent treatment, the fact that she joined the outpatient program at all indicates that she was ready for something. As her experience indicates, the type of treatment and the way it is presented to clients need to be tailored to each client's stage of change. Meg might have found the program more helpful if her providers had explored with her what made her unwilling to use the food-mood charts, respected her sense of timing about what she was ready to do, presented the charts as being in the service of something that mattered to her at that time (self-discovery rather than behavior management), and let her exercise some choice.

Overmanaged care impedes clinicians' ability to be empathically present with their clients, to be open and curious in their reception of them, to be creatively attuned and collaborative in their responses to them. In overemphasizing what clinicians do and deemphasizing how their attunement to states of being makes what they do effective, overmanaged care impairs therapists' use of some of their most powerful tools.

Being with Shame

Given that attunement to needs and yearnings ultimately brings a client into contact with her core sense of shame, one of the greatest challenges facing a psychotherapist is to help clients tolerate shame without being overwhelmed by it. Being able to tolerate shame and other painful feelings is arguably a prerequisite for all transformative learning, including that which happens in therapy (von Stade, 1986, 1988). Transformative learning requires that we tolerate the shame of feeling that we should have already known that which comes to feel so basic, and the shame of feeling inadequate to the task we are trying to master.

Of course it is important not to accentuate a client's shame. But it is equally important that the client's fear of shame—or the therapist's fear of feeling shame on behalf of the client—not leave the therapist so wary of eliciting shame that the therapy is rendered ineffective. Christopher von Stade (1986, 1988) notes that if we try to spare a learner any shame, we protect her from learning.

As discussed in Chapter 6, education about what to expect as they change appears to help women sense and tolerate self-experience, including the experience of shame. Using the story of Beauty and the Beast as a metaphor for a woman's bid for wholeness may not only demystify the process of change but also dignify the effort to bear the shame and distress inherent in the process.

Doing Enough and Being Enough

Everything I have just said about doing and being could be said of any good therapy, regardless of diagnosis. But in my experience, the countertransference in therapy with people with eating disorders typically takes the form of a painful sense of not being or doing enough. Unless therapists recognize that sense of inadequacy as countertransference, they, too, can find themselves overvaluing doing and devaluing being present with felt experience as a means of avoiding shame in their relationship with these clients. In trying to avoid rather than tolerate shame, they can perpetuate the dynamics of the disorder.

As I read the literature and attend conferences on eating disorders, I am often struck by the discrepancy between professionals' descriptions of seemingly straightforward, successful treatments and my own experience of how convoluted and complex therapeutic work with eating-disordered women is. It often requires extraordinary effort just to engage a client in the process of therapy, given how deeply ashamed, self-hating, and frightened she feels. As discussed in Chapter 4, resistance to attending to self-experience is a defining feature of bulimia nervosa. Some argue that the bulimic's defense against self-revelation and against working in the transference is itself the transference (Rizzuto, 1988; Sands, 1991). My efforts to care are apt to be met with contempt, the feeling that typifies my client's self-regard. Even once someone has engaged in therapy, progress is often plodding because learning to tolerate the feelings aroused by sensing self-experience is so difficult.

As caregivers, we feel inadequate when working with people who remain symptomatic despite our care. We fear that their symptoms are evidence of our inadequacy. We fear that we do not know enough, are not doing enough, and are not enough (Gans, 1989). To allow ourselves to be tyrannized by such fears is to accept a destructive assumption: the assumption that we should—and by implication *could*—be perfect, all-knowing, all-powerful, without limitations. It is an assumption born of and perpetuating a climate of shame and doubt, the very climate in which eating disorders flourish. To act as if I have power which I in fact do not have is arrogant, and arrogance is ultimately a defense against shame. If I try to do more and more and more in an effort to escape the sting of shame, I avoid learning all that I might from my clients. If I can let myself be with my countertransferential shame and with my urge to vanquish it, I can discover something of what my clients feel.

Just as I have been to conferences where presenters seemed over-confident, I have been to meetings where clinicians seemed to feel unduly powerless, saying, in effect, "There is nothing else I could do in this case." Like arrogance, feelings of impotence are a protection against shame. There are dangers both in overestimating my power and in discounting it. The challenge, as Suzanne Repetto Renna and I have pointed out, is not to take responsibility for things over which we have no power and to recognize those things over which we do have power.

I do not have the power to make another person change. She is a separate being with a right to self-determination.* I do have power to choose to be present to and curious about her experience, to express my concern for her safety and well-being, to confirm her sense of enoughness, to coach her to sense fundamental aspects of herself, to let her know how I experience her, to appreciate her complexity, and to offer her some sense of who she might be beyond someone with an eating disorder.

As Ana-Maria Rizzuto acknowledges, this is difficult, demanding, draining work: "In the countertransference, the analyst experiences exhaustion, discouragement, anger, humiliation and a wish to get rid of the patient . . . These patients do not develop a treatment alliance for a long time, even when they are paradoxically faithful to the treatment . . . The analyst must carry out his/her lonely interpretive task, surviving insults and rejections. He/she must remember that behind the bravado of tough words and the indifference of shrugged shoulders hide a person and a child who suffer alone in a world without communication" (1988, 372).

Clearly, this work keeps me humble: I, by myself, am not enough if "enough" means everything a client needs. But humility breeds wholeness. I may be just one member of a community of professional caregivers and others who help her treat herself with care and respect. As

---

*There are times when it may be appropriate to assume power and responsibility on behalf of a person with an eating disorder: for instance, if she is a child or is not able to keep herself medically safe.

Margaret McKenna has observed, a person with an eating disorder may have to hear the same message from forty-five different people before she can use it. If I am number eleven in that sequence, I will feel ineffective. But someone needs to be the eleventh in line, just as someone needs to be the tenth and the twelfth and so on to enable the forty-fifth person to be effective. Each of us must accept the limits of what is possible given our role and given that we can, at best, be only as helpful as the client allows us to be during the stretch of time in which we accompany her. We can hope that, collectively, the whole lot of us will be enough.

Humility breeds wholeness in another sense as well. It requires that we accept our own wholeness—limitations, imperfections, and all. We may work harder and harder in response to our fear that we are not a good enough therapist/physician/nutritionist (or parent or friend). But overwork, like other forms of striving for perfection, is ultimately a psychological defense against shame. If we do not respect the limits of our being and our time, we impair our ability to be wholly present with each client.

But while wholeness is a noble aim, we often miss our mark. We intend to be still enough, centered enough, and clear enough to attune to our clients, but clinical, administrative, and personal demands continually tap on our consciousness and tug at our attention. We are plagued by a persistent sense of not being enough and not doing enough for our clients, and yet we perpetually remind ourselves that it is humanly impossible to be either wholly perfect or perfectly whole.

That caregivers of people with bulimia nervosa inevitably encounter our own vulnerability to shame and perfectionism clues us in to what our clients need. Like our clients, when we try to be superhuman as a defense against shame, we treat ourselves inhumanely. Bulimic women embody the imperative to counter the internalized shame that makes it so difficult for them to embrace their complexity and bear their limitations.

Prizing and pride are fundamental antidotes to internalized shame. Bulimic women teach us that we need to prize each person's unique wholeness. Gershen Kaufman describes how such prizing is internalized: "Through having our unique differences valued by significant others, we begin to value them in ourselves. Once we do so, not only do we come to know who we are, but we also, and equally importantly, come to know who we are *not* . . . Only when we can stop trying to be all things do we become free to be who we are, and only as we move beyond shame and toward self-affirmation can we begin to relinquish this striving for perfection" (1974, 572–573). As Elizabeth Kensinger once put it, "It's one thing to try to be the best that you can be. It's quite another to try to be something that you're not meant to be."

When one prizes one's wholeness, one can more readily accept one's limitations because one's whole self is not at stake. *Humble* and *human* derive from roots that ultimately lead to "the earth or ground." We are inevitably humbled, or brought down to earth, by our human limitations. Yet, as discussed in Chapter 3, the women found others' acceptance of imperfection to be uplifting and healing. *Healing* derives from a word meaning "whole": we feel whole in the company of those who offer a humanizing regard by appreciating, in themselves and in others, the complexity of human nature and the reality of human limitation.

Being Safe Enough

Attention to a client's safety can be understood as a matter of attunement. The concept of enoughness helps us understand her lack of concern about her safety and communicate with her about our concerns.

Someone with bulimia nervosa is putting her health and life at risk. There are many medical complications of bulimia nervosa, which, in the worst case, can result in cardiac arrhythmia, cardiac arrest, and death. Someone with bulimia nervosa is apt to be unaware of when she is reaching a point of medical danger. She may assume that if she is in danger she will receive some physical warning sign, but in fact, in people with serious eating disorders, cardiac arrest and death can occur without warning.

Her inability to gauge what is safe enough has both psychological and physiological bases. Psychologically, she either does not attune to her internal states, whether psychic or physical, or she disregards them. If her body were to signal acute distress, she might not notice. Physiologically, purging and restrictive eating can result in dehydration and electrolyte imbalances, low blood glucose levels, and poor nutritional status generally. Her brain does not receive the nutrients it needs, and this biochemical impairment compounds her difficulty in perceiving her internal psychic and physical states and in gauging what is safe enough. She may also fail to perceive how dangerously depleted her body is because, in the short run, the body is able to compensate for the effects of disordered eating by borrowing from its reserves. As a result, she can get into serious, even mortal, medical danger abruptly, with no sense of warning.

Because a person with an eating disorder is unlikely to perceive the severity of her medical condition, her subjective assessment of her physical status, while important, is not sufficient. To ensure adequate care, she needs an objective medical evaluation and ongoing monitoring. Because she is not in a position to know that she is sick enough to need care and that she matters enough to be worthy of care, she needs others to keep speaking the language of enoughness with her so that eventually she can recognize and experience a felt sense of enough. Even if she is not concerned about her medical status and does not take her well-being seriously, she needs to hear that others are concerned and that they do take her health seriously enough to insist that her basic safety be assessed.

It is helpful for caregivers to speak about safety in concrete and specific terms. They must tell a bulimic woman not only the general statement that bulimia nervosa carries a risk of serious medical complications but the specific fact that her heart could stop and she could die. Hearing about medical dangers may not immediately lead her to seek help or change her behavior, but it is helpful for her to hear people repeat specific risks and facts because one day she may be able to act upon this knowledge. Written information about medical complications is especially useful, both because seeing the dangers in black and white makes the risks more real and because she can refer to the information again and again.

If adults have not consistently acted in her best interests, a person with an eating disorder may interpret efforts to care as efforts to control. Caregivers, friends, and family members need to continually take a stand on behalf of her safety by repeating the mantra that her safety is the top priority and by reframing safety limits as care rather than control. They also need to acknowledge that care and limits are for both her sake and their own: if people are scared that she may die, they cannot function well in their lives, nor can they attend fully to other legitimate concerns she may have about her life. She needs to hear that those who care for her and about her want to work *with* her rather than do things *to* her and that they will respect her pace and preferences but only within the bounds of safety.

GIVING RECOVERY ENOUGH OF A CHANCE

None of the women recovered while living in a four-year residential college. Recovering from bulimia nervosa requires an abiding context conducive to sensing self-experience. A residential college is arguably countertherapeutic in that it is a context conducive to sensing comparison and competition and in that it presents persistent pressures to stretch beyond one's limits. Recovering also requires that a woman invest substantially in her process of change. If she is heavily investing in her academic and extracurricular pursuits, she does not have enough personal resources to devote to the process of recovering: she is not able to give recovery enough of a chance.

I am not suggesting that colleges require every bulimic student to take a leave of absence to focus on recovering. I am saying that when a bulimic woman is not making recovering a priority, it is important to talk with her about the reality of what recovering requires. It is important to explore what would motivate her to give recovering enough of a chance. She may need to try half-hearted efforts at recovering for some time before she experiences the imperative to make recovering a priority. As William Perry observed, "Wisdom derives from the experienced defeat of all its enticing alternatives." The role of those who care about her is to help her reframe her failure to recover as her success in sensing just how much recovering requires.

IMPLICATIONS FOR RESEARCH

RECOVERING FROM ANOREXIA NERVOSA

According to Hilde Bruch (1973), recovering from anorexia nervosa involves developing a sense of enduring substance and worth and a sense of interoceptive awareness, meaning an ability to perceive internal states. It is by helping an anorexic woman make contact with the "impulses, feelings, and needs that originate within her" that a therapist helps her to experience "a self-directed identity" and to "recognize that she has substance and worth of her own, and that she does not need the strained and stressful superstructure of an artificial ultra-perfection" (1978, 135, 137).

Eugene Beresin, Christopher Gordon, and David Herzog (1989), in an interview study of thirteen women who had recovered from anorexia nervosa, describe the anorexic's experience of recovering as the process of becoming real after having had "no idea what it is like to be a real person with a cohesive sense of self, known and loved by others for herself" (127). The recovered anorexics said that the process required "getting to know themselves better" (120) and learning to tolerate uncomfortable feelings like anger, resentment, envy, and guilt. They found it helpful for a therapist to take an active role as they attempted to be in more intimate connection with self and other. They valued education about the disorder, coaching, and an expressed curiosity about their felt experience. Their accounts of pivotal experiences include taking self-initiated action and coming to feel sick and tired of the disorder. They found it helpful to talk to themselves, "particularly about their feeling states, desires, and body image" (120). Some talked to themselves in front of a mirror; some kept a journal and read it over and over again.

These processes sound essentially the same as the process of sensing self. Are both bulimia nervosa and anorexia nervosa fundamentally disorders of sensing self-experience? Given their different symptom patterns, how do the processes of recovering differ, both subjectively and objectively? Why do some people with anorexia nervosa have a binge-eating/purging subtype? Is recovering from this subtype of anorexia nervosa a different experience from recovering from the restricting subtype? Why do many people with anorexia nervosa, in their process of recovering, cross over to a diagnosis of bulimia nervosa, and why do some cross over from bulimia nervosa to anorexia nervosa? All these questions are worthy of further study.

GENDER, RACE, ETHNICITY, AND CLASS

There is relatively little research or clinical writing on men with eating disorders and, to my knowledge, none on men's recovery. Does men's experience of recovering differ from that of women, and if so, how is it different and how might we understand those differences? Similarly, we do not know how race, ethnicity, and class affect recovering. Given that recovering involves sensing self-experience, and given that internalized shame is one of the major impediments to sensing self-experience, we might look at how gender, race, ethnicity, and class affect a person's risk for internalized shame, ability to sense self-experience, risk of developing an eating disorder, and path toward recovery.

OTHER PSYCHOLOGICAL DISORDERS

No doubt some people who have difficulty sensing self-experience do not develop eating disorders. And no doubt much of what enables people to recover from bulimia nervosa also enables people to recover from other psychological disorders. What determines whether difficulty in sensing self-experience manifests in an eating disorder or in some other difficulty or disorder? How is recovering from an eating disorder different from and similar to recovering from other psychological disorders that derive from difficulty in sensing self-experience? How do men experience impairment in sensing self-experience? With what symptoms do they manifest this difficulty? Again, these are all questions worthy of exploration.

The lack of research on recovering is not limited to the field of eating disorders. Except for detailed psychoanalytic case studies, formal study of patients' experience of their disorder and of recovery is rare to nonexistent across all psychiatric diagnoses. One exception is the exploration of depression in women by Dana Crowley Jack (1991), who relied upon depressed women to provide "insight into the nature of depression in women . . . because they are the ones who know about their paths into depression as well as the ways that lead out of it" (24). Both Jack's work and my own reveal the power of combining a systematic research method with a detailed exploration of people's subjective experience. This combination allows us to bring experiential expertise to bear upon our understanding of etiology and change. As Beresin said to me, "Just imagine what we would learn if we asked people with schizophrenia what it is like to give up a long-held delusion or asked people with manic-depressive illness how taking lithium has changed their sense of self and their experience of themselves in relationships."

IMPLICATIONS FOR NOMENCLATURE

THE MISNAMING OF EXPERIENCE

It is commonly agreed that bulimia nervosa and anorexia nervosa are misnomers: the former is not characterized by ox hunger, nor the latter by a loss of appetite. Why, other than for reasons of custom and inertia, do we abide the misnaming of these disorders? And at what cost does misnaming come? Conversely, what difference would a name change make, given that bulimia nervosa and anorexia nervosa by any other names would be the same disorders?

Recovering from anorexia nervosa or bulimia nervosa requires coming to sense self-experience. The women I interviewed indicate that the accurate sensing of self-experience is fostered by, among many things, sensing voice, sensing that one matters, knowing what to expect in the process of change, and sensing others' (and one's own) curiosity about one's subjective experience. These phenomena suggest the following questions: Does the misnaming of bulimia nervosa contribute to disconnection from self-experience? Does the experience of people with bulimia nervosa matter enough for us to name it accurately? Can we choose a name that educates us about the fundamental psychic disruption to which disordered eating is a response and makes us curious to know more?

There is precedent for renaming psychiatric disorders. Dissociative identity disorder is the DSM-IV name for what was formerly called multiple personality disorder. The new name is arguably a more precise, descriptive term. The most recently identified eating disorder, binge-eating disorder, also has a straightforward, descriptive name.

Renaming is a complex task. A new name must have, to use the terms loosely, both face validity and construct validity. It must be concise. It must be compelling enough to motivate people to exchange the old name for the new one. It must not inadvertently accentuate the shame associated with the disorder. But neither can it be a euphemism, patronizing in its political correctness.

I believe that the terms *anorexia nervosa* and *bulimia nervosa* not only mystify but also romanticize these disorders. Eating disorders are a means by which women experience themselves as special, distinctive. To have a disorder with an exotic name reinforces the use of the disorder as a means of feeling special, when in fact the challenge for someone with an eating disorder is to discover the preferences, talents, capacities, sensibilities, and experiences that make her the singular person she is.

RECOVERING AND DISCOVERING

The women's accounts indicate not only what recovering might be but also what it might *not* be. When someone is ill, we assume that she wants to recover. Implicit in that assumption is the assumption that she wants to get *back* to a former state. But what I hear from the women is not metaphors of return, repair, mending, restoring something to an original state. While women who recover from bulimia nervosa reestablish healthy eating patterns and regain a sense of authenticity, what is most salient to them is not *re*covering something they once had but *dis*covering capacities they had never fully experienced and learning to acknowledge and accept aspects of themselves that had never been acknowledged or accepted. (Bruch, 1988, also noted that recovering involves discovering.)

Penelope Metropolis pointed out to me that these women struggle with "what can be held on to, in some cases very fiercely" (their bulimic symptoms, another person's voice) and "what is gotten rid of" (through the acts of purging and hiding). She noted that we come to discover a sense of self in part by discovering our answers to discriminating questions: "What is me? What is somebody else? What is society? What is a notion that I'm temporarily trying on versus something that is core and germane to who I am?" In learning to discriminate, the women come to discern what they want to take in and keep and what they want to reject and leave out. They no longer have to take in everything and keep next to nothing.

The concepts of discrimination and self-discovery shed light on the links between the physical and psychological symptoms of bulimia nervosa. The taking in of what is palatable and the rejection of what is not are manifest in the physical symptoms of bingeing and purging as well as in the psychological dynamics of the disorder. Bulimic women not only feel as if they are disgusting but, in vomiting, make clear that what they have taken in disgusts them. This phenomenon makes sense in terms of the dynamics of emotional invalidation: if a child's attempts to be close to the valued other repeatedly result in shame as a consequence of emotional invalidation, she learns that taking another in to meet an emotional need is distasteful and shameful. But if she cannot take in and psychically hold on to another person, her relational needs go unmet and she craves connection. How can she allow in and retain the good, palatable aspects of the relationship but not absorb the toxic shame with which the relationship is laced? How can she psychologically hold on to an other who is both good and bad? How can she discover, hold, and accept herself knowing that her self comprises both good and bad?

IMPLICATIONS FOR ETIOLOGY AND PREVENTION

Although the cure for a disorder does not necessarily point to its cause, much less untangle a complex causal web, the finding that recovering from bulimia nervosa requires coming to sense self-experience suggests that vulnerability to the disorder results from difficulty in sensing self-experience. We need to consider what risk factors impair girls' and young women's ability to sense self-experience. A core sense of shame is arguably a common link between risk factors and the development of bulimia nervosa. Many of the putative risk factors for bulimia nervosa—including vulnerability to childhood obesity, early menarche, parental absence or underinvolvement, parental criticism (especially about eating, shape, and weight), parental discord, high parental expectations, emotional abuse, physical abuse, and sexual abuse (Fairburn, 1994)—would leave someone at risk for internalized shame and/or body shame. The links between internalized shame and body shame deserve study, as do the links among risk factors, shame, deficits in self-structure and self-regulatory capacities, the use of dissociation as a defense, cultural influences, developmental demands, and biological vulnerability. We need to consider how the nature and severity of a given risk factor, its duration, and its timing in development affect internalized shame, body shame, and impaired self-sensing as well as the severity of bulimia nervosa, the course and chronicity of the disorder, the concomitance of other disorders, and the process of recovering.

I asked the women whether anything could have prevented their becoming bulimic. Many say that nothing short of an entirely different family experience could have prevented their eating disorder. Some are grateful for their eating disorder because it brought their psychological difficulties to such a pitch that they had to deal with them. For example, Leslie says: "It was definitely a catalyst for—it's funny, I think it was my bottoming out. These are alcohol terms. I needed to get that sick to realize I had a problem. And to realize that what I thought was normal and what was me was not normal . . . And that I needed to talk about it. So I guess it was a catalyst for all the recovery."

Abigail, too, is grateful that her symptoms got bad enough that she was motivated to do something to claim her life: "I wouldn't have wanted it. But I'd rather have it than thirty more years of misery. Of not living my life. So I guess what I would've preferred would be in some way to have had the knowing and the demand to live myself and not to have been so willing to put up with the things that discouraged and prevented me and tried to squelch that part of me."

When I ask Abigail what advice she has for parents, she replies: "Just to watch what your child experiences and feels and says and not to worry, just to notice that the child's different from you . . . It's hard to do. Allow the child to develop and express themselves as much as you can while also trying to guide them toward what you think is right."

Jill says parents need to let their child know that she is inherently okay: "I just wanted to know that my parents thought I was okay the way I was, and I didn't get that. And I think somehow, if you have a child that has an eating disorder, somehow they don't feel like they're okay. You've gotta let them know that they are. I don't know how you do that . . . If you can let your kids know that they're okay the way they are. I don't know what else you can do."

Amy advises parents to appreciate a child for who she is: "When I have children, I'm not gonna focus on whether, okay, they made it on the baseball team so they're successful. Just being who they are is gonna mean that they're successful. 'Cause I think that's what parents do a lot is judge their child's success by concrete, tangible type of things that they accomplish."

The women suggest that prevention efforts should focus on fostering and sustaining in girls and young women the capacity to sense self-experience. This effort needs to begin in infancy and continue through childhood, adolescence, and adulthood. We need to listen to these women when they say that early and chronic experiences in their families laid the foundation for their eating disorder. It is natural to point to culture as the culprit. But if we pin too much of the responsibility on culture, we ignore what we know about how early developmental experiences predispose a girl to develop an eating disorder. We fail to acknowledge what we know about the origins of shame and about how internalized shame diminishes a sense of personal worth.

It is fair to say that while culture alone does not cause eating disorders, it can and does foster them. Shame and self-doubt flourish in an environment in which people treat themselves and one another as objects, and in which people's worth is based on appearance, accomplishments, and other partial aspects of self rather than on character, authenticity, and fullness of being. In such an environment, a child does not learn to sense her wholeness and worth. She learns instead that her only chance of feeling worthy is to strive for some inhuman standard of physical perfection. When a young woman, already at risk for profound disconnection from self for the reasons discussed in Chapter 1, grows up in such a culture, she is at great risk for exacerbated shame, self-hatred, and self-destructive acts. She is apt to try to compensate for her sense of not being good enough by being perfectionist, competitive, driven, high-achieving, and people-pleasing. If she encounters a challenge to her already brittle sense of worth, she may start to diet in the hope that recasting her body will allow her to achieve even greater perfection and control, win her the approval of others, and thereby enable her to feel good enough. Dieting and other ways of striving for perfection are counters to, not means to, a sense of enoughness. Such striving knows no limits: a young woman who believes she needs to be perfect never feels she is beautiful enough, lean enough, toned enough, accomplished enough, desirable enough, good enough.

But not every young woman who grows up in this culture develops an eating disorder, and not every girl who develops eating-disorder symptoms develops a full-blown clinical disorder. The women's accounts suggest that the self-hatred that leaves a girl vulnerable to an eating disorder, while promoted and perpetuated by culture, is born of her experience in her family. I submit that culture is not the only or even the primary factor in the development of an eating disorder. Parents, often without realizing it and sometimes with the best of intentions, do participate in the development and maintenance of their daughter's disorder. Blaming parents for a child's eating disorder is unhelpful and even harmful, but sparing parents the knowledge of how they contribute to the disorder is also detrimental. Both assuming too much shame and guilt and trying to avoid those feelings are defensive maneuvers that protect one from learning. Protecting parents from learning about their role does a disservice to both the parents and their daughter.

Isabella, when asked what advice she has for parents, replies:

It's so hard. A lot of parents seem to think it's a reflection of themselves.

Is it?

It may be, but there's nothing you can do about the past, and I guess it's working on communicating now, and in the future, and expressing things to each other, and accepting. You can't do anything about the past . . . So you have to accept where you're at.

Ruth Striegel-Moore (1994) points out that prevention efforts need to target multiple populations at multiple points in development and multiple times. The women's experience suggests that prevention efforts also need to involve multiple generations, focusing not only on girls and young women but also on their parents and the many other adults in the village required to raise a child. Teachers, coaches, and other adults can play a protective role by helping girls sense their own worth. Adults can help girls and young women celebrate the natural growth and development of their bodies, grieve the loss of the bodies they have known, recognize continuities in themselves despite the changes of puberty and adolescence, and sense an internal gauge of "enough." The experience of both celebrating and grieving the changes in one's body is especially important to young women who once engaged in athletic activities, such as gymnastics and running, which their bodies literally outgrew. They need adults to help them know and bear their sense of loss, frustration, fear, injustice, anger, and shame and claim the grace and strength of their woman's bodies.

When I ask Meg whether, when her running times slowed, anyone acknowledged her experience of her body's growth and development, she talks about the reasons for her own decision to coach girls:

No. And if someone had been able to do it—but I don't think, there wasn't anyone who could have. Except for maybe my father. But he was so into me being an athlete that I didn't wanna disappoint him.

And your coach didn't—

No, no, no. No, and that's one of the biggest reasons I think that it's good for—I never had a female coach. And I really think it's important for women to coach girls. I think that there are men who can coach girls effectively if they understand well enough what's going on. But I think at that age particularly there's so much going on with girls' developing bodies and so much self-consciousness about their bodies that it's rare where you'll find a girl who will reach their potential, just because they're so uncomfortable with their bodies that they can't let themselves completely be free of their mind's control of their bodies.

When I speak of a multigenerational approach to prevention, I mean not only that we need to involve multiple generations in the lives of children today but that we need to think about how to prevent eating disorders in future generations of children. The emotional invalidation that contributes to shame and disconnection from self is no doubt transmitted across generations. How does one help someone attune to her experience of self if one is not able to attune to one's own self-experience? Kate suggests that for her parents to have been attuned and responsive to her, they themselves would have needed different childhood experiences:

Do you think anything could've prevented your developing bulimia?

A complete restructuring of my family life [*laughs*]. I think if my father had been a different person.

What kind?

A little more open. A little less critical. Both my parents are very critical.

But you target your father even more than your mother?

Yeah, I do actually . . . I think the problem, for myself, the problem can be traced back to my relationship with my father . . . I think if he were more open, more willing, or more able—I shouldn't say willing, he may have been very willing and just not able to express positive ideas. I always knew when he was angry, but I never knew when he was glad about something I did or when he thought something I did was really great . . . I think if that had been different. Which would mean their childhoods would have to have been different. It probably goes back a hundred years. Who knows how much further it goes back?

Our deepest knowledge of how a person senses herself, respects herself, and claims her wholeness necessarily derives from our own experience of who and what in our lives fostered and interfered with our capacity to sense and respect and be our whole selves. As Suzanne Repetto Renna has noted, we tend to treat others as we ourselves are treated. Therefore, in every encounter in which we promote a young person's capacity to sense and trust her own internal experience, our efforts will reach across time to touch the next generation, the children she will one day parent, as well as those she will teach, counsel, mentor, and befriend over the course of her life.

I hear many young women balk at the suggestion that their job is not to be a perfect person but to be authentically and fully the person they are. When I ask them what they fear, they reply, in effect, "If I were not trying to be perfect, I would have no motivation or standards. I would lose my drive and determination. I would become complacent. I would settle for mediocrity. I would be lazy. I would get fat. I would hate myself." Abigail says: "It's scary, what will happen if you're not a doctor or a lawyer or if you don't get all A's? Or the fear about being 300 pounds and undesirable. That's the fears . . . people think that they're gonna just turn into something horrible." They assume that motivation can derive only from obedience to external standards and from others' applause for what they do. They do not know that motivation can arise from within, from their own initiative, industry, playfulness, purpose, creativity, care, mastery, and meaning and from their own desire to make a difference. They do not know that they can strive for excellence while feeling connected to rather than dissociated from their sense of self. They do not know that striving for wholeness rather than perfection frees one to love, work, and play with zest.

One of the most important ways in which adults can promote children's ability to sense self-experience is by serving as models of people who are vitally connected to self and others; who try to integrate base and noble aspects of themselves; who can tolerate shame and guilt but are not ruled by shame and guilt; who have personal standards but accept themselves; who acknowledge their limitations but respect themselves;

and who feel free to create a life that is rich and meaningful, albeit imperfect. Adults must embody these fundamental antidotes to eating disorders. We must demonstrate by our own lives that an imperfect life is not only well worth living but preferable to a grim life devoted to the doomed pursuit of perfection. An imperfect life is as good as it gets. And as good as it gets has got to be good enough.

When I ask people what the opposite of an eating disorder is, they are typically stumped. "Not dieting?" someone will venture. "Healthy eating and normal weight?" I propose that the opposite of an eating disorder is accepting and respecting oneself as one is and yet striving to develop one's potential as an increasingly whole, complex person. Abigail recalls when she first began to wonder what else there was to her besides her beauty and her academic and professional success:

> There are a lot of things I remember Dr. Parker saying to me, but he would say to me something like, "Am I not lovable, do I have to be a successful person, a thin woman, do I have to be all those things to be lovable?" And I thought, "Yes, of course. What else is there?" And I remember going home, thinking, "There's nothing else. There's nothing else to me but that." And it didn't feel right, but I couldn't identify what he was talking about. People weren't happy with me if I wasn't successful, if I wasn't beautiful, if I wasn't thin. People wouldn't love me.

Abigail is asking the right question: What else is there? The "what else" is what Joan Erikson has called our fundamental capacities, among them our capacities for competence, creativity, gratitude, grace, love, loyalty, compassion, courage, playfulness, passion, intelligence, and integrity. We also have darker capacities, for greed, ungratefulness, envy, excess, disdain, deception, hatred, hostility, intolerance, indifference, resentment, and self-righteousness. To be whole, we do not need to let our darker capacities run amok in reckless action. But we do need to experience them in feeling and to appreciate the full range of our capacities. What Abigail calls "spirit" is the vitality that comes with claiming our capacities: "There's this spirit in people, and that's what makes people beautiful is when that spirit is fed and healthy." We must appreciate the human capacities of the young people we know if we are to help them rely upon their complexity, authenticity, and depth rather than upon disordered eating for a sense of mastery, specialness, and worth.

In transcribing the tapes of the women's interviews, I was sometimes moved to tears. My tears surprised me, for these women were, by and large, telling me stories of triumph. I came to understand that I was moved less by their pain than by their courage, their dignity, and the nobility of their struggle to know themselves, to accept themselves, and to live their lives with a fullness of spirit. That recovering is difficult was not news to me, but my respect for the strength and bravery it requires is all the greater for having heard these stories.

Appendix
References
Acknowledgments
Index

APPENDIX:
RESEARCH ON RECOVERY

Context of the Study

What we know about recovery from bulimia nervosa derives from research, clinical, and autobiographical perspectives on recovering. In this book I integrate those perspectives by bringing clinical experience to bear upon rigorous research on the subjective experience of change.

PROFESSIONAL PERSPECTIVES

There are three types of formal research on recovering: research on the course of the disorder, research on outcome, and research on the process of change. Studies of the course, or natural history, of the disorder aim to chart how symptoms manifest, progress, and remit over time. Such studies indicate that bulimia nervosa is a chronic and episodic disorder with high rates of relapse and recurrence, that some people with anorexia nervosa eventually "cross over" and develop a diagnosis of bulimia nervosa, and that some fewer people cross over from bulimia nervosa to anorexia nervosa.

Outcome studies aim both to assess outcome status—degree of recovery—and to determine to what extent specific predictor variables predict outcome status. Treatment-outcome studies aim to determine how effective different treatments are. It is hard to compare outcome studies because the populations under study may differ greatly depending upon selection factors, including diagnostic criteria, failure-to-participate rates, failure-to-trace rates, whether the subjects have ever had a diagnosis of another eating disorder or another psychiatric disorder, and whether subjects have different subtypes of an eating disorder (Herzog, Keller, and Lavori, 1988; Shaw and Garfinkel, 1990; Thompson and Gans, 1985). Even with similar populations, results may vary because of differences in study design: how recovery is defined; length of follow-up interval; methods of assessment (face-to-face interview, phone interview, questionnaire); and particular measures used.

The difficulty in comparing studies notwithstanding, researchers report recovery rates for people with bulimia nervosa ranging from 13 to 69 percent in studies of medium- to long-term follow-up. No factor consistently predicts recovery status, although alcohol abuse, suicide attempts, increased bingeing and vomiting at baseline, increased depression at follow-up, and coexisting personality disorder tend to be associated with poor outcome (Brotman, Herzog, and Hamburg, 1988; Fahy and Russell, 1993; Fallon et al., 1991; Fichter, Quadflieg, and Rief, 1992; Herzog, Keller, and Lavori, 1988; Herzog et al., 1991; Herzog et al., 1993; Keller et al., 1992; Mitchell et al., 1989).

Studies of process aim to discern the mechanisms, pathways, and experience of change. There are few studies of how people experience the process of recovering from bulimia nervosa, but themes from two such studies are congruent with my findings. Rorty, Yager, and Rossotto (1993) found that their subjects' "determination to recover grew out of being 'fed up' with the disorder and desiring a better life"; that "empathic and caring relationships" with therapists and others were essential; and that "more cognitive rather than behavior components of the disorder, such as distorted attitudes and perceptions toward food and body image, were the most difficult to change" (259). Peters and Fallon (1994) found that recovery from bulimia nervosa "is a process of human development and identity formation" (353), and identified three continua along which their subjects shifted as they recovered: "denial to reality," "alienation to connection," and "passivity to personal power." Themes identified within those continua include shifting from regarding the eating disorder as a solution to experiencing it as a problem, becoming more aware and accepting of their affective states, learning to assert their needs and preferences, and differentiating from family members.

Clinical writings are also sources of information on recovering (Boskind-White and White, 1983/1987; Geist, 1985, 1989; Goodsitt, 1983, 1985, 1997; Rizzuto, 1985, 1988; Sands, 1991; Sugarman and Kurash, 1982). While the clinical literature provides rich perspectives on the process of recovering, it tends to focus on theories, components, and techniques of treatment and to feature the therapist's role. Clients' own experience of change is rarely featured, and helpful experiences outside formal therapeutic contexts receive little or no attention.

With few exceptions, neither the research literature nor the clinical literature focuses on the subjective experience of the process of recovering or features the actual voices and narratives of women who have recovered. Researchers tend to approach interviews by coding themes, counting frequencies of a phenomenon, and converting narratives to numbers or summaries without analyzing how helpful phenomena were experienced as helpful or how those phenomena interacted in the process of change.

The voices of recovered anorexics are heard more frequently in the clinical literature than are those of recovered bulimics (Bruch, 1973, 1978, 1988; Claude-Pierre, 1997; Crisp, 1980; Orbach, 1986; Selvini-Palazzoli, 1985). But again, those voices are rarely heard in the research literature. Only three studies have begun with the premise that we have something to learn by listening to how recovered anorexics describe their experience of recovering (Beresin, Gordon, and Herzog, 1989; Hsu, Crisp, and Callender, 1992; Maine, 1985).

The near-absence of women's voices in the literature is especially striking given that eating-disordered women are often described in the clinical literature with metaphors of the unrecognized and unknown self; the silence of the self; difficulty knowing and voicing needs, desires, and feelings; and the absence of a sense of self-worth.

297

EXPERIENTIAL PERSPECTIVES

By definition, autobiographical accounts of recovery feature the voices of those who have recovered, consider the subjective experience of change, and describe the process of recovering. While such accounts by recovered bulimics (Hall and Cohn, 1992; Miller, 1988/1991; Rowland, 1984), recovered anorexics (Christian, 1986; Heater, 1983; Liu, 1979; MacLeod, 1982; O'Neill, 1982; Way, 1993), and those who have struggled with both anorexia nervosa and bulimia nervosa (Hornbacher, 1998) are detailed and compelling narratives of recovering, we would need a comparative analysis of the accounts to discover patterns among women's subjective experience of change. Even a comparative analysis could not avoid a critical limitation of autobiography: autobiographical narratives are likely to be more distilled and tidied up than interview accounts. Although interview participants also shape their responses, interviews allow the tracing of associations, the exploration of apparent contradictions and omissions, and other sustained and detailed inquiries, and consequently may yield rawer, richer data.

QUALITATIVE RESEARCH

In an effort to combine the power of research, clinical, and experiential forms of expertise, I used what Carol Gilligan, in a course at the Harvard Graduate School of Education, has called "clinical interviewing as a method of inquiry." While most research on recovery has focused on objective, quantifiable changes in behavioral symptoms, my effort was to explore subjective aspects of recovering that are not quantifiable but that are worthy of study. The term "qualitative research" is vague and problematic, often misunderstood as a definition-by-negation, used to indicate what the research is not—quantitative—rather than what it is. The very vagueness of the term contributes to the impression that qualitative methods are in essence unmethodical.

The question is not whether quantitative or qualitative research is better but rather which research methods best address which sorts of questions. For instance, prospective, naturalistic research on the course of an eating disorder necessarily relies upon observational, descriptive methods to address such questions as which aspects of the disorder change first and which aspects are most resistant to change. Experimental outcome research requires quantitative methods, standardized protocols, and statistical analyses to address such questions as whether the duration of the disorder when people present for treatment predicts how recovered they will be at a later time and whether one type of treatment is more or less effective than others. And research on process typically relies upon phenomenological interviews in which the researcher follows the threads of a participant's subjective experience. Analysis of those interviews enables a researcher to discern what phenomena are experienced as helpful in the process of recovering; how such phenomena are experienced as helpful; and how these phenomena interact with one another in real, lived experience.

Where experimental outcome research and quantitative methods assume that the research community has some agreement around what constitute meaningful outcome criteria and meaningful predictors of good and poor outcome, and where they aim to make connections between those variables more precise, phenomenological research attempts to discern new phenomena; to detail the actual events, mechanisms, and processes that link phenomena; and to challenge existing assumptions and understandings.*

I take issue with the methodological maxim that quantitative research is hypothesis testing while qualitative research is hypothesis generating. Both types of research yield, confirm, and disconfirm causal explanations. Maxwell (1996) argues that questions of *variance* ("whether

---

*Michael Basseches supplied this explanation, derived from the work of Jürgen Habermas, of the different interests—technical, practical, and emancipatory, respectively—of empirical/analytic, interpretive/hermeneutic, and critical research.

and to what extent variance in x causes variance in y") are best addressed with quantitative methods while questions of *process* ("*how* x plays a role in causing y") are best addressed with qualitative methods (20). Miles and Huberman (1994) describe how qualitative research can produce causal theories:

> We consider qualitative analysis to be a very powerful method for assessing causality . . . Qualitative analysis, with its close-up look, can identify *mechanisms,* going beyond sheer association. It is unrelentingly local, and deals well with the *complex* network of events and processes in a situation. It can sort out the *temporal* dimension, showing clearly what preceded what, either through direct observation or *retrospection.* It is well equipped to cycle back and forth between *variables* and *processes*—showing that stories are not capricious, but include underlying variables, and that variables are not disembodied, but have connections over time. (147)

Phenomenological research generates what Glaser and Strauss (1967) call "grounded theory," that is, explanation grounded in the rich data of interviews.

The in-depth analyses of cases that lead to the generation of theory about how something works do not require the large numbers of subjects that quantitative methods do. Qualitative studies aim to analyze a *process,* not a *population.* Where quantitative research relies on random sampling and large samples to be able to generalize from a representative sample to a population and to discern differences in populations, qualitative research relies on the exhaustive mining of a small number of carefully chosen examples to be able to generalize to the nature of a particular process.

Much of the research on girls and women with eating disorders has been done in medical contexts, funded by government agencies, and published in medical and psychiatric journals—all contexts and traditions dominated by men and by a research model which values quantitative data over qualitative data. In these contexts, objective, quantifiable data are generally referred to as "good, hard data," while subjective, narrative data are disparagingly called "soft." The language itself reveals the association of narrative with women and of women with inferiority. As research on women's development indicates, we misunderstand girls' and women's experience when we base our understanding on studies of boys and men, conducted by men, and fail to understand girls and women in their own terms (Chodorow, 1978; Gilligan, 1982/1993; Jack, 1991; Miller, 1976; Belenky et al., 1986).

INCLUSION CRITERIA AND RECRUITMENT

I recruited participants via referrals from colleagues, notices in a self-help group newsletter, and posters on health club bulletin boards. I screened for the following criteria:

1. *Diagnosis and duration:* full DSM-III-R criteria for bulimia nervosa for at least six months; no history or only a brief history of DSM-III-R anorexia nervosa.
2. *Age of onset:* 14–22 years.
3. *Definition and duration of recovery:* a Psychiatric Status Rating (PSR) of 1 ("usual self") or 2 ("residual") for bulimia nervosa for at least one and not more than four years, including at present. Both ratings specify that the person no longer binges or purges, although with a "residual" rating the person may still fight the impulse to do so (Herzog et al., 1993).

An exclusion criterion was that a participant not be a student at the university where I am a counselor. The women agreed to participate without remuneration. When I later received modest funding, I sent each a token sum.

INSTRUMENTS AND PROTOCOL

I interviewed each of the thirteen participants for three to four hours in one or two sessions in my office or in her home. I first asked participants to construct a chronology of their eating disorder. The balance of the interview included open-ended questions drawn from an interview guide which I adapted from Beresin, Gordon, and Herzog (1989). My interview questions derived from the following research questions:

1. What do formerly bulimic women regard as the most important changes they experienced in recovering?
2. To what do they attribute the changes they made in recovering?
3. What did they experience as helpful and harmful, both in and out of formal treatment? How were those contexts and factors experienced as helpful and harmful?
4. What experiences marked a shift in their readiness to change or in their belief that they could change? What made those pivotal experiences possible?
5. How did they experience their ambivalence about changing and recovering and continue to recover in the face of that ambivalence?
6. What features did they find easiest to change? Hardest to change?
7. What did they gain, or most appreciate, in recovering? What did they lose, or miss most?
8. What aspects of the eating disorder persist?
9. How do the women maintain the changes they made?
10. What do they understand to be the psychological function the eating disorder served for them?
11. What, to their minds, led to their developing bulimia nervosa?
12. Do they believe their disorder could have been prevented? How?

PARTICIPANTS

The informed consent form which each participant signed explained that my use of her interviews would protect her anonymity but not her confidentiality (Seidman, 1991). I have changed the names of all persons, schools, hospitals, cities, and countries, but I informed each participant that despite these measures, it is possible that someone who knows her well would recognize her from her story. I have edited excerpts for readability. Where I omit content and substance, I indicate the omission with an ellipsis, but where I omit "um," "er," repetition, and halting starts, I do not note the omission.

I conducted the interviews at a time when DSM-III-R criteria were the standard of diagnosis for bulimia nervosa. Those criteria have since been superseded by those of the DSM-IV, but from the information I have about participants' symptom histories, it appears that all of them met DSM-IV criteria for bulimia nervosa.

The DSM-III-R criteria are as follows (with DSM-IV revisions shown in brackets):

- Recurrent episodes of binge eating (rapid consumption of a large amount of food in a discrete period of time [two hours]).
- A feeling of lack of control over eating behavior during the eating binges.
- The person regularly engages in either self-induced vomiting, use of laxatives or diuretics, strict dieting or fasting, or vigorous exercise in order to prevent weight gain.
- A minimum average of two binge eating episodes a week for at least three months. [Compensatory behaviors also occur at least twice a week for three months.]
- Persistent overconcern with [self-evaluation unduly influenced by] body shape and weight.
- [The disturbance does not occur exclusively during episodes of anorexia nervosa. Also, DSM-IV differentiates between purging and nonpurging types of bulimia nervosa.]

All thirteen participants were Caucasian; twelve were from North America. (No people of color replied to my recruitment letters or ads although many women of color do have eating disorders.) Three were married. All had education beyond the high school level.

At the worst point of their disorder, all participants met at least "definite criteria" (a PSR score of 5); five would have had a score of 6, the highest PSR score, which corresponds to "definite criteria—severe" (Herzog et al., 1993). Most reported that their disorder was episodic, with a full-syndrome symptom level alternating with a subclinical level.

For eight women vomiting was the main means of purging; for three, laxatives; for one, both vomiting and laxatives; and for one, who is diabetic, vomiting and manipulation of insulin dosing. Most had tried both laxatives and vomiting at some point, and all had engaged in some additional compensatory behavior (fasting, diet pills, exercise). Two had a history of anorexia nervosa, but bulimia was their predominant eating disorder. Four reported childhood physical or sexual abuse, and two reported experiences of date rape in adolescence.*

I gathered demographic information, an eating-disorder history, and a treatment history by way of a questionnaire and the interview itself. The following sketches summarize the symptom and treatment histories of the thirteen participants.

———

Abigail, 30, works as a psychiatrist. She is single. She developed overconcern with her weight and shape around age 16, began bingeing at 17, dieting seriously at 18, and vomiting and using laxatives at 18, and at times also used diet pills, fasting, restrictive eating, and excessive exercise to counter the effects of bingeing. She met full DSM-III-R criteria for bulimia nervosa episodically at ages 18–26. Her bingeing and purging diminished gradually. She has met recovery criteria since age 26. Height 5'7", weight 135 lbs.

Her first psychotherapy referral was at age 23 to a therapist she found unattuned to her. Another referral at 25 was helpful, as was individual cognitive-behavioral therapy at 25–26 and psychodynamic therapy from age 26 to the present. She also found alternative healing methods—massage, bodywork, and yoga—particularly helpful. She is still somewhat compulsive about exercising.

———

Amy, 26, has a bachelor's degree and works as a supervisor in a corporation. She is married to Mark. She developed overconcern with her weight and shape around age 14, started bingeing at 13, dieting at 14, and using laxatives at 17, and at times also used diet pills, fasting, severely

———

*Some women with eating disorders have histories of trauma, including sexual abuse (Beckman and Burns, 1990; Connors and Morse, 1993; Welch and Fairburn, 1994; Pope and Hudson, 1992). I asked about sexual abuse only if a participant indicated that she had been sexually abused and was prepared to talk about it.

restrictive eating, and excessive exercise. She met full DSM-III-R criteria for bulimia nervosa at ages 17–18. She had a serious subclinical eating disorder at 18–22 and again, episodically, at 22–25. She stopped laxative abuse at age 25 and has met recovery criteria since then. Height 5'5½", weight 155 lbs.

She first sought help from a nutritionist, Monica, at 24, referred by a physical therapist, and found the sessions very helpful. The nutritionist referred her to a psychologist, Sally, whom she saw for only three months. Her exercising still verges on the excessive.

Several months after seeing the physical therapist, nutritionist, and therapist, Amy broke up with her boyfriend because she did not feel he cherished her. This self-affirming act followed her sister's having been hospitalized for a manic episode. As Amy was attending to her sister and her parents, she realized that no one had ever taken such good care of *her* or accepted *her* so fully. She made a vow to take care of herself and to accept her own needs and desires as legitimate.

Beth, 27, has a bachelor's degree and works as a case manager in a mental health clinic. She is married to Andy. She developed overconcern with her weight and shape around age 11, started bingeing at 12, dieting at 13, and vomiting at 14, and at times also used laxatives, diet pills, fasting, severely restrictive eating, and excessive exercise. She met full DSM-III-R criteria for bulimia nervosa at ages 18–22 (except during three months of hospitalization at age 21) and again for several months at age 25. She appears to have met DSM-III-R criteria for anorexia nervosa at about age 20. She episodically had a serious subclinical eating disorder at 14–18 and again at 22–24. She stopped bingeing and purging at 25 and has met recovery criteria since then. Height 5'2½", weight 111 lbs.

She first sought help from a counselor (Dr. Stahl) on her college campus, and later saw a second counselor (Dr. Locke) for both individual and group therapy (ages 20–21). While those were helpful experiences, Dr. Locke told her she needed to leave college to get treatment. She returned home and at age 20 began individual therapy with another therapist, who urged her to enter an inpatient treatment center. Just after her 21st birthday she overdosed on an antidepressant and was hospitalized overnight. She continued seeing the therapist, but did not enter inpatient treatment until several months later. The inpatient program included a twelve-step component (Overeaters Anonymous), which she eventually found helpful. After three months in that program, she returned home and resumed outpatient therapy. After several months she returned to college, continued group therapy on campus (ages 21–22), and irregularly attended OA meetings. She remained somewhat symptomatic. After a major relapse at 25, she decided to begin working the steps of OA. Since then she has not binged or purged. She is still active in OA. Medication: Imipramine, then Desipramine for depression and bulimic symptoms.

Claire, 25, is in a bachelor's program in psychology, having already been trained and employed as a registered nurse. She works in a psychiatric hospital on a clinical research team. She is single. She developed overconcern with her weight and shape around age 15, started bingeing at 16, dieting at 17–18, and using laxatives at 19, and at times also used fasting, severely restrictive eating, and excessive exercise. She met full DSM-III-R criteria for bulimia nervosa at ages 20–23; she had a serious subclinical eating disorder at 19–20 and again at 23–24. Her bingeing and purging diminished gradually. She has met recovery criteria since age 24. Height 5'4", weight 135 lbs.

She has had no psychotherapy. At age 23 she had surgery to remove benign ovarian and uterine tumors and says that her doctors' failure to heed her warnings about a heart condition and bleeding tendency caused life-threatening complications. This experience left her with indignation and a sense of self-determination: "Only you can look after yourself." During this time she lived with her boyfriend, Tom. Although the relationship was problematic and did not last, Tom did support her recovering by believing in her intellectual ability, encouraging her intellectual and poetic pursuits, and demonstrating care and affection. These efforts helped her to believe in and care for herself. She also found exercise helpful (swimming, aerobics, and martial arts), but exercise itself became excessive. She now uses laxatives only to relieve constipation, but says she must eventually stop using them altogether.

Claire reported childhood sexual abuse by a male relative and one incident of abuse by a male stranger at age 12.

———

Gita, 31 (32 by our second interview), works as an elementary school teacher. She has a master's degree in education. She is married to Paul, and they have one child. She developed overconcern with her weight and shape around age 15, started dieting at 17 and bingeing and vomiting at 19, and at times also used fasting, severely restrictive eating, and excessive exercise. She met full DSM-III-R criteria for bulimia nervosa at ages 19–20, 21–22, and approximately 25–28. After that she had subclinical symptoms. During and after college she developed a reliance upon alcohol. Her bulimic symptoms diminished gradually. She has met recovery criteria since age 30. Height 5'4", weight 117 lbs.

She had about five sessions of individual therapy at 25, as "a precursor" to group therapy for people with eating disorders (25–26). She found the group unhelpful, even harmful. During this time she lived with Paul and witnessed his healthy approach to eating. At age 30 she injured her back and saw an acupuncturist. His whole-person approach was helpful with some of her eating-disorder symptoms. Around this time she also had three sessions with a cognitive-behavioral therapist, in part to help her manage her expression of anger. She also cut out caffeine and reduced her alcohol consumption.

At age 30 she became pregnant. Her pregnancy marked the end of her bulimic symptoms. While pregnant and while nursing, she felt an imperative to nourish and care for herself so she could nourish and care for her child. She become more self-attuned, more accepting of her limitations, and clearer about what mattered to her.

Isabella, 31, has one master's degree and is about to begin a master's program in social work. She is divorced. She developed overconcern with her weight and shape around age 17, started dieting and bingeing at 18 and vomiting at 20, and at times used dieting, severely restrictive dieting, and excessive exercise. Having developed diabetes at 11, she also manipulated her insulin dosing to regulate her weight. She met full DSM-III-R criteria for bulimia nervosa at ages 18–28. Her bulimic symptoms diminished gradually. She has met recovery criteria since age 29. Height 5'7", weight 130 lbs.

Isabella's symptoms persisted despite several years of outpatient therapy. At 28 she was hospitalized for diabetic ketoacidosis resulting from intentional insulin manipulation. That hospitalization led to an inpatient hospitalization for her eating disorder. After hospitalization, she entered both group and individual therapy with Carol. She also separated from her husband, who had been emotionally and physically abusive. She also began meditating. Medication: Nortriptyline for anxiety.

Isabella reported sexual abuse at 14 by her sister's husband and at 15 by a friend's father.

Jessie, 25, works as a supervisor in a large corporation. She has attended some college. She is single with a serious boyfriend. At age 14 she developed overconcern with her weight and shape, started fasting and dieting, and developed anorexia nervosa. She received outpatient individual and group therapy, medical monitoring, and nutritional consultation at 14–16. By age 16 she had returned to a normal weight, but she began bingeing and vomiting. At times she also used laxatives to counter the effects of bingeing. She met full DSM-III-R criteria for bulimia nervosa at 16–23. Her bulimic symptoms diminished gradually. She has met recovery criteria since age 23. Height 5'7", weight 150 lbs.

In her early twenties Jessie developed a cocaine habit, which she kicked on her own. She sought outpatient therapy for bulimia nervosa (age 22 or 23), but did not click with the therapist. She was later referred to Helen, and found that therapy (ages 23–25) helpful. She still checks in with Helen occasionally. Through being mentored and believed in by her supervisor at work, she began to develop a sense of competence and worth.

Jessie reported childhood sexual abuse by her father from age 4 through 7 or 8.

———

Jill, 30, has a bachelor's degree and works as an officer in a bank. She is single. At age 16 she developed overconcern with her weight and shape and started fasting, dieting, bingeing, and vomiting. She also used laxatives, diet pills, fasting, and excessive exercise. She met full DSM-III-R criteria for bulimia nervosa at ages 16–24. Her bulimic symptoms diminished gradually. She has met recovery criteria since age 26. Height 5'7", weight 150 lbs.

At 22 Jill overdosed on alcohol and was hospitalized overnight. That experience led her to join Alcoholics Anonymous. She sought outpatient therapy for bulimia nervosa at 24 when she realized that her failure to progress in AA was due to her untreated eating disorder. Soon thereafter she sought group therapy as well. She found AA helpful in her recovering from bulimia nervosa. She attributes much of her recovery to the friends she knew through AA, particularly her sponsor, an older woman who offered her unconditional acceptance.

Jill alluded to a date rape during her college years.

———

Kate, 32, works as an administrative assistant and is attending college part time. She is single. She developed overconcern with her weight and shape around age 13 and began dieting, taking diet pills, and bingeing around 14 and taking laxatives at 17. She took laxatives at 17–21 and again at 25–28. At times she also used diet pills, fasting, restrictive eating, and excessive exercise. She met full DSM-III-R criteria for bulimia nervosa at 17–21 (some laxative abuse; largely bingeing and fasting) and again at 25–28 (laxative abuse). At 22–24 she was not bingeing or purging; this coincides with her relationship with a man to whom she became engaged (they later broke off the engagement). She stopped laxative abuse at 28 and has met recovery criteria since 29. Height 5'6", weight 143 lbs.

At 28 Kate began individual therapy and then group therapy with the same therapist, Linda. Both were very helpful.

———

Leslie, 25, has a master's degree and is in the first year of a doctoral program. She is seriously involved with Ted. She developed overconcern with her weight and shape and started dieting at age 17 and began bingeing at 19 and vomiting at 20. At times she also used diet pills, fasting, and excessive exercise. She met full DSM-III-R criteria for bulimia nervosa at 19–20 and again at 22. Her bulimic symptoms diminished gradually. She has met recovery criteria since age 23. Height 5'4", weight 125 lbs.

At 20 Leslie sought counseling at her college counseling center. When that therapist did not click with her, she sought a referral to a nutritionist. Her experience with the nutritionist was positive. She asked the nutritionist for a referral to a therapist, with whom she had several brief periods of therapy (21–22). At 23 she asked her family to participate in family therapy. Three months of family therapy proved especially helpful.

Leslie reported a date rape at age 16.

———

Meg, 23, has a bachelor's degree and teaches in a private secondary school. She is single. She developed overconcern with her weight and shape and began vomiting at age 15, and started fasting and dieting at 19. At times she also used laxatives. She met full DSM-III-R criteria for bulimia nervosa at 16–21. Her eating-disorder symptoms diminished gradually. She has met recovery criteria since age 22. Height 5'5", weight 135 lbs.

At 20 Meg participated in an intensive outpatient therapy program for people with eating disorders but did not fully commit herself to it. After a semester abroad, during which her symptoms worsened, she entered a residential eating-disorders program (age 20). The seven-week program, including group therapy, individual therapy (with Jennifer), and family therapy, was life-transforming. When she was back in college (age 21), she began to experience a relapse and moved back to her home state to finish college and to work with a psychiatrist. Medication: Prozac, for depressive and obsessive-compulsive symptoms.

———

Rebecca, 27, has a bachelor's degree in nutrition and psychology and is in a graduate program to become a registered dietitian. She is married to Robert. She developed overconcern with her weight and shape around age 15 and started fasting and dieting and using diet pills at 15 and bingeing and vomiting at 16. She met full DSM-III-R criteria for bulimia nervosa at 16–25. Her bingeing and purging diminished gradually. She has met recovery criteria since age 26. Height 5'5", weight 160 lbs.

At 17 Rebecca saw a psychologist but did not find the therapy helpful. During college she participated in an outpatient eating-disorder group at a hospital and a psychoeducational group on campus. The former was unhelpful; the latter interested her, though she felt unready to put what she was learning into practice. At 23 she sought outpatient therapy and group therapy with Susan. These were very helpful. Feeling stuck, she entered an inpatient eating-disorders program at 23. Several months later (at 24), she was hospitalized overnight for dehydration due to an overdose of alcohol compounded by use of diuretics, laxatives, and cocaine. She attributes that episode to Prozac. After that episode she returned to the inpatient eating-disorders unit and found the hospitalization very helpful. She discontinued group therapy at age 26 but still checks in with Susan occasionally, either individually or with her husband. Medication: Desipramine; Imipramine; Prozac; Lithium. She eventually stopped taking medication.

———

Sarah, 24, is a student in a master's degree program in psychology. (By our third interview she was 25, had completed her graduate program, and was working as a counselor.) She is single. She developed over-concern with her weight and shape at age 7 or 8, and began bingeing at 10, fasting and dieting at 14, and vomiting at 17. At times she also used laxatives and dieting/fasting. She met full DSM-III-R criteria for bulimia nervosa at 17–19 and had a subclinical disorder at 15–17 and at 20. She also had a recurrence of symptoms at 22. Her bulimic symptoms diminished dramatically on three occasions when she entered therapy. She has met recovery criteria since age 22. Height 5', weight 150 lbs.

At 19 Sarah sought counseling at her college counseling center. Her symptoms remitted almost immediately, but she then relapsed. At 20 she sought individual therapy with Sonya. Again her symptoms remitted. At 22, when she entered graduate school, she began therapy again, with Annie. Returning home for Christmas, she binged and purged. Annie responded with curiosity and concern and asked Sarah whether she wanted to meet more often. Sarah has not binged or purged since that time. As of our third interview, she had had twice-weekly therapy with Annie for three years and was continuing that therapy. Sarah has a history of panic attacks, beginning in childhood; her panic symptoms include non-induced vomiting.

Sarah reported physical abuse by her brother (13 months older than she) throughout most of her childhood and wondered whether she had been sexually abused.

Making Sense of the Data

I audiotaped the interviews and transcribed them in their entirety. These transcripts were my primary data. I applied the following analytical methods to the women's accounts.

I used *categorizing analysis* to identify common themes and phenomena *across* interviews (Maxwell and Miller, 1993). I derived my analytical method from methods described by Watkins (1977), Charmaz (1983), and Giorgi (1985). The ten-step method involves the progressive distillation and generalization of the interview data.

I also used *contextualizing analysis,* leaving transcripts intact to high-light narrative-structural connections *within* each participant's story (Maxwell and Miller, 1993). I adapted a method from those described by Miller (1991) and Mishler (1986) to write a narrative summary of each participant's experience, then traced the connections in the narrative.

Also following Miller (1991), I *combined* categorizing and contextu-alizing analyses. I moved among the narrative summaries, the categoriz-ing analyses, and the transcripts to learn how themes derived from categorizing analysis were connected in the women's actual experience.

ISSUES OF RELIABILITY AND VALIDITY

COMPARABILITY ACROSS INTERVIEWS

I addressed in four ways the issue of how to compare interviews in which participants might address very different content areas. First, after hav-ing each participant construct a chronology of her eating disorder, I asked a common question: "As you look back on your experience of recovering from bulimia nervosa, what stands out to you?" Second, I established common lines of inquiry and follow-up questions to guide me in the interview, although I was not wedded to the precise wording and order of those questions. Third, while in most of the interview I asked open-ended questions, if a participant did not spontaneously bring up areas of particular interest to me, I asked about them toward the end. And fourth, I was aware that themes and patterns might be more appar-ent in the structure than in the specific content of responses.

REPLICABILITY OF READINGS

In phenomenological research, "replicability of readings" does not refer to the goal that two researchers, given the same transcripts and nothing else, will see the same themes and patterns in the data. Rather, the goal is to describe what one sees and to delineate the steps by which one came to see what one sees so that another observer, equipped with the transcripts and with that description and delineation, could see the data in the same way (Glaser and Strauss, 1967). It is the detailing of one's approach that makes the analysis of transcripts an intentional and systematic method rather than a mere fishing expedition or a foregone confirmation of biases and beliefs.

RELIABILITY AND VALIDITY OF INTERVIEWS

The criticism that formerly eating-disordered people are especially poor informants about their experience is a reasonable one given that denial, distortion, and difficulties in knowing one's inner experience are symptoms of eating disorders. People with eating disorders tend to deny appetite, fatigue, thinness, specific behaviors (vomiting, laxative or diuretic abuse), certain feelings and attitudes, the seriousness of their condition, certain attributions for their symptoms, and even their denial itself (Vitousek, Daly, and Heiser, 1991). They are also considered to be "particularly ill-informed about the variables that shape their lives" and to have "difficulty in recognizing and expressing internal status," and they may be cognitively impaired because of the effects of starvation (650–651).

Recovered individuals are subject to some of the same problems as non-recovered patients. For instance, they may be prone to what Bruch (1978) calls "pseudoagreeing"—parroting the language and theories they have learned in therapy or reporting what they expect the researcher wants to hear, even if they privately see things differently.

I considered that participants might distort or deny or be reserved or overly compliant, but I assumed these difficulties would be less relevant with those who are recovered than with those still in the throes of an eating disorder and less relevant with participants at least one year into recovery than with those only recently asymptomatic.

Even with recovered subjects, how forthcoming they are depends upon the nature and structure of the interview. A subject may be more open in a less structured interview than in one in which she is asked to fit her experience into preconceived categories or hypotheses. In therapy, eating-disordered patients respond poorly when they feel the therapist is trying to see them as typical. They respond better to a collaborative approach which relies on the therapist's genuine curiosity about the patient's experience (Bruch, 1973, 1985; Orbach, 1986; Rizzuto, Peterson, and Reed, 1981; Selvini-Palazzoli, 1985). I aimed to approach the women with respect, curiosity, and gratitude throughout my research.

I also assumed that in a phenomenological interview I could counter distortion by employing Bruch's "constructive use of ignorance." When I suspected denial, oversimplification, or pseudoagreeing by a participant, I discussed my observations and questions with her. I found that my challenges were well received and worked to engage participants' own curiosity about the complexity of their experience.

No doubt the women's willingness to explore complexity was also fostered by their awareness that we had time (three to four hours) to do so. I prefaced interview questions with phrases such as "as you think about it," "in your experience," and "looking back" to help participants connect with their subjective experience. Participants said they welcomed the opportunity to think aloud about things they are rarely asked about and that they found themselves making new connections even as we spoke.

INTERPRETIVE VALIDITY

I addressed issues of interpretive validity using methods described by Maxwell (in a course at the Harvard Graduate School of Education, 1992) and Miles and Huberman (1994). I used the following questions to evaluate the validity of interpretations:

- Does this explanation or interpretation account for all of the data? Which data does it fail to account for?
- Are there other interpretations that could account for more of the data?
- Does any given interpretation or explanation compete with, supplement, or subsume other interpretations? How?

315

COLLABORATIVE INQUIRY

Further studies would do well to use standardized measures to gather a more detailed history of the course of symptom development and remission, assess past and current concomitant disorders, and chart a comprehensive treatment history. But in conducting semi-structured interviews prior to the phenomenological interview, one would need to address the risk of dampening a participant's readiness to describe the complexity of her experience. Standardized diagnostic instruments establish a cooperative rather than collaborative relationship. That is, the participant cooperates by giving information to a researcher who then categorizes it into an existing system of meaning. In a phenomenological interview, the parties collaborate to co-construct a new understanding that neither could construct alone. Even semi-structured diagnostic interviews are more cooperative than collaborative in nature in that they limit a participant's freedom to express her experience in her own terms.

The challenge would be to make clear to participants the distinction between the preliminary assessment measures and the heart of the study, which is the exploration of their actual experience. Each participant would need to know that the structured interviews serve to delineate her symptom and treatment histories in the formal way research requires but that in the balance of the interview she and the interviewer would shift gears and have a more expansive, exploratory conversation about how she experienced her recovering.

REFERENCES

Aisenberg, K. 1994. The fugue state of femininity: Development as dissociation. Paper presented at the Bureau of Study Counsel, Harvard University.

American Psychiatric Association (APA). 1987. *Diagnostic and statistical manual of mental disorders.* 3rd ed. rev. Washington.

———1994. *Diagnostic and statistical manual of mental disorders.* 4th ed. Washington.

Becker, A. E. 1997. Eating disorders and their cultural milieu. Talk presented at a public forum, Culture, the Media, and Eating Disorders, sponsored by the Harvard Eating Disorders Center, 3 Feb. 1997, Harvard University.

Beckman, K. A., and Burns, G. L. 1990. Relation of sexual abuse and bulimia in college women. *International Journal of Eating Disorders, 9,* 487–492.

Belenky, M. F., Clinchy, B. M., Goldberger, N. R., and Tarule, J. M. 1986. *Women's ways of knowing: The development of self, voice, and mind.* New York: Basic Books.

Beresin, E. V., Gordon, C., and Herzog, D. B. 1989. The process of recovering from anorexia nervosa. In J. R. Bemporad and D. B. Herzog, eds., *Psychoanalysis and eating disorders.* New York: Guilford.

Bettelheim, B. 1975/1977. *The uses of enchantment: The meaning and importance of fairy tales.* New York: Vintage.

Boskind-White, M., and White, W. C. Jr. 1987. *Bulimarexia: The binge/purge cycle.* 2nd ed. New York: Norton.

Brotman, A., Herzog, D., and Hamburg, P. 1988. Long-term course in 14 bulimic patients treated with psychotherapy. *Journal of Clinical Psychiatry, 49,* 57–160.

Brown, L. M., and Gilligan, C. 1992. *Meeting at the crossroads: Women's psychology and girls' development.* Cambridge, Mass.: Harvard University Press.

Bruch, H. 1973. *Eating disorders: Obesity, anorexia nervosa, and the person within.* New York: Basic Books.

———1978. *The golden cage: The enigma of anorexia nervosa.* Cambridge, Mass.: Harvard University Press.

———1985. Four decades of eating disorders. In D. M. Garner and P. E. Garfinkel, eds., *Handbook of psychotherapy for anorexia nervosa and bulimia.* New York: Guilford.

———1988. *Conversations with anorexics.* Ed. D. Czyzewski and M. Suhr. New York: Basic Books.

Brumberg, J. J. 1997. *The body project: An intimate history of American girls.* New York: Random House.

Burns, D. 1980/1999. *Feeling good: The new mood therapy.* New York: Avon Books.

Cardeña, E. 1994. The domain of dissociation. In S. J. Lynn and J. W. Rhue, eds., *Dissociation: Clinical and theoretical perspectives.* New York: Guilford.

Charmaz, K. 1983. The grounded theory method: An explication and interpretation. In R. M. Emerson, ed., *Contemporary field research: A collection of readings.* Boston: Little, Brown.

Chess, S., and Thomas, A. 1987. *Origins and evolution of behavior disorders from infancy to early adult life.* Cambridge, Mass.: Harvard University Press.

Chodorow, N. 1978. *The reproduction of mothering.* Berkeley: University of California Press.

Christian, S., with M. Johnson. 1986. *The very private matter of anorexia nervosa.* Grand Rapids, Mich.: Zondervan Books.

Claude-Pierre, P. 1997. *The secret language of eating disorders.* New York: Times Books.

Connors, M. E., and Morse, W. 1993. Sexual abuse and eating disorders: A review. *International Journal of Eating Disorders, 13,* 1–11.

Cooper, P. J., and Fairburn, C. G. 1993. Confusion over the core psychopathology of bulimia nervosa. *International Journal of Eating Disorders, 13,* 385–389.

Crisp, A. H. 1980. *Anorexia nervosa: Let me be.* London: Academic Press.

Demos, E. V. 1993. Developmental foundations for the capacity for self-analysis: Parallels in the roles of caregiver and analyst. In G. W. Barron, ed., *Self-analysis: Critical inquiries, personal visions.* Hillsdale, N.J.: Analytic Press.

Drewnowski, A., Hopkins, S. A., and Kessler, R. C. 1988. The prevalence of bulimia nervosa in the U.S. college student population. *American Journal of Public Health, 78,* 1322–25.

Drewnowski, A., Yee, D. K., and Krahn, D. D. 1988. Bulimia in college women: Incidence and recovery rates. *American Journal of Psychiatry, 145,* 753–755.

Emmett, S. W., ed. 1985. Theory and treatment of anorexia nervosa and bulimia. New York: Brunner Mazel.

Erikson, E. H. 1959/1980. *Identity and the life cycle.* New York: Norton.

———1963. *Childhood and society.* New York: Norton.

———1968. *Identity, youth, and crisis.* New York: Norton.

Erikson, J. M. 1988. *Wisdom and the senses: The way of creativity.* New York: Norton.

Everill, J., Waller, G., and Macdonald, W. 1995. Dissociation in bulimic and non-eating-disordered women. *International Journal of Eating Disorders, 17,* 127–134.

Fahy, T. A., and Russell, G. F. M. 1993. Outcome and prognostic variables in bulimia nervosa. *International Journal of Eating Disorders, 14,* 135–145.

Fairburn, C. G. 1993. Interpersonal psychotherapy for bulimia nervosa. In G. L. Kleman and M. M. Weissman, eds., *New applications of interpersonal psychotherapy.* Washington: American Psychiatric Press.

———1994. Genes and environment: A developmental, biogenetic model. Panel presented at the Sixth International Conference on Eating Disorders, sponsored by Montefiore Medical Center and Albert Einstein College of Medicine, April 29–May 1, 1994, New York.

———1997. Interpersonal psychotherapy for bulimia nervosa. In Garner and Garfinkel, eds., 1997.

Fairburn, C. G., Jones, R., Peveler, R. C., Carr, S. J., Solomon, R. A., O'Connor, M. E., Burton, J., and Hope, R. A. 1991. Three psychological treatments for bulimia nervosa. *Archives of General Psychiatry, 48,* 463–469.

Fallon, B., Walsh, B., Sadik, C., Saoud, J., and Lukasis, V. 1991. Outcome and clinical course in inpatient bulimic women: A 2- to 9-year follow-up study. *Journal of Clinical Psychiatry, 52,* 272–278.

Fichter, M. M., Quadflieg, N., and Rief, W. 1992. The German longitudinal bulimia nervosa study, I. In W. Herzog, H. C. Deter, and W. Vandereycken, eds., *The course of eating disorders: Long-term follow-up studies of anorexia and bulimia nervosa.* Berlin: Springer-Verlag.

Franko, D. L. 1994. Ready or not? Stages of change as predictors of treatment success in bulimia nervosa. Paper presented at the Sixth International Conference on Eating Disorders, sponsored by Montefiore Medical Center and Albert Einstein College of Medicine, April 29–May 1, 1994, New York.

Gans, M. 1989. Guilt and forgiveness: Spiritual and therapeutic perspectives in treatment of eating disorders. Paper presented at a conference, Eating Disorders: A Multidimensional Focus, sponsored by Anorexia Bulimia Care, April 29, 1989, Boston.

Garfinkel, P. E., and Walsh, B. T. 1997. Drug therapies. In Garner and Garfinkel, eds., 1997.

Garner, D. M., and Garfinkel, P. E., eds. 1997. *Handbook of treatment for eating disorders*. 2nd ed. New York: Guilford.

Garner, D. M., and Needleman, L. D. 1997. Sequencing and integration of treatments. In Garner and Garfinkel, eds., 1997.

Geist, R. A. 1985. Therapeutic dilemmas in the treatment of anorexia nervosa: A self-psychological perspective. In Emmett, ed., 1985.

———1989. Self psychological reflections on the origins of eating disorders. In J. R. Bemporad and D. B. Herzog, eds., *Psychoanalysis and eating disorders*. New York: Guilford.

Gendlin, E. T. 1974. Client-centered and experiential psychotherapy. In D. A. Wexler and L. N. Rice, eds., *Innovations in client-centered therapy*. New York: Wiley.

———1996. *Focusing-oriented psychotherapy: A manual of the experiential method*. New York: Guilford.

Gilligan, C. 1982/1993. *In a different voice*. Cambridge, Mass.: Harvard University Press.

Gilligan, C., Rogers, A. G., and Tolman, D. L., eds. 1991. *Women, girls, and psychotherapy: Reframing resistance*. Binghamton, N.Y.: Harrington Park Press.

Giorgi, A. 1985. *Phenomenology and psychological research*. Pittsburgh: Duquesne University Press.

Glaser, B. G., and Strauss, A. L. 1967. *The discovery of grounded theory: Strategies for qualitative research*. Chicago: Aldine.

Goodsitt, A. 1983. Self-regulatory disturbances in eating disorders. *International Journal of Eating Disorders, 2*, 51–60.

———1985. Self psychology and the treatment of anorexia nervosa. In D. M. Garner and P. E. Garfinkel, eds., *Handbook of psychotherapy for anorexia nervosa and bulimia*. New York: Guilford.

———1997. Eating disorders: A self-psychological perspective. In Garner and Garfinkel, eds., 1997.

Hall, L., and Cohn, L. 1992. *Bulimia: A guide to recovery*. Carlsbad, Calif.: Gurze Books.

Hartmann, H. 1958. *Ego psychology and the problem of adaptation*. New York: International Universities Press.

Heater, S. H. 1983. *Am I still visible? A woman's triumph over anorexia nervosa*. White Hall, Va.: White Hall Books.

Heatherton, T. F., and Baumeister, R. F. 1991. Binge eating as escape from self-awareness. *Psychological Bulletin, 110*, 86–108.

Herzog, D. B., Keller, M. B., and Lavori, P. W. 1988. Outcome in anorexia nervosa and bulimia nervosa: A review of the literature. *Journal of Nervous and Mental Disease, 176,* 131–143.

Herzog, D., Keller, M., Lavori, P., and Sacks, N. 1991. The course and outcome of bulimia nervosa. *Journal of Clinical Psychiatry, 52,* 4–8.

Herzog, D. B., Keller, M. B., Strober, M., Yeh, C., and Pai, S. 1992. The current status of treatment for anorexia nervosa and bulimia nervosa. *International Journal of Eating Disorders, 12,* 1215–20.

Herzog, D. B., Sacks, N. R., Keller, M. B., Lavori, P. W., von Ranson, K. B., and Gray, H. M. 1993. Patterns and predictors of recovery in anorexia nervosa and bulimia nervosa. *Journal of the American Academy of Child and Adolescent Medicine, 32,* 835–842.

Hornbacher, M. 1998. *Wasted: A memoir of anorexia and bulimia.* New York: Harper-Flamingo.

Hornyak, L. M., and Baker, E. K. 1989. *Experiential therapies for eating disorders.* New York: Guilford.

Hsu, L. K., Crisp, A. H., and Callender, J. S. 1992. Recovery in anorexia nervosa: The patient's perspective. *International Journal of Eating Disorders, 11,* 341–350.

Humphrey, L. T. 1988. Relationships within subtypes of anorexic, bulimic, and normal families. *Journal of the American Academy of Child and Adolescent Psychiatry, 27,* 544–551.

Jack, D. C. 1991. *Silencing the self: Women and depression.* Cambridge, Mass.: Harvard University Press.

James, W. 1890. *Principles of psychology.* New York: Holt, Rinehart and Winston.

Johnson, C. L. 1991. Treatment of eating-disordered patients with borderline and false-self/narcissistic disorders. In Johnson, ed., 1991.

———, ed. 1991. *Psychodynamic treatment of anorexia nervosa and bulimia.* New York: Guilford.

Johnson, C. L., and Connors, M. E. 1987. *The etiology and treatment of bulimia nervosa: A biopsychosocial perspective.* New York: Basic Books.

Johnson, C. L., and Sansone, R. A. 1993. Integrating the twelve-step approach with traditional psychotherapy for the treatment of eating disorders. *International Journal of Eating Disorders, 14,* 121–134.

Kadison, R. D. 1993. Square peg in a round hole: Eating disorders and managed care. Presented at a conference, Eating Disorders: A Multidimensional Focus, sponsored by Anorexia Bulimia Care, Inc., May 1, 1993, Boston.

Kagan, J. 1989. *Unstable ideas: Temperament, cognition, and self.* Cambridge, Mass.: Harvard University Press.

Kaufman, G. 1974. The meaning of shame: Toward a self-affirming identity. *Journal of Counseling Psychology, 21,* 568–574.

———1980/1992. *Shame: The power of caring.* 3rd ed. Rochester, Vt.: Schenkman.

Kegan, R. 1982. *The evolving self.* Cambridge, Mass.: Harvard University Press.

Keller, M. B., Herzog, D. B., Lavori, P. W., Bradburn, I., and Mahoney, E. M. 1992. The natural history of bulimia nervosa: Extraordinarily high rates of chronicity, relapse, recurrence, and psychosocial morbidity. *International Journal of Eating Disorders, 12,* 1–9.

Keys, A., Brozek, J., Henschel, A., Mickelsen, O., and Taylor, H. L. 1950. *The biology of human starvation.* 2 vols. Minneapolis: University of Minnesota Press.

Kilbourne, J. 1979. *Killing us softly.* Produced by Margaret Lazarus and Renner Wunderlich. Cambridge Documentary Films, P.O. Box 390385, Cambridge, Mass. 02139. 617-354-3677.

———1987. *Still killing us softly.* Produced by Margaret Lazarus and Renner Wunderlich. Cambridge Documentary Films, P.O. Box 390385, Cambridge, Mass. 02139. 617-354-3677.

Kohut, H. 1971. *The analysis of the self.* New York: International Universities Press.

———1977. *The restoration of the self.* Madison, Conn.: International Universities Press.

Levine, M. P. 1987. *How schools can help combat eating disorders.* Washington: National Education Association.

Levy, R. K. 1997. The transtheoretical model of change: An application to bulimia nervosa. *Psychotherapy, 34,* 278–285.

Linehan, M. M. 1993. *Skills training manual for treating borderline personality disorder.* New York: Guilford.

Lipson, A. 1989. School is hell. *Teaching and Learning: The Journal of Natural Inquiry, 4,* 11–20.

Liu, A. 1979. *Solitaire.* New York: Harper and Row.

MacLeod, S. 1982. *The art of starvation.* New York: Schocken.

Maine, M. 1985. Effective treatment of anorexia nervosa: The recovered patient's view. *Transactional Analysis Journal, 15,* 48–54.

Maxwell, J. A. 1996. *Qualitative research design: An interactive approach.* Thousand Oaks, Calif.: Sage Publications.

Maxwell, J. A., and Miller, B. A. 1993. Categorizing and connecting as components of qualitative data analysis. Manuscript, Harvard University.

Mayer, M. 1978. *Beauty and the Beast.* New York: Aladdin/Macmillan.

Mead, G. H. 1934. *Mind, self and society.* Chicago: University of Chicago Press.

Miles, M., and Huberman, A. M. 1994. *Qualitative data analysis.* 2nd ed. Thousand Oaks, Calif.: Sage Publications.

Miller, A. 1981/1994. *The drama of the gifted child: The search for the true self.* New York: Basic Books.

Miller, B. 1991. Adolescents' relationships with their friends. Doctoral diss., Harvard Graduate School of Education.

Miller, C. A. 1988/1991. *My name is Caroline.* Carlsbad, Calif.: Gurze Books.

Miller, J. B. 1976. *Toward a new psychology of women.* Boston: Beacon Press.

Miller, W. R., and Rollnick, S. 1991. *Motivational interviewing: Preparing people to change addictive behavior.* New York: Guilford.

Mishler, E. G. 1986. *Research interviewing: Context and narrative.* Cambridge, Mass.: Harvard University Press.

Mitchell, J. E., Pomeroy, C., and Adson, D. E. 1997. Managing medical complications. In Garner and Garfinkel, eds., 1997.

Mitchell, J. E., Pyle, R. L., Hatsukami, D., Goff, G., Glotter, D., and Harper, J. 1989. A 2–5 year follow-up study of patients treated for bulimia. *International Journal of Eating Disorders, 8,* 157–165.

Murray, C., Waller, G., and Legg, C. 2000. Family function and bulimic psychopathology: The mediating role of shame. *International Journal of Eating Disorders, 28,* 84–89.

O'Neill, C. B. 1982. *Starving for attention.* New York: Dell.

Orbach, S. 1986. *Hunger strike: The anorectic's struggle as a metaphor for our age.* London/Boston: Faber and Faber.

Oxford English Dictionary. Compact ed., 1971. New York: Oxford University Press.

Peters, L., and Fallon, P. 1994. The journey of recovery: Dimensions of change. In P. Fallon, M. A. Katzman, and S. C. Wooley, eds., *Feminist perspectives on eating disorders.* New York: Guilford.

Pipher, M. 1994. *Reviving Ophelia.* New York: Ballantine.

Pope, H. G., and Hudson, J. I. 1992. Is childhood sexual abuse a risk factor for bulimia nervosa? *American Journal of Psychiatry, 149,* 455–463.

Prochaska, J. O., and DiClemente, C. C. 1982. Transtheoretical therapy: Toward a more integrative model of change. *Psychotherapy Theory, Research and Practice, 20,* 161–173.

Prochaska, J. O., DiClemente, C. C., and Norcross, J. C. 1992. In search of how people change: Applications to addictive behaviors. *American Psychologist, 47,* 1102–14.

————1994. *Changing for good.* New York: Avon.

Pyle, R. L., Neuman, P. A., Halvorson, P. A., and Mitchell, J. E. 1991. An ongoing cross-sectional study of the prevalence of eating disorders in freshman college students. *International Journal of Eating Disorders, 10,* 667–677.

Random House College Dictionary. Rev. ed., 1975. New York: Random House.

Reindl, S. M., and Repetto Renna, M. S. 1991/2000. *What should I do? Guidelines for friends, lovers, roommates, and relatives of people with eating disorders.* Handout, Cambridge, Mass.

Rizzuto, A.-M. 1985. Eating and monsters: A psychodynamic view of bulimarexia. In Emmett, ed., 1985.

————1988. Transference, language, and affect in the treatment of bulimarexia. *International Journal of Psychoanalysis, 69,* 369–387.

————1991. Shame in psychoanalysis: The function of unconscious fantasies. *International Journal of Psychoanalysis, 72,* 297–312.

————1995. Sound and sense: Words in psychoanalysis and the paradox of the suffering person. *Canadian Journal of Psychoanalysis, 3,* 1–15.

Rizzuto, A.-M., Peterson, M. D., and Reed, M. 1981. The pathological sense of self in anorexia nervosa. *Psychiatric Clinics of North America, 4,* 471–487.

Romer, A. 2000. Only connect: Promoting meaning in the lives of patients with advanced dementia. In M. Z. Solomon, A. L. Romer, and K. S. Heller, eds., *Innovations in end-of-life care: Practical strategies and international perspectives.* Larchmont, N.Y.: Mary Ann Liebert, Inc.

Root, M. P. P., Fallon, P., and Friedrich, W. N. 1986. *Bulimia: A systems approach to treatment.* New York: Norton.

Rorty, M., Yager, J., and Rossotto, E. 1993. Why and how do women recover from bulimia nervosa? The subjective appraisals of forty women recovered for a year or more. *International Journal of Eating Disorders, 14,* 249–260.

Roth, G. 1982. *Feeding the hungry heart.* New York: Signet/New American Library.

————1984. *Breaking free from compulsive eating.* New York: Plume/Penguin.

Rowland, C. J. 1984. *The monster within: Overcoming bulimia.* Grand Rapids, Mich.: Baker Book House.

Sands, S. 1991. Bulimia, dissociation, and empathy: A self-psychological view. In Johnson, ed., 1991.

Schore, A. N. 1994. *Affect regulation and the origin of the self: The neurobiology of emotional development.* Hillsdale, N.J.: Erlbaum.

Schupack-Neuberg, E., and Nemeroff, C. 1993. Disturbances in identity and self-regulation in bulimia nervosa: Implications for a metaphorical perspective of "body as self." *International Journal of Eating Disorders, 13,* 335–347.

Seidman, I. E. 1991. *Interviewing as qualitative research.* New York/London: Jason Aronson.

Selvini-Palazzoli, M. 1985. *Self-starvation: From individual to family therapy in the treatment of eating disorders.* New York/London: Jason Aronson.

Shapiro, E. R. 1982. On curiosity: Intrapsychic and interpersonal boundary formation in family life. *International Journal of Family Psychiatry, 3,* 69–89.

Shaw, B. F., and Garfinkel, P. E. 1990. Research problems in the eating disorders. *International Journal of Eating Disorders, 9,* 545–555.

Steiner-Adair, C. 1984. The body politic: Normal female adolescent development and the development of eating disorders. Doctoral diss., Harvard University.

Stern, D. N. 1985. *The interpersonal world of the infant: A view from psychoanalysis and developmental psychology.* New York: Basic Books.

Striegel-Moore, R. H. 1994. Genes and environment: A developmental, biogenetic model. Panel presented at the Sixth International Conference on Eating Disorders, sponsored by Montefiore Medical Center and Albert Einstein College of Medicine, April 29–May 1, 1994, New York.

Strober, M. 1991. Disorders of the self in anorexia nervosa: An organismic-developmental paradigm. In Johnson, ed., 1991.

————1994. Genes and environment: A developmental, biogenetic model. Panel presented at the Sixth International Conference on Eating Disorders, sponsored by Montefiore Medical Center and Albert Einstein College of Medicine, April 29–May 1, 1994, New York.

Sugarman, A. 1991. Bulimia: A displacement from psychological self to body self. In Johnson, ed., 1991.

Sugarman, A., and Kurash, C. 1982. The body as a transitional object in bulimia. *International Journal of Eating Disorders, 1,* 57–67.

Swift, W., Ritholz, M., Kalin, N., and Kaslow, N. 1987. A follow-up study of thirty hospitalized bulimics. *Psychosomatic Medicine, 49:* 45–55.

Taft, J. 1933/1973. *Dynamics of therapy in a controlled relationship.* Gloucester, Mass.: Peter Smith/Dover.

Thompson, M. G., and Gans, M. T. 1985. Do anorexics and bulimics get well? In Emmett, ed., 1985.

Tobin, D. L., and Johnson, C. L. 1991. The integration of psychodynamic and behavior therapy in the treatment of eating disorders: Clinical issue versus theoretical mystique. In Johnson, ed., 1991.

van der Kolk, B. A. 1996. The complexity of adaptation to trauma: Self-regulation, stimulus discrimination, and characterological development. In B. A. van der Kolk, A. C. McFarlane, and L. Weisaeth, eds., *Traumatic stress: The effects of overwhelming experience on mind, body, and society.* New York: Guilford.

van der Kolk, B. A., Weisaeth, L., and van der Hart, O. 1996. History of trauma in psychiatry. In B. A. van der Kolk, A. C. McFarlane, and L. Weisaeth, eds., *Traumatic stress: The effects of overwhelming experience on mind, body, and society.* New York: Guilford.

Vitousek, K. B., Daly, J., and Heiser, C. 1991. Reconstructing the internal world of the eating-disordered individual: Overcoming denial and distortion in self-report. *International Journal of Eating Disorders, 6,* 647–666.

von Stade, C. 1986. Shame and its implications for psychotherapy. Qualifying paper, Harvard Graduate School of Education.

———1988. Shame and the learning process: An exploration of shame, learning, and group dynamics in a course for counselors. Doctoral diss., Harvard Graduate School of Education.

Watkins, M. 1977. A phenomenological approach to organismic developmental research. Manuscript, Cambridge, Mass.

Way, K. 1993. *Anorexia nervosa and recovery: A hunger for meaning.* New York: Harrington Park Press.

Welch, S. L., and Fairburn, C. G. 1994. Sexual abuse and bulimia nervosa: Three integrated case control comparisons. *American Journal of Psychiatry, 151,* 402–407.

White, M., and Epston, D. 1990. *Narrative means to therapeutic ends.* New York: Norton.

Wilson, G. T., Fairburn, C. G., and Agras, W. S. 1997. Cognitive-behavioral therapy for bulimia nervosa. In Garner and Garfinkel, eds., 1997.

Winnicott, D. W. 1958/1975. *Collected Papers: Through Paediatrics to Psycho-analysis.* New York: Basic Books.

———1965/1994. *The maturational processes and the facilitating environment: Studies in the theory of emotional development.* Madison, Conn.: International Universities Press.

ACKNOWLEDGMENTS

Although much of the process of researching and writing a book is necessarily done alone, this book simply would not exist without the help of many generous, caring people in my life. That family, friends, and colleagues have found ways to support me during this process means more than I can say. But I will try.

First, I want to thank the participants in my study for the courage and honesty with which they spoke to me about their experience of recovering. I am also grateful to my clients, who have taught me much of what I know about eating disorders and about recovering. My thanks also go to Virginia Demos for treating my roughest drafts with the greatest respect and for her writing on the development of a sense of agency, which illuminated my understanding of participants' narratives and—to my delight—marked an intersection of our intellectual paths; to Carol Gilligan for teaching me to ask real questions and for encouraging me to explore the seemingly self-evident; to Gil Noam for challenging me to nail key points; to Joe Maxwell for his inspired and informed teaching and writing about qualitative methods; to the American Psychological Association, Radcliffe College, and the Harvard Graduate School of Education for their support of my research; to Joe Guido, Toni Tugenberg, and Sally Walker for their company and wisdom as I considered two possible topics; and to the late Joan Erikson for urging me to choose this one, for her abiding wisdom on the senses, and for continually bringing me to my senses with her "Now look" and "Now listen."

I am thankful to David Herzog for including me in discussions of research on recovering; to Eugene Beresin for our many enlightening conversations about recovering and for an invaluable tutorial on Winnicott; to Ingrid Ott and Michèle Flournoy for the timely and attuned gifts of the coffee grinder and cappuccino maker and for their abiding love and friendship; to Alexandra Myles, Becky Reynolds, Elaine Schenot, and JoAnn Ellsworth for understanding my near unavailability during long seasons of immersion and for welcoming the sound of my voice when I surfaced; to Leora Heckelman for her enthusiasm about my work and for her empathy and friendship; to Margery Gans for grounding and inspiration via our talks about our work and for her devotion to detail as she commented on draft after draft; to Michèle LaCroix for appreciating the unabridged version and for joining in the deliberations about a title; to Robin Rosenberg for guidance from a fellow psychologist and writer; to Laura Weisberg for her ever encouraging words and voice; to Richard Kadison for his observations on windows of opportunity and for all he has taught me about working with people with eating disorders; to Anna Romer for practical wisdom and guidance in qualitative data analysis, for thoroughly commenting on drafts, and for her unflagging faith in me and in this project; and to my colleagues in three networks of eating disorders professionals—at Harvard, at MIT, and in Greater Boston—for encouragement and for creating environments in which it is safe to talk about what we do not know.

I am most grateful to Charles Ducey for his observations on intersubjectivity and on the process of becoming more fully oneself, for his respect for my work, and for practical support in the form of time and flexibility; to Suzanne Repetto Renna for commenting on excerpts of interviews and drafts of the manuscript, for drawing my attention to shame in the women's accounts, and for serving as a model of what it means to be humanizing; to Abigail Lipson for encouraging me to start with the obvious, for asking questions that helped me discover what I was hearing in the women's narratives, for building the desk in the cupola, and for responding to many drafts and emails; and to my other colleagues and friends at Harvard's Bureau of Study Counsel for being all one could ever hope for in a holding environment.

I thank Aida Donald, formerly of Harvard University Press, for her initial interest in this book; my editor, Elizabeth Knoll, for her commitment to this project, for her patience, and for her questions and challenges that led me to refine my thinking; Camille Smith for editing my manuscript with extraordinary skill, care, and respect (the manuscript could not have been in better hands) and for her thoughtful attention to detail; and my agent, Doe Coover, for her steadiness and clarity.

My mother, Phyllis Reindl, and my father, the late Donald Reindl, have always believed in me, and I am eternally grateful. I thank them as well for the timely, attuned, and enormously generous gift of the Power-Book, for prayers said on my behalf, for phone calls of support, and for the many other ways they found to send their encouragement, cheer, and love across a distance we all wished were shorter.

I thank my stepdaughters, Holly and Lee Reichhold-Caruso, for sharing me with this book and for being such wonderful reasons to take breaks from it (never mind finish it altogether). And I thank Frank Caruso for being such a devoted and generous husband to me and such a devoted and generous stepfather to this book. His countless, daily acts of love and care, as well as his sense of playfulness and perspective, continually brought (and bring) me home and have enabled me to send this book on its way in the world.

INDEX

Abiding context, 54, 79–81, 83, 91, 92, 278

Abigail, 9–10, 44, 69–70, 73, 80, 90, 96, 97, 104–105, 108–109, 111–112, 115, 120–121, 140–141, 163, 176–177, 181, 188–189, 194–195, 206, 222, 228–229, 237–238, 244, 249–250, 285, 289, 290

Abuse, 30. *See also* Emotional abuse; Physical abuse; Sexual abuse

Acts of care, authentic and attuned, 205–208

Adequacy, sensing, 109–110

Adolescence, developmental demands of, 13, 42–43

Agency. *See* Self-agency

Aggression, 6. *See also* Beast within

AIM: and development of sense of agency, 57, 94; and bingeing and purging, 95; and anger, 96–97

Aisenberg, K., 45–46

Alcoholics Anonymous, 34, 59, 63, 110, 195

Ambivalence, 1, 190–194, 266–267

Amy, 32, 51, 59, 60–61, 63, 81, 87–89, 175, 186, 197, 206, 207–208, 209–210, 225–226, 231–232, 240–241, 248, 267, 285, 304–305

Anger, 3, 68, 70; and enoughness, 95–98; and rage, 97. *See also*

Emotional pain; Felt sense of enough

Anorexia nervosa: women with, 6; recovery from, 7, 279–280, 297; crossover between bulimia nervosa and, 133n, 295; vs. bulimia nervosa, 133–134; misnaming of, 281

Anxiety. *See* Emotional pain

Attunement, 8; in early development, 17; to self, 137; and implications for treatment, 268–278

Attunement, lack of: and shame, 14, 17; in abusive families, 30; and deficits in self-structure and self-regulation, 38–40; examples of, 89–91

Authenticity, 4, 80, 110–112, 134, 291; and naturally maintainable weight, 4, 183, 248–249; and fidelity to self, 50; and loss, 159. *See also* Identity; Separateness; Wholeness

Autobiographical accounts of recovery, 298

Basseches, M., 299n

Baumeister, R., 33–34

Beast within: behavior of, 129–131; birth of, 131–138; banishing of, 138–139; badness of, 139–146; befriending of, 146–150; sensing respect for, 151–156; sensing wholeness of,